The Third
Indochina Conflict

Westview Replica Editions

This book is a Westview Replica Edition. The concept of
Replica Editions is a response to the crisis in academic and
informational publishing. Library budgets for books have been
severely curtailed; economic pressures on the university presses
and the few private publishing companies primarily interested in
scholarly manuscripts have severely limited the capacity of the
industry to properly serve the academic and research communities.
Many manuscripts dealing with important subjects, often representing the highest level of scholarship, are today not economically viable publishing projects. Or, if they are accepted for
publication, they are often subject to lead times ranging from
one to three years. Scholars are understandably frustrated when
they realize that their first-class research cannot be published
within a reasonable time frame, if at all.

Westview Replica Editions are our practical solution to the
problem. The concept is simple. We accept a manuscript in camera-
ready form and move it immediately into the production process.
The responsibility for textual and copy editing lies with the
author or sponsoring organization. If necessary we will advise
the author on proper preparation of footnotes and bibliography.
We prefer that the manuscript be typed according to our speci-
fications, though it may be acceptable as typed for a disserta-
tion or prepared in some other clearly organized and readable
way. The end result is a book produced by lithography and bound
in hard covers. Initial edition sizes range from 400 to 800
copies, and a number of recent Replicas are already in second
printings. We include among Westview Replica Editions only works
of outstanding scholarly quality or of great informational value,
and we will continue to exercise our usual editorial standards
and quality control.

The Third Indochina Conflict
edited by David W.P. Elliott

The Third Indochina Conflict (1975-) is seen by some as the escalation of a local quarrel between Vietnam and Kampuchea; others attribute it to the attempts of external powers to advance their own interests by encouraging conflict among the various Indochinese states; most agree that it is a logical--but not inevitable--consequence of the First (1946-54) and Second (1959-75) Indochinese conflicts. The contributors to this book analyze the origins and development of the Third Indochinese Conflict and the problems posed by the complex issues involved.

Dr. Elliott is assistant professor of government and international relations, Pomona College, and has also taught at Cornell University. He spent six years in Vietnam with the Rand Corporation.

The Third
Indochina Conflict

edited by
David W.P. Elliott

Westview Press / Boulder, Colorado

A Westview Replica Edition

Copyright © 1981 by Westview Press, Inc.

Published in 1981 in the United States of America by
     Westview Press, Inc.
     5500 Central Avenue
     Boulder, Colorado 80301
     Frederick A. Praeger, Publisher

Library of Congress Cataloging in Publication Data
Main entry under title:
The Third Indochina conflict.
  (A Westview replica edition)
  Based on a panel discussion at the annual meeting of the Association
for Asian Studies, held Mar. 1979.
    1. Cambodian-Vietnamese Conflict, 1977-   --Congresses. 2. Indo-
china--History--1945-   --Congresses. I. Elliott, David W. P.
II. Association for Asian Studies. III. Series: Westview replica
edition.
DS554.842.T47   959.704'4   81-2736
ISBN 0-89158-739-X   AACR2

Printed and bound in the United States of America

Contents

Preface

The Third Indochina Conflict was the subject of a
panel at the annual meeting of the Association for Asian
Studies held in late March 1979. Shortly thereafter a
group comprising all but one of the contributors to the
present volume explored the topic further at the "Conference on the Third Indochina Conflict" held at Pomona
College on April 2, 1979 under the joint sponsorship of
the International Relations Program of Pomona College and
the International Relations Program of Claremont Men's
College.

The inspiration for these panels came from George
McT. Kahin of Cornell University, and Josef Silverstein
of Rutgers University. They had the foresight in the
Fall of 1978 to see that the tensions in Indochina would
become even more serious -- as events in late 1978 and
early 1979 were to confirm -- and were instrumental in
initiating the idea of organizing a panel of scholars to
assess this disturbing development. The focus of this
book is largely on the origins and development of the
crisis up through the Chinese invasion of Vietnam in
February 1979. The related problem of the subsequent
diplomatic attempts to deal with the conflict constitutes
a separate, and equally complex, area of inquiry. Nonetheless, understanding the causes of the conflict is
essential to dealing with its consequences, and it is our
hope that this book will contribute to that end.

Because of various conflicting commitments and communications problems, it proved to be difficult to allow
all contributors to revise their manuscripts to take into
account subsequent events. This did not prove to be a
significant handicap, since most of the major facts and
events were known to the authors as they prepared their
papers. The exception was Stephen Heder, who was unable
to revise his presentations at the panels. Through the
permission of Singapore University's Institute of Southeast Asian Studies, we were able to use Heder's contribution to the annual publication of that Institute,

<u>Southeast Asian Affairs</u> (1979), and it is here presented in its original form. The prescience of his analysis and careful research in this article makes it a particularly valuable contribution to this volume. Charles Benoit, who was not a member of the original panels, kindly consented to the inclusion of his unique and perceptive report on the boat people, which filled a crucial gap in the analysis of the conflict.

Timely assistance **from** the International Relations Programs of Pomona College and Claremont Men's College made the conferences -- and therefore this book -- possible. Pomona's research committee approved funds for the preparation of the typescript, which was the product of the combined efforts of Beverly Biedenbach, Marge Twydell, and Penny Arnn. A special debt of gratitude is owed to Mervyn Seldon, whose support was instrumental in completing this project.

David W.P. Elliott

Contributors

CHARLES BENOIT is a Ph.D. candidate at Harvard in East
Asian Languages and Civilizations. He is the former
head of Ford Foundation programs in Vietnam (1973-75)
and subsequently program officer of the Asia and Pacific
section of Ford Foundation's International Division. His
article is based on interviews conducted in the major
centers for Indochinese refugees in Hong Kong and Southeast Asia. He is fluent in both Vietnamese and Chinese.

DAVID W.P. ELLIOTT is assistant professor of government
and international relations at Pomona College, and a
former staff member of the Rand Corporation in Vietnam.
His recent publications include "Vietnam: Institutional
Development in a Time of Crisis," Southeast Asian Affairs
1979 (Institute of Southeast Asian Studies, Singapore),
and "Institutionalizing the Revolution: Vietnam's Search
for a Model of Development," Vietnamese Communism in
Comparative Perspective (Westview, 1980).

BANNING GARRETT is Senior Foreign Policy Analyst at Harold
Rosenbaum Associates Inc., (Arlington, Virginia), and
Research Associate of the Institute of International
Studies at the University of California, at Berkeley. He
is the former president and co-editor of Internews, and
is a Ph.D. candidate at Brandeis University. His articles
include "China Policy and the Strategic Triangle," in
Kenneth Oye et.al. Eagle Entangled: U.S. Foreign Policy
in a Complex World (Longman, 1979). He is also the author
of The China Card and its Origins: U.S. Bureaucratic
Politics and the Strategic Triangle (Berkeley, forth-
coming).

STEPHEN P. HEDER is a Ph.D. candidate in the Department
of Government and affiliated with the Southeast Asia Program at Cornell University. From 1973 to 1975 he lived in
Phnom Penh, where he worked for Time magazine and NBC
news. He is fluent in Khmer (as well as Thai and Chinese)
and has conducted extensive interviews with Kampuchean

refugees. He is the author of a number of articles on Kampuchea including "Origins of the Conflict" in the Southeast Asia Chronicle, No. 64, September-October 1978, and Kampuchean Occupation and Resistance, Asian Studies Monographs No. 027, Institute of Asian Studies, Chulalongkorn University (Bangkok, Thailand), January 1980.

GARETH PORTER is a professorial lecturer at Johns Hopkins School of Advanced International Studies, and a staff member of the Center for International Policy. His most recent trip to Indochina was in January 1981. He is the author of numerous articles on Vietnam as well as A Peace Denied: The United States, Vietnam, and the Paris Agreements (Indiana, 1976), and was editor of The Vietnam War, A Documentary History (New American Library, 1980).

ROBERT G. SUTTER is an Asian affairs analyst in the Congressional Research Service of the Library of Congress, and a former research analyst in Chinese foreign affairs in the U.S. Central Intelligence Agency. He is the author of several books on China's foreign policy, including China-Watch: Sino-American Reconciliation (Johns Hopkins University Press, 1978), and Chinese Foreign Policy After the Cultural Revolution (Westview Press, 1978).

The Third
Indochina Conflict

1 | The Third Indochina Conflict: Introduction

David W.P. Elliott

There seems to be an iron law regulating events in Indochina: nothing is ever simple, and things can always get worse. The First Indochina War, fought by France from 1945-54 to retain its colonial possessions there, was a contest between the forces of empire and the aspiration for independence complicated by its linkage to larger international issues. United States involvement in Vietnam led to the Second Indochina War (1959-75), initially construed as an effort to defend the interests of the "Free World" against a monolithic communist bloc. By the time this rationale had lost its relevance the changes that had occurred in Indochina and in the world had prepared the ground for another round of conflict, this time between allies who had stood together in the earlier contests. No sooner had the Second Indochina War ended in 1975 with the victory of the revolutions in Vietnam, Kampuchea and Laos, than the hitherto submerged antagonisms between three parties -- China, Vietnam, and Kampuchea -- came to the surface. These tensions ultimately led to open armed hostilities and ushered in the Third Indochina Conflict.

This book is an attempt to examine the causes and con-sequences of the Third Indochina Conflict. It tries to unravel the tangled knot of issues involved in this analysis by following two principles: proceed from the basic to the more complex aspects of the problem, and take the perspective of each participant in the conflict as a starting point. Stephen Heder, in an article completed just prior to the Vietnamese invasion of Kampuchea and republished here in its original form, explicates the historical and political factors under-lying the conflict between the two countries. Gareth Porter examines the Vietnamese view of the deteriorating relations between Vietnam and Kampuchea and the escalat-ing involvement of China. Charles Benoit discusses the problem of the "boat people" and the position of the

1

ethnic Chinese in Vietnam, which became the focal center
of a major turning point in the escalation of hostilities. His article is based on interviews conducted with
refugees from Vietnam in various locations throughout
Southeast Asia in 1979. Robert Sutter then explores
China's motivations in intervening in Indochinese
affairs, and discusses the internal political factors
that affected the decisions on policy toward Vietnam, as
well as the general foreign policy context in which
these decisions were made. The final author, Banning
Garrett, looks at the conflict from a broader international perspective, analyzing the ways in which the
regional issues of the Indochina conflict intersect with
those on the larger chessboard of global politics.

Given the complexity of the conflict, finding
definitive answers to the fundamental questions of
causation and responsibility is not an easy task. The
major events in the conflict are clear enough. Vietnam
invaded Kampuchea in December 1978 and China invaded
Vietnam in February 1979. The connections between the
key events, and the chain of cause and effect that produced them are not so easily discerned, however.
Briefly, the basic positions of each of the major actors
may be summarized as follows: Pol Pot's Kampuchea
pointed to a long history of Vietnamese aggression and
encroachment on Khmer sovereignty and maintained an
inflexible diplomatic stance based on the view that
compromise would lead to capitulation to the stronger
power. Vietnam found it difficult to comprehend this
rigid stance, was critical of the Kampuchean revolutionaries' independent strategy which Hanoi felt undermined
the struggle against a common enemy, and ultimately came
to see Kampuchea as a pawn of Chinese interests at a time
when China had clearly signalled its hostility to
Vietnam. Having led the anti-colonial struggle and having been the principal resistance force against the
United States intervention in Indochina, the Vietnamese
felt that they had a right to be the senior partner in a
"special relationship" with Kampuchea as well as Laos.
China, for its part, saw Vietnam as a potential rival in
Southeast Asia as well as an instrument of Soviet policy
in a region which China regarded as its sphere of influence, and as a link in the Soviet effort to surround
and "contain" China with a ring of anti-Chinese states.

Vietnam's connections with the Soviet Union were regarded by Beijing as the root of the problem, and China
moved to establish close ties with the Pol Pot government to counterbalance the "Cuba of Southeast Asia."
The superpowers played a critical, if indirect role in
the escalation of the conflict. Vietnam's friendship

treaty with the Soviet Union preceded its invasion of
China's ally Kampuchea by one month, and China's attack
on Vietnam followed shortly after signing the normalization pact with the United States.

What, then, are the issues raised by the Third
Indochina Conflict? One crucial issue is the role of
diplomacy in avoiding or defusing such conflicts. Was
the conflict inevitable, or could it have been forestalled by more skillful diplomacy and a better understanding of the fundamental problems? What implications
does this have for the resolution of the conflict and the
prevention of future hostilities in the region? A
related problem is the linkage between regional and
global politics. Was this a local conflict which in-
advertently escalated into an international crisis? Or
did the structure of global international relations, in
particular the triangular relationship between China,
the United States, and the Soviet Union, exacerbate a
potentially manageable problem by grafting extraneous
issues onto the existing tensions of local disputes? Is
the Third Indochina Conflict, then, a local quarrel which
spun out of control, becoming in the process a component
of a larger global conflict, or was it a "proxy war" that
inflamed the frictions of the local actors into open
warfare? And, from the standpoint of resolving the
conflict, does it make any difference which of these
interpretations is correct?

An equally important question is why the causes and
consequences of the Third Indochina Conflict have been
the object of disputation. Is it the basic facts that are
in question? Or do the values and sympathies of the
proponents of the various positions influence their conclusions? To some extent, both of these problems have
complicated the analysis of the conflict. But the main
problem is not one of facts or values, but of interpretation and perspective. There are so many variables and
possible connections between events, that even establishing a chronology of events is difficult. Relating causes
to effects, and highlighting of crucial turning points in
the evolution of the conflict involves not simply the
cataloguing of facts, but also establishing the relationships between them. Presenting a chronology implies that
a judgement has been rendered on what elements constitute
the key links in the causal chain. In addition, the
problem of perspective is vitally important. Kampuchea
saw the problem in terms of national survival and was
mainly preoccupied with its immediate problems with
Vietnam. Vietnam viewed Kampuchea as a secondary problem
whose main importance lay in its connection with China.
Beijing, in turn, regarded Vietnam as a relatively minor

irritant made intolerable only by its ties to the Soviet
Union. There is an ironic parallelism here. In the
ascending hierarchy of size and power, each actor regarded its own relations with the lesser power as
reasonable and innocuous, and ascribed the source of
conflict to the threatening behavior of the greater
power. Only Kampuchea, at the bottom of this ladder,
had no such bifarious view. Indeed it is precisely its
weak and exposed position, and its single minded obses-
sion with Vietnam that led to policies and actions that
are not easily explained by conventional diplomatic
analysis or by imperatives of revolutionary strategy.

Two analytic orientations have dominated the discussion of the Third Indochina Conflict; the "national
interest" approach stressing reasons of state, and a
focus on decision making which emphasizes the importance
of perceptions and misperceptions and the range of
choices available to the political leadership of each
country. The national interest view points to the
geopolitical realities of the region and the inherent
conflicts of interest between the parties to the conflict. The rivalry between Vietnam and China for
influence in Laos, Kampuchea, and the rest of Southeast
Asia is frequently cited as a basic ingredient of the
conflict. Another key element is the dynamics of the
US-China-Soviet Union strategic triangle. As several
contributors have demonstrated, these factors are
indispensible to understanding the bilateral conflicts
between Vietnam-Kampuchea and China-Vietnam, as well as
the diplomatic-strategic interplay that fueled the
escalation of the conflict.

At the same time, it would be a mistake to under-
emphasize the alternative options available to each
national leadership, and the predispositions that made
one choice seem better than another. Also, internal
considerations such as divergences within the leaderships
and responses to the expectations of non-elites cannot
be overlooked. We are not dealing with the classic
"unitary actor" of traditional statescraft, but with an
extremely complex series of cross pressures that combine
to produce decisions. And, as many recent studies of
decision making would predict, often decisions are
reactive, partial, and incremental, rather than part of
a "game plan" concocted by a team of "rational actors."

Historical factors weigh heavily among the deter-
minents of the decisions affecting relations between the
antagonists. Not only are there general ethnic-
cultural antagonisms between Vietnam and Kampuchea and
Vietnam and China, but the experiences of each revolu-

tionary leadership with its counterpart left a legacy
of mistrust and ill will. Heder's article reveals how
crucial the discord between the Kampuchean and Vietnamese
Parties over revolutionary strategy was in precipitating
open conflict between them. Porter likewise shows the
strains that have existed between Vietnam and China
since at least 1954. Both cases illustrate the necessary linkage between the national interest and
decision making approaches. Without the inherent conflicts between their mutual stategic objectives,
cultural and ethnic tensions would not have led to open
conflict, nor would the differences in revolutionary
line have been as potent a contributing factor in fuel-
ing the conflict. As it was, however, Pol Pot's forces
ultimately accused the Vietnamese of genocidal designs
against Kampuchea. Vietnam, in turn, revived the
spectre of Great Han chauvinism, as is evidenced in
Premier Pham Van Dong's scathing attack on Mao Zedong
as "a former Chinese emperor" who had always been
obsessed by a dream of "expansion" and "hegemony." No
doubt the traditional Vietnamese hostility to China
exacerbated the conflict once it had occurred, as did
the traditional Chinese view of Vietnam as an in-
significant but insubordinate troublemaker in its rightful sphere of influence.

During the 19th century Vietnam and Thailand contested
for power in Vietnam. One account of the period notes,
"The almost total control exercised over Cambodia by the
Vietnamese at this period set the stage for a struggle
by Siam to regain its influence. ....The Vietnamese,
following the stern policies of Emperor Minh Menh,
attempted to change the face of Cambodia. Vietnamese
provincial administration was substituted for the
Cambodian, and an attempt was made to impose Vietnamese
patterns of dress on the Cambodians. It is difficult to
exaggerate the searing effect of the Vietnamese occupation." [1] As Heder observes, the fear of national
extinction at the hands of more powerful neighbors
prompted the Khmers to approach questions of territorial
sovereignty with an uncompromising rigidity. Even the
supple Sihanouk made the nonnegotiability of Kampuchea's
borders a major object of his diplomacy in the 1960s.

    An example of the importance of the historial and
psycho-cultural background of antagonism between Vietnam
and Kampuchea is a relatively minor episode in the
gradual escalation of hostilities between the two
countries, the breakdown in April 1976 of the technical
talks between them that led to the collapse of higher
level substantive discussions scheduled for the following month. The specific point of contention was the

delineation of the boundary between the two countries,
but this was quickly overshadowed by much broader
questions involving the fundamental bases for relations
between them. As Heder observes, the Kampucheans "saw
the Vietnamese proposals at the technical conference as
an attempt to undermine the principle of non-negotia-
bility of the borders" backed up by a military presence
in areas claimed by Kampuchea" in order to negotiate in
a big power way, from a position of strength." The
abortive technical talks of April 1976 marked the last
time that territorial issues were diplomatically discussed between the two sides. According to Democratic
Kampuchea sources, an anti-government plot was crushed
in that month. Subsequently, it was charged that
Vietnam (and CIA) agents were collaborating to overthrow Pol Pot. Whatever the truth of this allegation
it did, as Porter notes, lead to an intensification of
Pol Pot's concern with "insuring security and loyalty
of the Party and army itself." This, in turn, probably
contributed to the escalation of the conflict by
exacerbating Pol Pot's already intense concern about
internal and external security and the link between
them. Porter concludes that the internal purge in
Kampuchea which began in 1976" was accompanied by a new
policy of military initiative on the border with
Vietnam and a propaganda campaign in the villages to
portray Vietnam as Kampuchea's enemy," leading to
escalating Kampuchean military attacks across the
Vietnamese border from January 1977 on. Although the
exact connection between the purges and the accelera-
tion of Kampuchean military activity along the
Vietnamese frontier is unclear, the probable connection
of these internal upheavals with the expanding conflict between the two countries should caution against
analyzing the conflict purely in terms of an action-
reaction cycle based on decisions made by unitary actors
in response to external stimuli.

Nonetheless, such a cycle is discernable in the
events that followed. Heder writes that in early 1977
the Kampucheans increased their pressure on the disputed
zones, which led to a Vietnamese reinforcement of their
military position along the frontier. Shortly thereafter the "escalating spiral in the military sphere
gained momentum in April and May 1977. The Kampucheans
who had previously only wanted to suggest that they
could make things costly for the Vietnamese and who had
probably sent in patrols with orders to fire only in
self defense, now began to initiate military activies."
Heder feels that these Kampuchean military initiatives
were part of a negotiation strategy aimed at convincing
the Vietnamese to acknowledge the Kampuchean

definition of an acceptable framework for negotiations. Whatever the intent, it led to a further intensification of hostilities and hardening of positions.

Heder observes that the "border conflict alone probably would not have had the same profound consequences had there not existed other fundamental conflicts that poisoned the diplomatic atmosphere." In the area of revolutionary strategy Vietnam and the Khmer Rouge stood at opposite poles. Conflict and tension between the two revolutionary movements of Vietnam and Kampuchea emerged at the Geneva Conference of 1954 when Vietnam, under pressure from China and the Soviet Union dropped its insistence that the Khmer People's Party be legitimated within the framework of the settlement. Subsequently, a revolutionary leadership independent of the Vietnamese emerged, and the strategy of the Communist Party of Kampuchea (founded in 1960 as the successor to the KPP) diverged sharply from that of the Vietnamese Party. Vietnam saw Sihanouk as a valuable (if untrustworthy) ally and gave its support to Sihanouk as long as his policies excluded US influence from Kampuchea. The CPK, on the other hand, found that its own revolutionary requirements necessitated going into armed revolt against Sihanouk and pursuing the "anti-feudal" task of class struggle and the transformation of society even though the "anti-imperialist" struggle suffered in the process.

Vietnam viewed this as a short sighted policy, a threat to its own interests, and a renunciation of the obligations of "proletarian internationalism". As Porter's article suggests, the Ho Chi Minh legacy led Vietnam to take the idea of solidarity in the world revolutionary movements very seriously, even though they had more often been the victims than the beneficiaries of this policy.[2] Comintern shifts in strategy embarrassed the Vietnamese Party more than once and, like Kampuchea, they were pressed to compromise crucial objectives in the Geneva conference of 1954. This is now blamed on China, but it seems clear that it was, in fact, the Soviet Union that pressured Vietnam, just as it was the Soviet Union that nearly undermined Vietnam's unification struggle by proposing admission of both North and South Vietnam into the United Nations in 1957, and pressed Hanoi to pursue a policy of non-violent struggle in line with the dialectics of "peaceful coexistence" until the pressure on and from the southern revolutionary movement forced a change of line. Vietnam's stress on the united front as a crucial element of the anti-imperialist struggle was rejected by the CPK. As Heder has written elsewhere, the

8

divergent policies constituted "an implicit mutual
critique" in which "each revolutionary model points out
the real or imaginable shortcomings of the other and
thereby questions its legitimacy."[3] From critique to
armed conflict was a long step, but the groundwork had
been laid by the contrasts in revolutionary experience.

For Kampuchea, the concept of proletarian internationalism was merely semantic covering for the idea
of a Vietnamese dominated Indochina Federation. From
1930 to 1951, the Indochinese Communist Party had placed
the communist movements in Kampuchea and Laos under the
aegis of the Vietnamese leadership on the theory that
the French colonial regime constituted a common enemy
against which coordinated action was required. Subsequently the Vietnamese continued to play the lead role
against the United States intervention. Porter points
out that, "The more troubled relations between Vietnamese and Cambodian parties became, the more the
Vietnamese turned to the relationship between the Vietnamese and the Laotian parties as a model of Indochina
unity...The Vietnamese regarded their military presence
as a normal form of cooperation between stronger and
weaker states required by Indochinese revolutionary
solidarity."[4] The Vietnamese first employed the term
"special relationship" to describe their view of the
ties between the Indochinese combatants which "must be
close to each other, although each country is
independent."

To the Kampucheans, the "special relationship:
meant Vietnamese hegemony, while to the Vietnamese it
was a statement of self-evident strategic necessity
which was vital to the security of all three states.
This is a particularly apt illustration of the complexity
of the two frameworks of analysis noted earlier. From
the strategic, geo-political perspective, the divergence
between the Vietnamese and Kampuchean position reflects
an inevitable clash of state interests. The relationship
of Kampuchea to Vietnam (and of Vietnam to China) simply
illustrates the sardonic Vietnamese folk wisdom that
"the big fish eat the little fish" - each larger power
strives for hegemony where it can. It is, however,
necessary to add the role that political, cultural and
historical factors play in tempering or exacerbating
this simple rule of international politics. Had not the
Vietnamese amd Kampuchean revolutionary experiences been
so markedly different, it is quite conceivable that the
events which led to an armed Vietnamese intervention
might not have taken place. In this case, the two
perspectives complement each other. One explains the
necessary structural preconditions for conflict, the
other the sufficient motivating perceptions that pushed

the situation over the brink.

Can the same analysis be applied to Vietnam's relations with China? The parallels are suggestive but limited. Vietnam's historical experience with China has not been a happy one. Clearly the harshness of Vietnam's post-1978 policies toward overseas Chinese in Vietnam is in some measure due to ethnic hostilities which are an outgrowth of that historical experience. Yet Vietnam had used Chinese culture and institutions in its efforts to strengthen itself and throw off Chinese domination and had also had close and cordial relations with China at critical junctures in its own revolution. Although Vietnam's post-1954 internal development model was an implicit critique of China's, this never became a major point of contention between them. And although China's revolutionary strategy significantly diverged from Vietnam's strategy from 1965 onward, the contrast was not absolute. China's revolutionary model stressed the idea of the united front which Vietnam favored and Kampuchea distrusted. China supported and played a major role in the Indochina conference of 1970 held in Southern China which, as one author characterized it, "would symbolize the unity of the revolutionary movements in Indochina" - albeit with China as the major coor- dinator of the conference while the Vietnamese "assumed a modest role."[5] But if the principle of a special unity of Indochinese revolutionary movements was acknowledged, could it be expected that the major force in Indochina would stay in the background for long?

Some prescient analysts of the Vietnam war pointed out that both the domino theory and the containment policy ignored the diversity of the communist movements in Asia as well as the inherent conflicts of interest between Vietnam and China in Southeast Asia. These conflicts have indeed come into the open and, far from vindicating the domino theory, are evidence of the asser- tive nationalism within the region which the domino theory overlooked. Another assumption of the domino theory, that each communist revolutionary movement in the region represented an aggressive projection of a global communist monolith, has been invalidated by the current internecine conflict among the communist states. In addition, the domino theory assumed that the dynamics of regional international relations are the result of superpower contention in a vacuum devoid of indigenous power and interests. Here too, as will be discussed below, the evidence is at best mixed.

A further question is, does the conflict between Vietnam and China reflect a predictable, even inevitable, clash of ambitions and interests between two active and

powerful forces in the region, or is there another
dimension that provided the sufficient condition to
supplement the necessary precondition? The analyses of
Porter and Garrett demonstrate the importance of looking
beyond Indochina to locate the main sources of conflict.
The Chinese suspicion that Vietnam was acting as a
surrogate for the Soviet Union inflamed existing tensions
between China and Vietnam which might, in isolation,
have been contained. Like the situation between Vietnam
and Kampuchea, border tensions were the symptoms of
deeper conflicts. But unlike Kampuchea, Vietnam did not
regard its national survival at stake in the border
dispute. There was not, therefore, as tight a linkage
between the symptom and the underlying cause of conflict
in the case of Vietnam and, therefore, more room for a
diplomatic solution. How was it, then, that at this
critical juncture, escalation of the conflict was not
contained?

Robert Sutter's analysis indicates that China's
policy of maintaining correct party and state relations
with Vietnam and avoiding "raising Sino-Vietnamese
disputes or publicly pressing Vietnam into allying more
closely with the Soviet Union" changed abruptly in May
1978. This change was, in Sutter's view, part of "a
series of Chinese foreign policy initiatives demonstrating a more assertive approach to international
affairs." As Sutter points out, China's policy in Asia
has been motivated "in large measure by a strategic
concern to promote a balance of influence in the region
that is favorable to China and to block what Peking sees
as Soviet efforts to 'contain' the spread of Chinese
influence." Even after the first large scale clashes
between Kampuchea and Vietnam in late 1977 China's policy
toward Vietnam remained restrained and flexible. Why was
it, then, that Peking's view of the threat posed by Hanoi
changed so abruptly? In part, Sutter speculates, the
change was due to the growing power of Deng Xiao-ping in
the Beijing leadership, and the initial predilection of
Deng to take a harder line toward Vietnam. Having, in
Sutter's view, helped push relations with Vietnam to a
state of crisis, Deng drew back and tried to exert a
moderating influence against other elements in the
Chinese leadership which were urging prompt punitive
action against Vietnam.

A central event in the rapid deterioration of China-
Vietnam relations was the question of Vietnam's hua qiao
or resident Chinese population. In south Vietnam a new
government policy nationalized the bulk of the commercial
sector of the economy - a policy whose weight fell
heaviest on the hua qiao who had concentrated their
economic activities in this area. In the north a rumor

campaign (whose origins are still unclear) frightened
the hua qiao with the prospect that Beijing's support
for Kampuchea would leave all Chinese in Vietnam open to
charges of being a fifth column in the event full scale
war broke out between Vietnam and Kampuchea. The resulting exodus of boat people and refugees attempting to
flee into China prompted a strong response from the PRC.

Sutter dates China's increased pressure on Vietnam
from late May when the People's Republic of China (PRC)
publicly accused the Vietnamese of persecuting their
Chinese residents. Porter concurs, noting that it "was
not Kampuchea that triggered the crisis in Sino-
Vietnamese relations but the massive exodus of the Hoa
(hua) from Vietnam which began in April 1978." This
exodus was stimulated by a variety of factors. In
south Vietnam, the attempt to bring the private commercial sector under state control fell especially hard on
the Chinese community there. But it was in the north
that the problem was most serious. Charles Benoit
concludes from his interviews with both hua qiao and
ethnic Vietnamese that the motives of those who fled
from the north were "fear of their fate in the
increasingly likely event of war between China and
Vietnam, sentimental attachment to their nationality,
which they feared losing, concern regarding their
ability to maintain what they considered an acceptable
standard of living and in general an increasing perception of the erosion of privileges they had enjoyed as
foreign residents." Benoit concludes that "except in
the border areas, where the Vietnamese had begun to
implement security measures, their exodus was not yet,
as China charged in May 1978, the result of "ostracising,
persecuting, and expelling the Hoa."

On May 26, 1978 Beijing unilaterally escalated the
conflict by announcing a decision to send ships to
Vietnam to "bring home the persecuted Chinese residents"
without prior approval from Vietnam. The polemics
triggered by this action included a Chinese charge that
Vietnam was "adopting anti-China policies at the behest
of the Soviet Union," while "Hanoi responded by directly
identifying Beijing as Cambodia's patron." Sutter
concludes that by "failing to mention Hanoi's offer to
accommodate the Chinese ships, and raising the Soviet
connection, Beijing appeared to have deliberately mapped
out a collision course with Hanoi."

The decisive turning point in the conflict appears
to have accured in the late spring and summer of 1978,
when the local and regional dimensions of the conflict
became fused. Vietnam had, according to Gareth Porter,

decided to encourage the overthrow of Pol Pot by supporting Khmer dissidents in early February 1978. An abortive uprising by Vietnam's prime candidate for the job was crushed in late May, thus ending Hanoi's hopes of engineering an internal coup against Pol Pot. In conjunction with the tensions with China, this led Hanoi's leadership to make a series of new decisions which, in Porter's view, "constituted a historic turning point of the Vietnamese revolution." These included: branding China as the main enemy, initiating planning for the military overthrow of Pol Pot, establishing closer ties with the Soviet Union, and accelerating efforts to improve relations with ASEAN and the United States.

China's allegations linking Indochina events to outside forces soon took on an ominous reality. Hanoi announced in late June 1978 that it had requested to join COMECON, the Soviet dominated economic bloc. The spiral of escalation accelerated. China terminated its aid programs to Vietnam and withdrew its advisors, a move ironically reminiscient of a similar Soviet action directed against China in the early stages of the Sino-Soviet conflict. Border clashes between China and Vietnam intensified. Negotiations resumed in the summer of 1978 but soon became mired in polemics and were terminated in September. Talks between the United States and Vietnam on normalization of relations were also suspended in September by the United States. Hanoi's overtures to ASEAN did not evoke a positive response. On November 3, 1978 the Vietnamese and the Soviet Union signed a friendship treaty. These events raised the conflict to a new plateau. The local conflict between Vietnam and Kampuchea had escalated to a regional conflict in the spring of 1978 and by the fall of that year had begun to involve the superpowers. Vietnam sought Soviet protection against China in preparation for its assault on Kampuchea aimed at removing Pol Pot. The rapidly concluded normalization of relations between China and the United States culminated in the visit of Deng Xiao-ping to Washington and the establishment of formal diplomatic relations in January 1979 checkmated the Vietnamese move by posing the implicit deterrence of the US connection as an impediment to a Soviet challenge to any Chinese reaction to Vietnam's invasion of Kampuchea.

The framework of analysis thus shifts from the perceptions and miscalculations of the frontline antagonists to the broader structure of the international relations which not only intensified the local conflict, but threatened to destabilize an entire region and invite

superpower confrontation. Banning Garrett's essay
examines the dynamics of the triangle of the United
States-China-Soviet Union and the implications of the
triangle for the Third Indochina Conflict. The period
1976-79 was characterized by the deterioration of
US-Soviet relations, the increasing importance of China
in US foreign policy, an intensified Chinese interest in
normalization with the US as a strategic counter-weight
to the Soviet Union, and a continued freeze in Soviet-
Chinese relations. Sutter observes that Chinese foreign
policy was becoming more assertive in the spring of 1978,
and this increased activism provided the framework in
which Beijing's decisions regarding Hanoi, Moscow, and
Washington were being made. From China's vantage, the
trip to Beijing by Presidential Special Advisor
Zbigniew Brzezinski in May 1978, signalling a shift
in US attitude toward the PRC, could not have been more
opportune. Garrett shows that this visit laid the
groundwork for the US to "play the China card," that is,
departing from a position of "even handedness" in
dealing with China and the Soviet Union in favor of
cultivating a quasi-alliance relationship with the PRC.
Brzezinski noted that the US saw its relationship with
China not as a tactical expedient, but as being "derived
from a long term strategic view." The US, he said,
shares "China's resolve to resist the efforts of any
nation which seeks to establish global or regional
hegemony." "Global hegemony was the standard Chinese
code word for the Soviet Union's actions while, as
Garrett points out "regional hegemony" referred to "US
support for Chinese action against Vietnam, viewed by
China as a Soviet surrogate." "For Vietnam" says
Garrett, "there was also a clear message: the US was
now backing China in its dispute with Hanoi as part of
a common Sino-American opposition to "global and
regional hegemony." He cites the fact that China made
its first public denunciation of Vietnam the day after
Brzezkinski's departure from Beijing, as an indication
of China's belief that it had US support for escalating
the conflict with Hanoi.

Seeing its borders with Kampuchea under increasing
military pressure, its negotiations with the Kampuchean
government forestalled and China forging a quasi
alliance with the United States and increasing its
pressure, Vietnam moved in the only remaining direction -
toward the Soviet Union. Following its entry into
Comecon in late June 1978, and the intensification of
border clashes with China, the Vietnamese signed a
treaty of "peace and friendship" on November 3, 1978.
(On the same day, US Secretary of State Cyrus Vance
acknowledged that the Vietnamese had earlier attempted to
break the impasse in relations with the United States by

dropping their previous preconditions for normalization, and announced that the US would no longer oppose any arms sales by third countries to China - another move toward the "China card."

Although this treaty provided only for "consultations" in the event of an attack on Vietnam, the Vietnamese evidently felt that it would be an adequate deterrent against a major Chinese invasion. In Porter's analysis, the threat of Chinese punitive action against Vietnam had lost its effectiveness by the summer of 1978 because Hanoi had become convinced that a military confrontation with China was now inevitable and, by fall 1978, the efforts of Democratic Kampuchea to improve its international image led Vietnam to conclude that the costs of intervention would grow if they delayed their planned military attack.

The SRV invasion of Kampuchea began on December 25, 1978 and had accomplished the seizure of most major cities in Kampuchea by early January 1979. This came at a time when some of the Chinese leaders had become increasingly concerned with the prospect of a Soviet "encirclement" and naturally intensified their alarm about Vietnam's actions. During his January visit to the United States, Deng Xiao-ping called the Vietnamese the "Cubans of the Orient" and suggested that China might have to teach them "some necessary lessons." As Garrett notes, the communique from this visit added the phrase "or domination" to the anti-hegemony clause, broadening the document to include Vietnam's actions in Kampuchea. With US support against Vietnam presumed, implied or explicit, Deng felt that he had checkmated the Vietnamese link with the Soviets by the acquiescence of US to his Indochina policy. China's invasion of Vietnam on February 17, 1979, while clearly motivated by Vietnam's prior invasion of Kampuchea (and indirectly their ties with the Soviet Union), was justified on the more limited grounds of punishing it for "wanton incursions into Chinese territory", and, less plausibly, the necessity of showing that China could "not be pushed around."

Guaging the success of the Chinese "lesson" is a complex matter. In the broadest terms they did succeed in manoeuvering the United States into support of the anti-Soviet position in Indochina, and demonstrated the limitations of Soviet support to Third World Allies. On the debit side, the operation revealed serious military deficiencies in the People's Liberation Army (PLA) while at the same time raising some concern in Southeast Asia about China as a neighbor. Sutter speculates that there was high level disagreement on the wisdom and success of this policy, and that Deng appears to have reversed his earlier hawkish stand on Vietnam. (It may not be accidental that shortly after the PLA withdrawal from Vietnam China initiated a sweeping reappraisal and retrenchment of its ambitious modernization program, possibly due in part to the impact of the invasion on the political debate within Beijing's leadership). Finally, the invasion did not force a Vietnamese withdrawal from Kampuchea or reinforce China's credibility as a patron.

China's invasion of Vietnam was the culmination of a dual process of polarization and escalation that had progressively eliminated diplomatic options and spread the conflict beyond the confines of indochina. A major analytic problem in understanding the dynamics of the conflict is whether or not the polarization was cause or effect of the escalation, or whether the two proceeded in tandem. The initial conflict between Vietnam and Kampuchea can be viewed as an extension of historical hostilities and inter-party grievances. One of the most crucial factors in the escalation of the conflict toward open armed confrontation was the overseas Chinese problem in Vietnam which inflamed sensibilities on both sides in a way that could have been predicted on the basis of historical patterns of behavior. Yet the bilateral issues between each pair of antagonists did not dictate the inevitability of military confrontation. The general consensus of the contributors is that it was the catalytic reaction caused by the superimposition of several larger frameworks (such as the Chinese-Vietnamese rivalry in Indochina and Southeast Asia, and the strategic triangle of the major powers) on the bilateral conflicts.

Does this conclusion, then, vindicate the view of presidential advisor Brezezinski, expressed in early 1978 prior to the subsequent dramatic escalation of the conflict, that the fighting between Vietnam and Kampuchea was "the first case of a proxy war between China and the Soviet Union" and that the "larger international dimension of this conflict speaks for itself"?[6] Certainly Brzezinski was correct, though premature, in pointing to the larger international dimension of the problem. Yet at this stage (January 1978) the Chinese were still attempting to avoid a total rupture with Vietnam, the Soviet Union had not become directly involved, and Washington preferred to sit back and enjoy the spectacle of this falling out between countries formerly allied against the United States. It is certainly wrong to call the Third Indochina conflict a proxy war in the sense of Vietnam and Kampuchea fighting merely to serve the interests of patrons in Moscow and

Beijing and this, indeed, was acknowledged in a subsequent State Department clarification which noted that "the main point is that the conflict involved age-old animosities and a border conflict. Overlying it are great power rivalries."[7] Paradoxically, this recognition of the larger dimensions of the problem was not accompanied by any response to the dangers posed by the potential for escalation of hostilities, nor did it lead to a diplomatic strategy aimed at blunting the polarizing forces at work in the conflict.

The argument that polarization pushed the escalation process could point to the intensified Chinese effort to force Vietnam to choose sides in the Sino-Soviet dispute in 1975, increased Chinese military support to Kampuchea during the escalation of attacks against Vietnam in late 1977 and early 1978, the growing rapprochement between China and the United States on the basis of an increasingly explicit shared anti-Soviet sentiment, the US rejection of Vietnam's attempts to improve relations and Vietnam's turn toward the Soviet Union in the summer and fall of 1978. This scenario clearly points to the PRC as the principal instigator of the polarization process and would ascribe the escalation of the conflict, in part at least, to Beijing's attempt to place the Vietnam-Kampuchea problem in the larger framework of the global strategic triangle. Implicit in this analysis of both Porter and Garnett, in fact, is the possibility that the PRC may not have been entirely displeased with the Vietnamese invasion of Kampuchea, since it could be used to move the US to a position in the strategic triangle more favorable to China and hostile to the Soviet Union. The irony, in this view, is that China engineered a self-fulfilling prophecy: by treating Vietnam as a client of the Soviet Union it increasingly forced Hanoi to become one.

There are, however, some elements of the escalation process that do not fit neatly into this picture. First, there is the problem of subjective perceptions (and misperceptions). Porter suggests that the Vietnamese perceived Kampuchea's military harassments as being instigated by the PRC, and part of a Chinese plot to destabilize Vietnam. Heder points out that within the Kampuchean frame of reference, there were compelling reasons to take an inflexible and even aggressive stance toward the Vietnamese. Second, there is another problem of perception, that of China reacting to Vietnam's policies as they affected the overseas Chinese. It appeared to the Chinese that the Vietnamese actions were caused by a pro-Soviet orientation, despite the fact that the nationalization of commerce that heavily contributed to the hua qiao crisis had also been carried out in China as an integral part of the process of "building socialism," and that the discriminatory treatment of the hua qiao came after relations with China had reached the breaking point. Also, China's unilateral action in response to the crisis of sending boats to evacuate Chinese without prior permission from the Vietnamese was an exacerbating factor which lies more within the traditional framework of Sino-Vietnamese relations than the structure of the strategic triangle.

Then there is the scenario of Vietnam as the main instigator of the conflict and the principal cause of its escalation. It is certain that Vietnam attachment to the concept of proletarian internationalism influenced its behavior in three important ways. First, it inclined the leadership toward a view that the Soviet Union still represented the vanguard of world revolution, and led Vietnam to accept the broad outlines of Moscow's foreign policy. This did not mean, as the Chinese and the U.S. felt, that Vietnam had accepted a client relationship with the Soviet Union, and was acting as a Soviet proxy. Such a view is unsustainable in the light of Vietnam's longstanding struggles for independence, and fails to see the extent to which Vietnam's commitment to "proletarian internationalism" (to which, ironically, their own interests had been sacrificed many times) was the product of deeply held convictions of a generation of leaders formed in the 1920s and 1930s. Second, it embittered the Vietnamese when the Kampucheans refused to coordinate revolutionary strategy and act in the wider interests of revolution in Indochina rather than pursuing their own parochial aims. Third, proletarian internationalism justified the Vietnamese view that they had a rightful role to play in defending the interests of world revolution in Indochina, thus legitimizing their intervention in Kampuchea (and Laos). The Vietnamese concept of a "special relationship" came from the idea that all the states in Indochina had shared a common enemy, and Vietnam's leading role in that relationship was viewed as natural in terms of its greater capacity to contribute to the struggle against that common enemy. Nonetheless, to the Chinese and the Kampucheans all this added up to a Vietnamese scheme to set up an "Indochinese Federation" of the three states under its dominance.

At the same time, Vietnam at first was not flexible in its dealings with the United States, preferring to adhere to its fixed demands (however justified they might have been) rather than taking the more expedient position of dropping its preconditions in order to normalize relations with the United States when it was possible to do so. When they finally reversed this position, it was

too late. The US had already decided to play the China
card and considered that a move toward Vietnam would
disrupt this ploy. Similarly, Vietnam's diplomacy
toward China and Kampuchea (while less well documented)
was probably not without fault. In each case, however,
it is difficult to argue that the cause of diplomatic
failure lay solely with Vietnam.

The Soviet role is probably the least clear.
Certainly the Russians viewed Vietnam as an important
element in their Asian strategy of encircling China with
a containment belt of "collective security" pacts. And
certainly the Russians must have pressed Vietnam hard
for a quid pro quo for the vital military and economic
assistance they offered. But the Russians (paradoxically
in view of their activism in other areas of the world)
appear to have played a relatively passive role here.
They were the losers in the US "China card" shift in the
strategic triangle. They did not move to counteract the
Chinese invasion of Vietnam. And while they stood
available for a closer relationship with the Vietnamese,
it seems to be more of a push from other sources than
a pull from the Soviet Union that drew the Vietnamese
closer to Moscow.

It may be that it was the least motivated actor
which had the greatest opportunity to prevent the
polarization and the escalation. Had the United States
moved to normalize relations with Vietnam, the Vietnamese
might have had an option that would have stemmed their
movement toward the Soviet Union. It might have
assuaged China's fears and avoided the self fulfilling
prophecy. Had China not hardened its stance toward
Vietnam, it might be that Kampuchea would not have been
viewed as a tool of Beijing by Hanoi, and the local conflict contained at the level of a sporadic border war.
This "for want of a shoe" logic is, for practical
purposes, idle speculation. Too much has happened, the
battles lines are too hardened, to unravel what has taken
place. Yet it is crucial to try to reconstruct the
causes and consequences of the Third Indochina Conflict
both for the lessons it offers, and the possibility that
it might offer some insights into a possible basis for a
solution of the conflicts and stabilization in Southeast
Asia. To this we will return in the concluding chapter.

NOTES

1. Milton Osborne, The French Presence in Cochinchina and Cambodia, (Ithaca: Cornell University Press, 1969), p. 10.

2. For a more detailed treatment of the Vietnamese view of "proletarian internationalism" see Gareth Porter, "Vietnam and the Socialist Camp: Center and Periphery", in William S. Turley ed., Vietnamese Communism in Comparative Perspective, (Boulder: Westview Press, 1980), pp. 225-264.

3. Stephen R. Heder, "Origins of the Conflict", Southeast Asia Chronicle, No. 64, September-October 1978, p. 7.

4. Gareth Porter, "Why Vietnam Invaded Cambodia", The Nation, June 9, 1979, p. 699.

5. Jay Taylor, China and Southeast Asia, (New York, Praeger, 1976), p. 155.

6. Murray Marder, "Soviets Assail Brzezinski on Indochina War Views", The Washington Post, January 10, 1978.

7. Ibid.

2 | The Kampuchean-Vietnamese Conflict

Stephen P. Heder

On 31 December 1977 Radio Phnom Penh denounced as an aggressor what it termed the so-called Socialist Republic of Vietnam (SRV). It alleged the SRV had expansionist designs on Kampuchean territory, and plans to incorporate Kampuchea into a Vietnamese controlled Indochina Federation.[1] The broadcast came at a time when elements of eight divisions of the Vietnam People's Army (VPA), operating with co-ordinated air, armour and artillery support, were engaged in vicious fighting with the Kampuchean Revolutionary Army on Kampuchean territory.[2] This large scale battle was only the culmination of an escalatory spiral of armed clashes that had in fact begun during the time of these two armies' war against the U.S. and its client regimes in Kampuchea and Vietnam. The war had continued sporadically, but with ever-increasing scope and intensity, since the victories of Vietnam and Kampuchea over these enemies in April 1975. In his statement, Khieu Samphan announced a temporary suspension of Kampuchean diplomatic relations with Vietnam and exhorted Kampuchean armed forces to fight a "people's war" to throw back the Vietnamese.

It was obvious from Khieu Samphan's 31 December statement that, although a border conflict was a crucial element of the hostilities, more fundamental issues revolving around the nature of the proper relationship between Kampuchea and Vietnam as communist and Indochinese states and of these two countries' relations with other communist as well as noncommunist states were also deeply involved. Indeed, it seems that, although the border conflict was a critical irritant that eventually sparked an explosion, the more basic issues of the subsequent war were to be found elsewhere: in the contradictions between two very different models of revolution and two very different views of the world scene, and against a background of conflicting interests between two communist movements originating in different historical eras and operating in different socio-economic

21

and political settings. These problems created profound
suspicions that exacerbated the border conflict and
transformed it into a violent struggle for survival,
especially in the case of Kampuchea.

THE BORDER DISPUTE

Let us begin with the spark. There has been much
confusion concerning the background of the territorial
and border disputes between Kampuchea and Vietnam.
Therefore, it must be stressed that neither the
Kampucheans nor the Vietnamese had made major claims on
the land territory of the other. Both sides had agreed
in principle on a land border--that drawn by the French
colonialists--and a map to represent its general outline—
that published by the French administration in 1954. The
dispute was not over vast tracts of land, but over the
precise delineation and demarcation of a land border,
the location of which both sides recognized in principle.[3]
The total area of problematic zones appeared to be less
than 100 square kilometers. The Vietnamese talked of
approximately 70 square kilometers.[4] The Kampucheans of
an unspecified number of zones with areas of "a dozen to
several dozen square kilometres.[5] On the other hand,
there was a true territorial dispute concerning the
maritime border. The two sides did not even agree
whether a maritime border exists, much less on its location. However, this territorial dispute involved only
territorial waters, not offshore islands in the Gulf of
Siam. Both sides agreed on the existence and location
of a line -- the so-called Brevie line drawn by the
French Governor General of Indochina as an administrative
boundary in 1939 -- which determines sovereignty over
the islands, including the most important island, Vietnam's Phu Quoc. The disagreement came over whether
the same line determined the division of territorial
waters.[6]

These differences developed out of a complex historical context, with currents running from the ancient past
up through the late 1960s. This context explains the
intractability of the border conflict. It was the different approaches to the problem as much as the territorial disagreements that brought about armed clashes.

The Kampuchean approach to the border question was
deeply influenced by the memory of precolonial and
colonial era history and by the diplomatic position on
frontiers that was developed and refined by Prince Norodom Sihanouk and his foreign policy advisors from 1953
to 1970. As is well know, the ancient Khmer empire
gradually lost political influence over territory in the
Mekong delta to Vietnamese courts and local elites.
This process of loss of territory to Vietnam was not
halted by the French colonialists. Rather, the French

arbitrarily annexed to what is now Vietnam large tracts of land that, at the time of their conquest of the region, were inhabited primarily by Khmers or similar ethnic groups and were either under the administrative influence of or owed some form of fealty to the Khmer court.[7]

Kampuchea's historical territorial losses to Vietnam -- and widespread popular awareness of them -- contributed to the emergence of a particular diplomatic strategy regarding the frontier issue in the Sihanouk era. At the time of Kampuchea's independence from France, the Sihanouk regime maintained that Kampuchea continued to have a right of sovereignty over what came to be known as the "lost territories" of Kampuchea Krom ("lower Kampuchea", that is, the lower Mekong delta), and officially protested their incorporation into the State of Vietnam.[8] Gradually, however, this position was abandoned in favor of one in which Kampuchea would renounce its claims and agree to the "unjust and illegal" French frontiers, but only on the condition that Vietnam agree to two principles: first, that the frontiers are nonnegotiable, and, second, that Kampuchea, and Kampuchea alone, had the right to ask for minor readjustments in the French delineation of the frontiers or to resolve any ambiguities that might exist in that delineation. The principle of nonnegotiability required Vietnamese recognition of the inviolability, immutability, and intangibility of the borders (that is, recognition that Vietnam could not "touch" the borders by calls for negotiated readjustments in its favor. This policy was consciously and explicitly designed to put a definitive end to what were perceived as Vietnam's "traditional" tactics of making a series of ostensibly reasonable demands, backed up by superior military force and diplomatic leverage, for minor territorial readjustments that nevertheless ultimately cumulated into significant territorial losses. The Kampuchean policy meant that "negotiations" with Vietnam could not involve any mutual give-and-take; rather, they could only involve Vietnamese acceptance or rejection of border definitions presented by the Kampucheans on a take-it-or-leave-it basis. If the Vietnamese rejected the Kampuchean definitions, the Kampucheans would cut off talks in order to maintain the credibility of their insistence upon the principle of the nonnegotiability of the borders. The likelihood that the Vietnamese would reject the Kampuchean definition of the borders was always high, because the Kampucheans also unswervingly maintained that only they had the right to make small, rationalizing changes in the French delineation and to decide, within the general parameters of the line appearing on French administrative maps, the exact meaning of vague or ambiguous French delineations. On the basis of this claimed right, the Kampucheans obviously would make readjustments in their favor, but these would necessarily be minor, because the French delineation in most areas was quite clear. The Kampucheans felt that, in return for these minor Vietnamese concessions of territory, they were making a much greater one by first renouncing Kampuchea's claims on vast "lost territories."

It cannot be emphasized too greatly that by the mid 1960s this posture had become defined, both in Kampuchea's diplomacy and in terms of popular domestic political perceptions, as a minimal position. This theme was repeatedly hammered home in the Sihanouk era press and in the frequent and lengthy speeches of Sihanouk himself. At both the elite and the mass levels, anything less than this posture came to be associated with national betrayal. It became almost universally accepted that if Kampuchea were to abandon its historical claims on Kampuchea Krom, it had to receive something in return in order to demonstrate that the renunciation of these claims did not involve a sellout of national interests. This put very severe domestic constraints on Kampuchea's frontier diplomacy. These constraints operated on the Pol Pot regime despite the many radical and violent changes that had occurred in Kampuchean society. Moreover, in some ways these constraints operated more strongly than in the past because the Pol Pot government claimed to be, and perceived itself as, a regime of national liberation that was more capable of protecting Kampuchea's national interests than its predecessors. Thus, for it, as for its predecessors, the position adopted on the frontier issue was a key barometer, both at the elite and the mass levels, of its fidelity to Kampuchean nationalism and therefore is related to its nationalist legitimacy.

The Vietnamese approached the frontier issue very differently. The territorial gains that Vietnam made at the expense of Kampuchea in precolonial and colonial times naturally have not been made into a major domestic political issue by any modern regime. The frontier issue has therefore had a much lower salience in Vietnam, and a regime's position on this issue has certainly not become such a crucial indicator of the validity of its nationalist credentials as in Kampuchea.

As a result, Vietnamese regimes operated with fewer domestic constraints when negotiating frontier issues: for this reason, in turn, the Vietnamese negotiating position was less completely solidified and apparently more flexible. This apparent flexibility is related to a very different set of feelings about the border when it does become salient as an issue. For the Vietnamese, the border was a product of French colonialism, an historical monstrosity that was imposed by the French upon both Vietnam and Kampuchea, with equally disastrous effects upon both. The border issue was not viewed

as a crime against Kampuchea, but as a crime against both
Vietnam and Kampuchea. Its criminality, moreover, is
not seen in its general favoritism for Vietnam, but in its
many specific irrationalities. In other words, when the
Vietnamese look at the frontier, they see a collection
of colonial quirks, some of which greatly inconvenience
Vietnam, others of which greatly inconvenience Kampuchea.
The Vietnamese negotiating stance, therefore, always
stressed the possibility for mutual benefit through
territorial exchanges that would eliminate these quirks.[9]

The incompatibility of the Kampuchean and
Vietnamese approaches to the border question had
always bedeviled relations between the two countries.
The Kampucheans approached the question as the sole
aggrieved party, and expect a certain recompense for their
historical losses and their willingness to cease contest-
ing them. They offered not negotiations in the regular
sense, but unilateral resolutions of outstanding problems
that provide such recompense in a minor way. They
demanded that the Vietnamese either accept or reject their
proposals and not attempt to tinker with them. The
Vietnamese, by contrast, expected a mutual bargaining
process in which the borderline was to be readjusted and
rationalized to the benefit of both sides, without either
side making unilateral gains.

These problems complicated negotiations between the
Sihanouk regime and the Vietnamese communists, represented by the National Liberation Front (NLF) in the
mid 1960s. Sihanouk had found the Saigon regime completely intransigent on the frontier issue, but the Vietnamese
communists, who were cultivating Sihanouk diplomatically
in order to encourage his anti-U.S. stand (and thus
to protect the flank of their struggle to liberate
southern Vietnam) were more amenable to his negotiating
stance. Nevertheless, when Sihanouk's negotiators, in
their talks with the NLF, made demands for readjustments
of the land frontier based on ambiguities in the French
line, the Vietnamese rejected these demands as arbitrary
and unacceptable. Similarly, when Sihanouk's negotiators
went somewhat beyond the minimal position publicly
defined by Sihanouk and asserted Kampuchean sovereignty
over several offshore islands in the Gulf of Siam to
the south (that is, on the "Vietnamese" side of the
Brevie line) the Vietnamese strenuously rejected these
claims. [10]

Faced with this situation. Sihanouk made it increasingly clear that continued Kampuchean diplomatic support
for Vietnam against the U.S. and, after 1965, acquiescence to a Vietnamese troop presence on neutral Kampuchean
territory were dependent upon a Vietnamese acceptance of
some kind of border settlement. In early May 1967, he
offered a solution. He demanded that the Vietnamese make
a unilateral declaration of respect for an recognition of

Kampuchea's "existing borders." Placed in a diplomatic
bind, the Vietnamese responded with the required statements: one from the NLF in late May, one from the Democratic Republic of Vietnam (DRV) endorsing the NLF statement in early June.

Sihanouk portrayed these statements as a great
diplomatic victory for Kampuchea. He interpreted them
as Vietnamese acceptance of the fundamental principles
upon which the Kampucheans had always based their border
stand. He declared that, by these statements, the
Vietnamese had renounced any right to future renegotia-
tion of the borderline and thus that the border's
nonnegotiability had been established He also argued
that, because the Vietnamese had made a unilateral
statement recognizing Kampuchea's "existing borders" --
whereas Kampuchea had made no parallel statement --
Kampuchea, as the recipient of recognition, had been
granted the unique right to interpret any ambiguities
in the "existing borders." In other words, Kampuchea
had been granted the unique right to interpret any
ambiguities in the French line and to make appropriate
readjustments. In practice, this meant that Sihanouk
interpreted "existing borders" to mean the borders as
his negotiators had defined them in previous talks with
the Vietnamese, including the readjustments that the
Kampucheans had proposed and the Vietnamese had
rejected. Sihanouk therefore published official maps
of Kampuchea with the land frontiers "corrected" in
Kampuchea's favor. On the other hand, although the
Vietnamese statements could clearly be interpreted as
recognition of the Brevie line -- the only "existing"
maritime frontier despite its originally "administrative"
character -- Sihanouk instructed his cartographers
to design their maps in such a way as to leave off
all but those offshore islands most proximate to the
coast and also to omit the Brevie line. Sihanouk
apparently hoped to renew Kampuchea's historical claims
on several small and more distant islands south of the
Brevie line at some future point, and wanted to leave
the maritime situation ambiguous in order not to rule out
such claims." The Vietnamese, for their part, evidently
originally saw their statements as implying recognition
of the Brevie line as a complete maritime frontier,
but did not immediately realize the full significance
of this position. Thus a high Vietnamese official would
later comment that "at the time we agreed to the Brevie
line, we were not aware of the problems of the territorial water, continental shelf, etc. -- these new
phenomena".[12]

It is doubtful whether the Vietnamese were ever
happy with Sihanouk's version of the significance of
their 1967 statements. They did not, however, publicly
contradict him, or evidently even make private protests,

because they recognized that such actions might
seriously undermine, or possibly destroy, his
willingness to support and facilitate their struggle
against the U.S. On the contrary, their public
propaganda gave every implication that the NLF and
the DRV fully supported Sihanouk's position on the
frontier issue, and that they had no disagreements with
his interpretation of their statements or with the on-
the-map conclusions he had drawn from them.

This was the diplomatic legacy that faced the
victorious revolutionary regimes in April 1975. There
was also a legacy of small scale armed hostility.
During the liberation wars, there had been clashes
between the armed forces of the two sides. These
probably began as early as late 1971, when the Kampucheans decided that it was necessary to assert the political supremacy of their own administrative and military
organizations in areas on Kampuchean territory where
Vietnamese armed forces and political cadres had organized local anti-Lon Nol governments and militias and
maintained strong political influence.[13] This decision
came at a time when the Lon Nol regime was having
considerable success in mobilizing opposition to the
Kampuchean communists on the basis of their apparent
dependence upon and subservience to Vietnamese forces.
In 1972, the clashes became more frequent, as the
Kampucheans attempted to demonstrate Kampuchean
sovereignty over Vietnamese base camps and along
Vietnamese military supply lines on the Kampuchean side
of the frontier by strictly enforcing the requirement
that Vietnamese forces seek permission from local
Kampuchean authorities before setting up encampments
or transiting Kampuchean territory.[14] In 1973, following
a post-Paris Accords reduction in the quantity of
military supplies that the Kampucheans had been
receiving from the Vietnamese in exchange for Kampuchean
rice and other foodstuffs,[15] there were clashes involving
these exchanges.[16]

The two legacies combined to produce a number of
clashes in the immediate aftermath of April 1975. There
were clashes on land, in the sea, and on offshore
islands. The land clashes were apparently very small
scale. They seem to have been skirmishes involving
the local border security forces of the two sides. The
causes of these skirmishes appear to have been threefold.
First, although the Vietnamese had withdrawn or were
withdrawing from most of their wartime camps and logistics
lines on Kampuchean territory, this withdrawal does not
seem to have been either immediate or complete, especially
in the so-called Parrot's Beak province of Svoy Rieng
and in the far northeastern provinces of Ratanakiri and
Mondulkiri.[17] Therefore, there was a continuation of
the wartime problems concerning relations between local

Kampuchean authorities and Vietnamese forces. Second, it seems that, for the most part, Vietnamese forces did not evacuate from zones that the Kampucheans considered theirs as a result of the Vietnamese statements of 1967.[18] This seems to have resulted in small firefights when Kampuchean military units attempted to enter zones controlled by Vietnamese forces. It must be emphasized, however, that the Kampucheans apparently made no full scale attempt to forcibly evict the Vietnamese either from the remnants of their base camps and logistic lines or from the zones of Sihanouk era readjustments. Rather, the Kampucheans apparently hoped to achieve Vietnamese withdrawals through negotiations. A third and final precipitator of minor skirmishes was crossings by Kampuchean forces into recognized Vietnamese territory. Some of these crossings were probably inadvertent. Others, however, were probably conscious tests of Vietnamese defenses near certain problematic areas.[19]

There were larger and more immediately significant clashes in the sea and on offshore islands. Factors involving both sides probably contributed to bringing about these clashes. First, Sihanouk had left behind much confusion. The Vietnamese could not be sure that the new Kampuchean communist regime would not do what Sihanouk had apparently planned to do: reassert historical claims on islands south of the Brevie line. Second, in late 1974, the Lon Nol and Thieu regimes had almost engaged in hostilities over an oil exploration rig that was located southwest of the Kampuchean offshore island of Poulo Wai at a point just north of the Brevie line. When this dispute became public, the clandestine propaganda outlets of the Kampuchean revolutionaries had asserted Kampuchean sovereignty not only over Poulo Wai, but also over the spot in the Gulf where the oil rig was located.[20] Vietnamese communist sources, however, took no position.[21] This implied to the Kampucheans that the Vietnamese might be planning to take advantage of the ambiguities of the situation to make claims on territory north of the Brevie line. These two factors heightened both sides' sensitivities and suspicions and resulted in intensive patrolling by their navies.

It was in the context of these suspicions that, at the beginning of May 1975, Kampuchean and Vietnamese patrol vessels exchanged fire off the coast of the island of Phu Quoc,[22] the largest offshore island. Most of Phu Quoc lies north of the Brevie line, but Brevie placed the entire island under Vietnamese administration, and Sihanouk explicitly did not contest Vietnamese sovereignty over it. However, Brevie had decreed that Phu Quoc's administrative territorial waters would extend only three kilometres from the coast. The

Vietnamese had never been happy about this,[23] and their vessels were very possibly patrolling beyond the three kilometres limit when the first clashes occurred,[24] indicates where the Vietnamese felt they had a right to patrol   Kampuchean forces then shelled the patrol boats' bases on Phu Quoc, and may even have attempted a commando raid against them. This was followed by a Kampuchean landing on the island of Tho Chau (also known as Poulo Panjang and, in Kampuchean, as Koh Krachak Ses), which lies south of the Brevie line and about 155 kilometers from the coast, and which had been claimed by Lon Nol and Sihanouk. These forces were in turn attached and pushed into the sea by local Vietnamese units at the end of May. In early June, the leader of the Communist Party of Kampuchea (CPK), Pol Pot, met with a high-ranking Vietnamese communist official, Nguyen Van Linh, and discussed these incidents. He condemned the Kampuchean landings as errors resulting from ignorance of geography on the part of the Kampuchean forces involved, and at least implicitly recognized Vietnamese sovereignty over both Phu Quoc and Tho Chau. Even if the Tho Chau landings had in fact resulted from Kampuchean probing actions and had not been the result of independent acts by ignorant local Kampuchean forces attempting to implement Lon Nol or Sihanouk era claims, the matter might have ended here. A few days after Pol Pot's assurances, however, Vietnamese naval units launched attacks on Kampuchean naval bases on Poulo Wai island, which lies north of the Brevie line and about 110 kilometres from the coast.[25] Then, on 10 June, the evening before Pol Pot and two other top CPK leaders, Nuon Chea and Ieng Sary, were scheduled to leave Phnom Penh for talks in Hanoi, reinforced Vietnamese units, with heavy air support, launched new attacks on Poulo Wai.[26] When the Kampuchean leaders arrived in Hanoi on 11 June[27] the Vietnamese had fully occupied the island. Naturally, under these circumstances, border problems were one of the major topics of discussion. However, the Kampucheans did not allow the Vietnamese occupation of Poulo Wai to ruin the talks. Rather, they downplayed the seriousness of the problem and instead proposed a friendship treaty with Vietnam. Discussion of the proposed treaty, however, apparently remained in the preliminary stage.[28]

After this summit meeting, the land skirmishes and the sea and island battles virtually ceased. Poulo Wai remained in Vietnamese hands until August when, following a visit to Phonom Penh by Vietnamese Communist Party leader Le Duan[29] the island was returned to Kampuchean control in an apparent Vietnamese goodwill gesture.[30] Thereafter, the border question was a relatively dormant issue until April 1976. Neither side took any significant military initiatives, and the Kampuchean side made the only diplomatic moves by protesting Vietnamese presence along old logistics lines in the rugged Northeast of Kampuchea. The Vietnamese rejected the protests.[31] Then, in April 1976, the two sides agreed to hold another high-level meeting in June 1976 to discuss outstanding problems. To prepare for this meeting, a technical conference was scheduled and held in Phnom Penh in May.

During the conference, the two sides reiterated the Sihanouk era agreement in principle on the validity of the French-drawn land boundary and of French colonial administrative maps.[32] The Vietnamese side, however, either made no mention of their 1967 statements or took the position that they were legally meaningless and had been misinterpreted by Sihanouk. They thus negated the recompensatory elements of Sihanouk's minimal border package and, either implicitly or explicitly, proposed mutual readjustments instead. The Kampuchean side, on the other hand, apparently steadfastly attempted to maintain the integrity of Sihanouk's package; they continued to renounce Kampuchea's historical claims to "lost territories" and took the position that Sihanouk's recompensatory readjustments should not be challenged either by calls for renegotiations or by what the Kampucheans saw as de facto Vietnamese agression against Kampuchea in the form of military (or civilian) occupation of zones shown on Sihanouk's late 1960s maps as within Kampuchean territory.

Moreover, they apparently demanded that Vietnamese forces both stay permanently away from old base areas and communications routes and withdraw from Sihanouk's recompensatory zones in order to improve the climate for subsequent talks. The Vietnamese position was apparently that any withdrawals should take place only after the talks had resolved outstanding disputes and mutually beneficial territorial exchanges had been agreed to. In other words, the Vietnamese held that withdrawals should be the result of, and not the prelude to, negotiations. The Kampucheans demanded preliminary withdrawals first because they felt that the Vietnamese had no right to be in these zones, which they felt the Vietnamese had recognized as Kampuchean since the Sihanouk era, and second because they felt that even if there were legitimate differences between the two sides, it was improper for the Vietnamese to take advantage of the opportunities provided by their period of wartime refuge and by their superior military strength to establish a presence -- and thus a strong argument for de facto sovereignty -- in disputed zones.

Discussion of the maritime frontier revealed even more problems.[33] The Kampuchean side made what it certainly felt was a major concession. It renounced the claims Sihanouk had implicitly attempted to maintain on islands south of the Brevie line. Instead, it maintained

that the Brevie line should be taken as a border delineating sovereignty over both offshore islands (with
Phu Quoc remaining in Vietnamese hands) and territorial
waters. This position could not only be justified by
reference to the Vietnamese statements of 1967 (and
was evidently in line with the Vietnamese understanding
of the import of those statements at the time), it
also finally brought the Kampuchean position on the
maritime border in line with Sihanouk's minimal policy
on the land frontiers. The Vietnamese, however,
rejected the Kampuchean position and instead proposed
that the Brevie line be readjusted in Vietnam's favor
at least in order to allow Vietnamese vessels easier
access to Phu Quoc and in order to expand Phu
Quoc's territorial waters further than three kilometres.
Instead of receiving recompense for their renunciation
of claims on islands south of the Brevie line and on
Phu Quoc, the Kampucheans were asked to give up
territorial waters north of it.

The Kampucheans saw the Vietnamese proposals at the
technical conference as an attempt to undermine the
principle of the nonnegotiability of the borders,
to deny the existence of the recompensatory elements
that Sihanouk had linked to his renunciation of
historical claims on Kampuchean Krom, to take advantage
of the Kampuchean renunciation of historical claims
on islands south of the Brevie line and on Phu
Quoc by annexing territorial waters north of it,
and to rely on their military presence in a number
of Kampuchean zones in order to negotiate, in a big
power way, from a position of strength. Acceptance
of the Vietnamese proposals would have made the Kampuchean
regime vulnerable to charges of lack of fidelity to
and inability to protect Kampuchea's national interests.
Therefore, it is not surprising that the Kampuchean
negotiating team announced a suspension of the talks.
This suspension was designed to demonstrate to the
Vietnamese the unacceptability of their negotiating
stance, as well as of their concrete proposals, and
to reaffirm the principles of nonnegotiability of the
borders, unique Kampuchean rights to recompensatory
readjustments, and rejection of any talks so long as
the Vietnamese continued to occupy Kampuchean territory
or disputed zones.

The Kampuchean suspension of the technical talks
resulted in a cancellation of high level discussions
scheduled for June. In the meantime, liaison committees
along the frontier handled border incidents, which
were apparently infrequent and small scale affairs.[34]
As the months passed, however, both sides became more
and more impatient with the deadlock: the Kampucheans
realized that the suspension of the talks had not
persuaded the Vietnamese to revise their negotiating

stance, while the Vietnamese realized that the Kampucheans were not going to reconsider and reopen the dialogue. Growing impatience and continuous friction over unresolved frontier problems probably resulted in mounting tension and more frequent and violent incidents along the border, especially in and near zones that the Kampucheans considered illegally occupied by the Vietnamese. In early 1977, the Kampucheans increased their pressure on these zones. This pressure probably involved the dispatch of Kampuchean patrols into the zones, where they were supposed to demonstrate a Kampuchean presence. They were probably not ordered to initiate hostilities, but were given permission to fire if fired upon by "Vietnamese troops or village militias.[35] From the Kampuchean point of view, this intensified patrolling was an attempt to show the Vietnamese that they could not continue to commit what the Kampucheans considered de facto aggression without facing a Kampuchean challenge. The Kampucheans probably saw themselves attempting to break the deadlock by suggesting that they were willing to make it costly, rather than territorially profitable, for the Vietnamese to rely upon their superior military strength to maintain the status quo. For the Vietnamese, however, the Kampucheans, who had cut off negotiations, were now increasing their intransigence with intensified patrolling. The Vietnamese therefore did not soften their negotiating position, and instead of withdrawing, they reinforced their military position along the frontier.[36]

The escalatory spiral in the military sphere gained momentum in April and May 1977. The Kampucheans, who previously had only wanted to suggest that they could make things costly for the Vietnamese and who had probably sent in patrols with orders to fire only in self-defense, now began to initiate military activities. During this period, Kampuchean forces in some localities resorted to artillery barrages and occasional small scale forays into what the Kampucheans regarded as Vietnamese territory. As before, these Kampuchean military initiatives were part of a negotiation strategy.[37] The Kampucheans were not making any new territorial claims nor were they trying to permanently occupy any of the targets of their attacks. Rather, they still believed themselves to be responding in kind to what they saw as longstanding de facto Vietnamese aggression against Kampuchean territory. Now they wanted to demonstrate that the Kampucheans had a capability to strike at Vietnamese territory. They were trying to show the Vietnamese that both sides had the option of reliance upon military force and therefore the Vietnamese stood to gain if they would negotiate on modified terms.

However, the Vietnamese communists responded to the

April and May Kampuchean shellings and raids by sending thousands of reinforcements to the border zone to launch counterattacks into Kampuchean territory.[38] The diplomatic denouement came in June. On 7 June 1977, the Vietnamese sent the Kampucheans a letter, proposing high level talks, but making no change in Vietnam's negotiating stance and accusing the Kampuchean raiders of attacks on civilians.[39] On 18 June 1977, the Kampucheans responded with a letter of their own, with a proposal for a mutual disengagement of military forces, to be achieved through a pullback of both sides to a distance of 0.5 to 1.0 kilometers, thus creating a 1-2 kilometer demilitarized zone. This proposal was apparently intended not only to achieve a partial Vietnamese withdrawal from problematic zones, but also to allay Vietnamese fears that Kampuchea would then simply move into these zones by promising a simultaneous Kampuchean withdrawal. The mutual withdrawal proposal was coupled with a Kampuchean request for a combination cooling off and good faith period to precede the resumption of talks.[40] The Vietnamese evidently ignored the Kampuchean disengagement proposal, however, and therefore the Kampucheans felt justified in ignoring the Vietnamese proposal for a high level meeting. The diplomatic initiatives of both sides thus came to naught, and both sides apparently began preparing for a military confrontation. In mid-July, the Kampuchean administration of the country's Eastern Region, which is responsible for much of the frontier with Vietnam, decided that if the Vietnamese committed any new aggressions against Kampuchean territory, Kampuchean forces would respond with co-ordinated forays across the frontier into Vietnam. Kampuchean military units were not ordered to launch any unprovoked attacks, but their commanders were instructed to prepare their units for co-ordinated counterraids into Vietnamese territory if they were attacked on what the Kampucheans considered Kampuchean territory.[41] The purpose of these counterraids was to show the Vietnamese that military initiative and the power of intimidation did not rest in Vietnamese hands alone.

The Vietnamese, meanwhile, had apparently decided that earlier Kampuchean military actions and continued refusal to negotiate on what the Vietnamese felt were reasonable terms had gone unpublished for too long, and that it was time to unleash some strong retaliatory operations. Thus, in late July and early August, the Vietnamese took a series of battlefield initiatives against the Kampuchean armed forces, and struck into Kampuchean territory.[42] These initiatives coincided with a visit by Vietnam's top military strategist, General Vo Nguyen Giap, to the frontier areas. This was clearly an attempt to warn the Kampucheans that the

Vietnamese were serious about major military action.[43]
In early September, the Vietnamese indeed launched new
raids into Kampuchea.[44]

This series of Vietnamese moves triggered implementation of the Kampuchean decision to launch co-ordinated
border raids in response to new Vietnamese aggression
In late September 1977, Kampuchean forces carried out
a number of simultaneous quick raids into Vietnamese
territory, penetrating as far as seven kilometres.[45]

The Vietnamese decided to launch a massive invasion
of Kampuchea's eastern frontier zones. They marshalled
an estimated 30,000 to 60,000 troops with complete
air, armor and artillery support to carry out this
invasion.[46] They apparently hoped that such a massive
and well-supported invasion force would be capable
of destroying the Kampuchean Revolutionary Army's
effective forces in the frontier areas. They also
evidently hoped that their large scale attacks would
be so devastating that they would smash the Kampuchean
political administration along the border, and that in
many places it would be possible for the Vietnamese to
begin replacing it with a new administration that would
be willing and able -- with Vietnamese protection and
support -- to resist the reestablishment of political
elements loyal to Phnom Penh.[47] The Vietnamese
probably calculated that under these circumstances
the Kampucheans would see themselves as having only
two choices: either to back down and negotiate on
Vietnamese terms or to face the destruction of a major
part of their army and the disintegration and replacement
of their frontier zone administration with a new and
hostile one. If the Kampucheans refused to negotiate,
they would be so weakened as to no longer pose a threat
to Vietnamese forces and settlements along the frontier.

The Vietnamese invasion, which reportedly began on
16 December[48] raised the level of the border fighting from
skirmishes and small unit raids to divisional level war
engaging the most important main force units of both
sides. The Vietnamese initially advanced rapidly and
with relative ease as Kampuchean border forces and backup
divisions either were overrun or withdrew. However,
the Kampucheans did not accept defeat but decided to
fight back and not give an inch diplomatically. They
began reorganizing their forces, carrying out guerrilla
counter-attacks and publicly condemned Vietnam and
suspended diplomatic relations.

THE POLITICAL DISPUTE

The border conflict between Kampuchea and Vietnam
thus had its own logic. Yet the border conflict alone
probably would not have had the same profound consequences
had there not existed other fundamental conflicts that

poisoned the diplomatic atmosphere. The essence of these
conflicts must be extracted from two propaganda lines:
the Kampuchean allegation that Vietnam would like to
establish an "Indochina Federation" under Vietnamese
domination and the Vietnamese claim that Vietnam
merely desires a "special relationship" between Kampuchea
and Vietnam. It seems that the Kampuchean allegation is
an exaggeration, at least if it is taken literally.
The Vietnamese claim, however, is euphemistic and
rationalizes Vietnamese national interests in the
existence of a regime in Phnom Penh that has no important
disagreements with the Vietnamese communists concerning
the meaning of socialism in a domestic context or the
interpretation of the international situation. These
conflicts do exist, however, and multiplied because the
two sides also differ fundamentally over how much they
should co-operate and co-ordinate in domestic and
foreign policy matters.

The roots of Kampuchean and Vietnamese disagreements
over the meaning of socialism and the interpretation
of the international situation are deep. The most
important of them stem from the contrasting socio-
economic and political settings that faced Kampuchean
and Vietnamese communists in making their revolutions
and from differences in the historical eras during which
these two groups entered the more and more nationally
divided ranks of a disintegrating world communist
movement.

The formative period of the Vietnamese revolution
involved classically colonial circumstances in which
the main task of the revolution was not the destruction
of "feudal" society and "feudal" traditions, but the
formation of an antiforeign united front to win
national independence and, later, reunification. By
contrast, the formative period of the Kampuchean
revolution involved an attenuated "neocolonial"
setting in which the main task of the revolution was
the destruction of a colonially ossified and neocolonially
modernized "feudal-bureaucratic," but indigenous and
nationalist regime. In Vietnam, the communist movement,
while retaining its commitment to a socialist transformation of Vietnam, became the essentially unrivalled
representative of Vietnamese nationalism during the
colonial period, when its main opponent was the French
colonial administration. Early in the colonial period,
the French had undermined or displaced many elements of
the old Vietnamese "feudal" society by reducing the royal
court to insignificance and by imposing an extensive
commercialization of agriculture. This disestablished
"feudalism" without consolidating a modern capitalist
regime. In this setting, the Vietnamese communists
tended to deemphasize class conflict and class struggle
and to emphasize continuity with premodern traditions

of gentry-led peasant opposition to foreign rule. These
emphases continued even after 1954 during the stage of
building socialism in the liberated north, because this
socialist construction had to be carried out without pan-
icking the elements of the southern population who were
sympathetic to the nationalist goals of expulsion of the
U.S., destruction of the political regimes so obviously
dependent on U.S. power, and national reunification,
but who were hostile to socialism. Socialism had to be
built cautiously and with a minimum of provocative
class conflict in order to preserve the national
liberation united front in the south. These circumstances injected relatively high degrees of traditional-
ism and class caution into the praxis and the theory of
Vietnamese revolution. In praxis, the Vietnamese prefer
to rely upon relatively mild administrative measures
rather than upon relatively violent mass movements
in the resolution of social contradictions. In theory,
they believe that the forces of production (that is,
science, technology, and large scale capital investment), and not the relations of production (that is,
class struggle and class conflict) should be emphasized
in the postliberation stage of socialist construction.
Moreover, Vietnamese communism, while strongly nationalist,
never had to face anything more formidable than the Bao
Dai, Diem, and Thieu regimes. It thus did not have to
go especially far in order to successfully demonstrate
its nationalist credentials.

The setting in which the CPK made revolution was
quite different. This Party was founded in 1960 and
launched its armed struggle to make revolution in 1968,
that is, in neither the colonial era nor the Lon Nol
years, but during the Sihanouk period. The Party's and
the revolution's opponent during its formative period
was a highly nationalistic and indigenously rooted
autocracy, based on a monarchy that had been symbolically
strengthened by the French and on a rural economy that
had been only minimally developed or commercialized.
Sihanouk, and not a communist-led independence movement,
had credibly claimed the mantle of national liberator.
He was eventually supported not by the U.S., but with
diplomatic, economic and military aid from the DRV,
the USSR, the PRC and Third World neutralists.
Internally, Sihanouk's "Buddish Socialist" regime was
based on an amalgamation of strong "feudal" remnants and
a modernized state bureaucracy. This regime was
viciously repressive and failed to solve any of the major
socio-economic problems in the countryside, but it
co-opted many nationalist and antiimperialist themes and,
with its vaguely anticapitalist ideology, a good number
of social reform themes as well. In this setting,
the Kampuchean communists could not draw upon mildly
nationalist and reformist themes and policies in their

attempts to build up a popular base for revolution. They
tended to emphasize the strongly classist and anti-
traditional elements of a struggle aimed against deeply
rooted class enemies with nationalist legitimacy.
Moreover, the Party's nationalist line had to outdo
that of the Sihanouk regime if it were to avoid being
tarred as antinational by Sihanouk, who already kept
Kampuchea a relatively closed country and preached
self-reliance. Thus, radical class and nationalist
elements were deeply implicated in the Kampuchean communist movement in the period before 1970, when the great
bulk of the CPK's present higher level cadre was formed.
These cadres were the nucleus around which the Party and
a full-sized Revolutionary Army were constructed after
the March 1970 Lon Nol coup. Although this coup
catapulted Sihanouk and many members of his personal
and political entourages into a temporary united front
with the communist, the CPK's classist and extraordinarily strong nationalist tendencies were not
undermined or diluted by this front. On the contrary,
the Party further radicalized its class and nationalist
standpoints in order to strengthen its own social base
and prevent a capture of the leadership of the anti-U.S.,
anti-Lon Nol movement by Sihanouk and Sihanoukism.
    This socio-economic and political setting helps to
explain the more radical social and nationalist tendencies
in the postliberation praxis and theory of the Kampuchean
revolution. In praxis, class radicalism is manifested
in a reliance upon disruptive and violent mass-based
class struggles in the resolution of social contradictions.
Nationalist radicalism is reflected in an intensification
of Sihanouk's closing off of the country to a point
where almost all foreign elements are excluded. In
theory, the class radicalism is manifested in a belief
in the primacy of mass and class mobilization,
subjective resoluteness and learning through practical
work over technology, theoretical sophistication,
and capital investment in the postliberation stage of
socialist construction. The nationalist radicalism is
reflected in devotion to the principles of independence,
self-reliance, and nonalignment.
    The intellectual-historical factors related to the
evolution and disintegration of the international communist movement reinforce the difference between the two
parties. Today's Vietnam Communist Party (VCP) is
descended from a Party of the 1930s and 1940s, while
today's CPK is a Party of the 1960s and 1970s. The VCP
was born and its main cadres formed in an era when
socialism, existing in only one country, had only one
center, however imperfect. Its leaders experienced the
era of the Comintern which, despite internal disagreements and factional infighting, gave an institutionalized
legitimacy to worldwide co-ordination of communist move-

ments. The Vietnamese communist leadership that was
formed in the 1930s and the 1940s later received aid
from the USSR and PRC, both for its struggle against
the French and the U.S. in the 1950s, 1960s and the
first half of the 1970s and for its socialist construction projects in the north. Although the quality
and the quantity of aid from the USSR and PRC varied
considerably during these years, sometimes dropping to
near zero, the overall flow maintained a credible
picture of international communist solidarity with
Vietnam. During this period, the Vietnamese communists believed that Sino-Soviet differences reflected
a minor split within the world communist movement and
not a definitive splitting up and disintegration of the
movement. Furthermore, after the fall of Khrushchev,
who had virtually ceased giving Soviet aid to Vietnam,
and his replacement by Brezhnev and Kosygin, who greatly
increased aid, the Vietnamese essentially abandoned
polemics against "revisionism" internationally and
rejected any idea of an all out struggle against
"revisionist" tendencies within Vietnam.

As a result of these historical experiences and
their relationship to changing currents in Marxist-
Leninist thought, the Vietnamese have continued to place
relatively strong emphasis on the concept of a socialist
bloc, while deemphasizing the threat of "revisionism"
as a Thermidorean force. The Vietnamese have continued
to believe that Vietnam is a member of a cohesive world
communist community, which forms -- or should form --
a real socialist bloc. The existence of this bloc --
and its confrontation with a capitalist bloc -- requires
a certain amount of cooperation and coordination among
communist states, despite their national divisions.
This cooperation and coordination is a matter of
principle that cannot be denied without excluding oneself
from the socialist bloc (and thus from Marxism-Leninism)
and inviting worldwide capitalist victories. Of course
the Vietnamese recognize disagreements and flaws, but
they do not reject the concept involved. Even war with
Kampuchea and polemics and hostilities with China
have not shaken this conceptual framework. Rather,
Kampuchea and China have simply been defined out of the
picture.

Strong belief in the concept of a socialist bloc has
a paradoxical double effect: first, it juxtaposes
the Vietnamese communists' relatively mild nationalism
(when compared to that of the Kampucheans) with nonexclus-
ivist policies vis-a-vis other communist nations to
produce a Vietnamese communist cosmopolitanism; second,
it rationalizes policies that serve Vietnamese national
interests (for example, the extension of Vietnamese
influence over other countries and communist movements)
as performance of communist internationalist and socialist

bloc duties. At the same time, deemphasis on revisionism as a Thermidorean threat dovetails with the relative
complacency the Vietnamese communists have displayed over
the issue of class struggle in both the liberation
war and socialist construction stages of the Vietnamese
revolution.

The Kampuchean Party, by contrast, was born and
began to grow in the 1960s, with the Sino-Soviet split
had already created two communist centers and demolished
the socialist bloc, and when rightism in the form of
revisionism was seen among most new communists as the
main internal threat to "true" Marxism-Leninism.
Moreover, during its formative period, the CPK experienced a situation in which the socialist bloc seemed to
have very little meaning. At no point in the 1960s did
the CPK receive significant materials or propaganda
support from the Soviet Union, China, or Vietnam. On
the contrary, such support went to the Sihanouk regime.
When the CPK launched an armed struggle against Sihanouk
in early 1968, it found that China disagreed with its
action and that the USSR and Vietnam opposed it. This
lesson in the practical unreliability of the socialist
bloc was soon followed by one in its hypocrisy: the
Soviet invasion of Czechoslovakia. The Kampucheans cannot
have failed to notice that this application of the
doctrine of limited sovereignty was supported by Vietnam.

The lessons that the CPK learned in the 1960s fit
well with its radical nationalist tendencies. A
communist Kampuchea would not be part of the socialist
bloc; it would be an independent revolutionary
Kampuchea. Because Kampuchea could not depend on or
trust in proletarian internationalism, it would have
to be as self-reliant as possible. At the same time,
the CPK would be on guard against agressive nationalism
disguised as internationalism. Finally, the 1960s upsurge
in emphasis on radical and sometimes violent anti-
revisionist action within communist parties, especially
in newly formed parties and especially in Asia, also
fit well with the radical socio-economic tendencies of
the CPK. Just as the socio-economic setting of the
Sihanouk regime pushed the CPK towards radicalism in its
struggle against that regime, the antirevisionist ideological climate in the 1960s suggested to the CPK
that radical policies, including struggle against
revisionists within the Party, were necessary if the
revolution was not to be subverted by bourgeois restor-
ationists.

Thus, contrasting socio-economic and political circumstances and different experiences with international
communism in different eras have combined to make the
Kampuchean and Vietnamese revolutions very different
affairs, with different domestic policies and different
views of the international scene. These differences

render cooperation and coordination between Kampuchea and Vietnam very difficult. Worse yet, the Vietnamese insist upon such cooperation and coordination as a matter of socialist bloc principle, while the Kampucheans reject both the bloc and the principle.

For the Kampucheans such close links are all the more unacceptable in view of repeated Vietnamese communist betrayals of the interests of Kampuchean revolutionary movements.[49] These begin in the 1960s, when the Vietnamese communists, then organized as the Indochinese Communist Party (ICP), failed to recruit any Kampucheans into their party, but instead concentrated on ethnic Vietnamese living in Kampuchea. After 1945, the Vietnamese did recruit Kampucheans, but did not allow them to operate as a truly autonomous Communist Party. The Vietnamese then sacrificed the Kampuchean communist movement at the Geneva Conference in 1954, when the Vietnamese delegation abandoned demands for representation of the Kampuchean communists at the Conference and for the establishment of regroupment zones for their forces within Kampuchea. After Geneva, the Vietnamese advised Kampuchean communists either to take refuge in Hanoi, or, if they decided to stay in Kampuchea, to rely upon unarmed struggle to protect the revolutionary forces there. This strategy resulted in the virtual annihilation of the communist movement in Kampuchea. After the formation of the CPK in 1960, the Vietnamese opposed its increasingly anti-Sihanouk regime position, apparently because the Vietamese found it more in the interests of their struggle in South Vietnam to cultivate the Sihanouk regime and its anti-U.S. foreign policy than to support internal opposition to it. The Lon Nol coup of March 1970 brought about a temporary alliance between the Kampuchean and Vietnamese communists, but there appear to have been significant disagreements about the terms of this alliance. Serious strains then developed in the alliance in 1974, when it became clear that the two parties differed over whether there should be a ceasefire in Indochina. When the Vietnamese signed a separate ceasefire agreement with the U.S. in January 1973, the Kampucheans found themselves battling U.S. power alone. They also suffered, as noted above, from a reduction in Vietnamese logistic support, which seemed designed to pressure the Kampucheans into ceasefire talks.

Given this history, the Kampucheans could hardly be confident that close links with Vietnam in the postwar period would be in their interests. The Vietnamese, however, insisted that such links were in fact a necessity if liberation war victories in both Vietnam and Kampuchea were to be safeguarded against imperialist reaction and if postwar reconstruction was to be successful. Thus, while the existence of a socialist bloc

was to be the basis for close links, the existence of an
Indochina bloc was to be the basis for even closer links
and even greater cooperation and coordination in the form
of a "special relationship." For the Vietnamese, even
if Indochina need not be formally federated, it must
operate as a regional bloc in order to best serve the
interests of the region's peoples and revolutions.[50]
The exact nature and parameters of the "special relationship" desired by the Vietnamese are unclear, but their
relationship with Laos gives some indication of how
intensive and extensive the relationship is supposed to
be. The Kampucheans naturally had even less enthusiasm
for an Indochina bloc and a special relationship than
they had for a socialist bloc.

For the Kampuchean leadership, the Vietnamese
insistence on a special relationship was -- and is --
a double threat. On the one hand, if a special relationship is accepted, it necessarily implies a modification of Kampuchea's domestic and foreign policies to
make them more compatible with those of Vietnam. By
thus undermining Kampuchea's autonomy, a special relationship with Vietnam would undermine the CPK's
nationalist legitimacy. It would expose the CPK to
charges of being a Vietnamese lackey, and this, in turn,
would expose it to the threat of being overthrown
by rivals who could base their opposition to the CPK
on appeals to Kampuchean nationalism. On the other
hand, if a special relationship is rejected, the CPK
makes itself the enemy of Vietnam and invites Vietnamese
action against it. This action can take not only the
form of external diplomatic -- and military -- pressure,
but also of internal subversion. In 1975, the CPK
leadership knew that, despite the long history of discord between the CPK and the Vietnamese communists,
there were elements within the CPK and within the
Kampuchean army and civil administration who had been
trained and influenced by the Vietnamese either under
the auspices of the old ICP, in the period 1954-70 (when
200 Kampuchean communist cadres were in exile in
Hanoi), or in 1970-72, when Vietnamese forces carried
out military training on Kampuchean soil. Some of these
Vietnamese trained personnel could be expected to share
Vietnamese ideas concerning proper Kampuchean domestic
and international policies and to form a potential
nucleus of Vietnamese-backed political oppositon to
the CPK leadership. Indeed, when significant political
strife broke out within the Kampuchean Party and army
in late 1976 and early 1977, the Kampucheans perceived
this as Vietnamese subversion. These internal political
conflicts in Kampuchea followed the Kampuchean suspension
of frontier talks in May 1976 and coincided with
escalatory skirmishes along the border. The Kampucheans,
who believed the Vietnamese had tried to subvert the

CPK since the mid 1960s[51] who probably knew that the
Vietnamese had considered overthrowing the CPK leadersship
in 1970 - 72[52] and who had already weathered one apparent
coup attempt in September 1975 [53] saw the conflict
as Vietnamese-inspired activities intended at least to
put pressure on them to change their negotiating position and at worst to overthrow their regime. The
Vietnamese, whether or not they had in fact instigated
the troubles, saw elements more friendly to them defeated
and purged.[54] These events greatly exacerbated an
already bad diplomatic atmosphere and helped further to
convince each side of the futility of dealing with the
other through negotiations. These feelings undoubtedly contributed to the failure of the two sides'
June 1977 diplomatic initiatives. This failure, in turn,
suggested to the Kampucheans that the Vietnamese might
escalate their involvement in attempts to subvert their
regime and Phnom Penh therefore treated the Vietnamese
with according hostility. This suggested to the
Vietnamese that they faced a situation in which force
might be the only language the CPK leadership could
understand. When the Vietnamese invasion came in December, the Kampucheans saw their suspicions confirmed.
This was obviously no simple border clash but an attempt
to destroy their army and their administration along the
frontier, and thus to undermine their regime. And,
indeed, the Vietnamese, seeing themselves as having
exhausted every other option, probably expected the
Kampucheans to perceive such a threat, because they had
apparently calculated that it would take such a threat
to convince the Kampucheans of the necessity of negotiations on Vietnamese terms. What they did not expect
was that the Kampucheans would neither be frightened
nor easily defeated. Nor did they apparently realize
that the Kampucheans would interpret the Vietnamese
threat to their regime not as an incentive to sue for
peace and negotiate, but instead would increasingly
demand an end to all such threats -- including Vietnam's
insistent calls for a special relationship -- as a
new precondition for negotiations.

THE INTENSIFICATION OF CONFLICT

The Vietnamese responded to Khieu Samphan's 31 December
1977 statement announcing the suspension of relations
with Vietnam by calling for immediate and unconditional
high level talks on the frontier issue.[55] Since the
Vietnamese had not modified their previous negotiating
position, and since a large scale Vietnamese invasion
force was still in place on Kampuchean territory, the
Kampucheans rejected these unconditional talks. On
3 January 1978, the Kampucheans made the obvious
counterproposal: negotiations could begin only after a

Vietnamese withdrawal. They added what had been a part
of their June 1977 proposal: that negotiations should
also await the lapse of a period of time after the
Vietnamese withdrawal, during which the Vietnamese must
demonstrate their good faith and peaceful intentions by
refraining from further military initiatives. The
Kampucheans made it clear that, if the Vietnamese
refused to withdraw, the Kampucheans would rely on
military means to smash the Vietnamese invaders. They
implied that, if they had to force a Vietnamese
withdrawal, the prospects for future negotiations would
be greatly reduced. Heavy fighting would continue --
and the level of mutual hostilities would be further
raised -- as the Kampucheans demonstrated to the
Vietnamese that the Kampucheans still had military
options of their own.[56]

At first, the Kampuchean position was seen abroad --
perhaps in Vietnam -- as one of desperate bravado,
Kampuchean claims of having inflicted serious military
reversals on the Vietnamese by 6 January -- and thus
having "basically defeated" the Vietnamese invasion --
were dismissed as baseless war propaganda.[57] These
dismissals seemed justified a few days after 6 January
when Vietnamese attacks on Kampuchea's far northeaster
provinces were reported.[58] However, by mid January it
was clear that Vietnamese forces, while still on
Kampuchean territory, had fallen back from their most
forward positions after having suffered unexpectedly
heavy losses of men and equipment and, moreover, that
Kampuchean forces had been able to regroup and launch
strong counterattacks on Vietnamese territory. These
attacks were aimed at weak points along the frontier and
apparently caught the Vietnamese by surprise. The
most successful attacks were launched against Vietnamese
territory near the town of Ha Tien, at the point where
the Kampuchean-Vietnamese frontier reaches the Gulf
of Siam.[59] The Kampuchean recovery on the battlefield
was celebrated in a self-confident speech by CPK Secretary and Kampuchean Prime Minister Pol Pot on 17
January 1978, the tenth anniversary of the foundation
of the Revolutionary Army of Kampuchea. Pol Pot
reiterated Kampuchea's preconditions for an end to
hostilities with Vietnam: withdrawal of Vietnamese forces
from Kampuchean territory (presumably including the
problematic zones defined by Sihanouk as Kampuchean) and
cessation of all Vietnamese attempts to undermine or
overthrow the CPK regime, presumably including calls for
the establishment of a special relationship.[60]

It was in this context that the PRC apparently made
an attempt to ameliorate the dispute by encouraging
the Kampucheans to negotiate. The outbreak of war between
Kampuchea and Vietnam had put the Chinese in an extremely
difficult position. Since 1975, the Chinese had been

trying to maintain a precarious diplomatic stance between
Kampuchea and Vietnam. The Chinese wanted simultaneously
to strengthen and consolidate their anti-Soviet alliance
with Kampuchea and to prevent a deterioration of
their relations with Vietnam, which would prevent a
strengthening and consolidation of a potentially anti-
Chinese alliance between the USSR and Vietnam. A
major conflict between Kampuchea and Vietnam would
obviously make it impossible for the Chinese to continue
this balancing act by forcing the Chinese to make a
choice, either in words or in deeds, between Kampuchea
and Vietnam. Heading off such a conflict had therefore
been a goal of Chinese policy in Southeast Asia since
April 1975.[61] Yet Chinese attempts came to naught.
Rather, the conflict eventually drew the Chinese in
deeper and deeper and finally forced them to make a
choice they would have preferred not to make.

   The development of Kampuchean-Chinese relations after
1975 has to be understood in the context of what had
happened in previous years. In the 1960s, the Chinese,
including the Cultural Revolutionaries, had disagreed
with the tactics the CPK adopted in its intensifying
struggle against the Sihanouk regime. After the Lon
Nol coup, the CPK saw the Chinese moving rapidly towards rapprochement with the U.S., and, in 1972-73,
the Chinese had recommended that the CPK seek a negotiated ceasefire and a temporary political settlement
with Lon Nol rather than fight on. However, the
Chinese (unlike the Soviets) continued to give the
Kampucheans full diplomatic support, and (unlike the
Vietnamese) stuck to their military aid commitments.[62]
Therefore, although the bases for a postwar relationship
were shaky, they were better than those for relationships
with the USSR or Vietnam. After April 1975, the
Chinese attempted to cement the relationship by
agreeing to provide Kampuchea with U S $200 million worth
of aid per annum over a five to six year period.[63] (By
comparison, the Chinese provided Vietnam with more than
US $300 million per annum in the immediate postwar
period.[64] Although the absolute amount was greater, the
per capita amount was considerably lower.)

   In August 1975, the Kampucheans signed a joint
communique with China which condemned "hegemony"
several times.[65] Thereafter, however, they refrained
from public polemics against either the USSR or
hegemonism, and generally adopted a foreign policy
position that avoided the seamier aspects of China's
indiscriminately anti-Soviet world diplomatic strategy.
In early 1976, even before the death of Mao and the fall
of the Cultural Revolutionaries in China, the Kampucheans
privately expressed reservations about their relations
with China.[66] After the emergence of Hua Kuo-feng and

the reemergence of Teng Hsiao-ping, more strains
appeared, as the new Chinese leadership repudiated the
radical path of socialist construction that the
Kampucheans favored. Meanwhile, in early 1977, the
Chinese made it clear that they would prefer that the
Kampucheans agree to talks with Vietnam on frontier
problems, rather than try to pressure them into a
modification of their negotiating position.[67] Even
in the midst of a gala welcome for Pol Pot on the occasion
of his first public visit to China, in late September and
early October 1977, there were signs of a discord. In
his implicit but obvious references to border conflicts
with Vietnam, Pol Pot seemed not to be preaching to the
converted, but to be attempting to convince the Chinese
of the justice of Kampuchea's case.[68] The Kampucheans
later indicated that they had tried to convince Peking
that Vietnam was an aggressor at this time, but China
was "unwilling to listen."[69] After Pol Pot's visit,
but almost certainly without Kampuchea's approval, the
Chinese approached the Vietnamese with an offer to
mediate the border conflict. (According to a source in
contact with Vietnamese and Chinese officials in August
1978, the Vietnamese reportedly turned the offer down
because it came with conditions they found unacceptable).

The Chinese attempted to maintain their contradictory
policy after the December 1977 Vietnamese invasion. At
first, when Vietnamese forces were still advancing,
China's propaganda apparatus displayed obvious favoritism
towards Kampuchea. Then, as the Kampucheans recovered
on the battlefield and, following a Vietnamese protest
against the bias, the Chinese coverage of the charges and
countercharges became decidedly more evenhanded.[70] On
10 January, the Chinese signed a new economic aid agreement with Vietnam in an attempt to demonstrate that the
fighting would not necessarily prejudice Chinese support
for the postwar reconstruction of Vietnam.[71]

Having thus moved to a relatively neutral position,
the Chinese Government dispatched Teng Ying-ch'ao, the
widow of Chou En-lai, to Phnom Penh on 18 January.
Teng Ying-ch'oa's emergency visit coincided with a
trip to Peking by Vietnamese border negotiations expert
Pham Hien. It seems that, during her visit, Teng
probed the Kampucheans' diplomatic position and suggested
they might now consider becoming more flexible in their
preconditions for negotiations, but found the Kampucheans
unwilling to modify their negotiation stance.[72] At some
point during her talks with Kampuchean leaders on 19
January, Teng, evidently made some indiscreet remarks
about Chinese aid to Kampuchea and implied that
Kampuchea should weigh the potentially negative effects
of an unchanged diplomatic position on the provision of
Chinese aid. The Kampucheans apparently saw the Chinese
attempting to do what the Vietnamese had done in 1973:

use military aid leverage to prod them towards negotiations. This perception provoked an extraordinary
Kampuchean radio broadcast on the morning of 20 January.
This broadcast implicitly warned the Chinese that
Kampuchea had not fought the U.S. and was not fighting
the Vietnamese in order to become a Chinese puppet. It
further explained that Kampuchea's

> friend-making criterion is not based on whether this
> or that friend can provide material aid; it is
> based on the principles of equality, mutual respect
> and mutual benefit, on sentiments of solidarity in
> accordance with the principle of respecting the
> right of each country, be it large or small, to
> manage its own destiny, and in accordance with the
> principle of protecting justice against injustice,
> interference and agression.[73]

Because the Kampucheans had refused to modify their
stance and had rejected the probes of Teng Yin-ch'ao,
the Chinese apparently felt they had little choice but
to implement an essentially bankrupt policy: give
preferential, including military, aid to Kampuchea but
continue to cultivate Vietnam, both by giving economic
aid and by avoiding public condemnation of it or repetition of Kampuchean charges against it.

In late January, the Kampucheans increased the
intensity of their counteroffensive, especially in the
Ha Tien area. The Kampuchean counteroffensive demonstrated that the Vietnamese invasion had not been a
military success; it showed that the Vietnamese
had not destroyed Kampuchean military effectiveness in
the frontier areas.[74] Meanwhile, there was of course
no sign of any movement of the Kampuchean negotiating
stance in a direction acceptable to the Vietnamese, with
or without Chinese mediation. Faced with a renewed
military and diplomatic impasse, the Vietnamese turned
more toward political struggle against the Kampuchean
regime. Even before the Kampuchean counteroffensive,
the Vietnamese had been referring to the CPK leaders
either as "reactionaries"[75] or simply as "authorities" (a
term previously used to refer to the Thieu and other
"puppet" regimes).[76] Now, at the end of January, Hanoi
Radio began broadcasting statements by Kampuchean refugees
and prisoners of war calling for the overthrow of the
Kampuchean regime and its replacement by one that
would be friendly to Vietnam. On 26 January, one
Kampuchean POW was reported to have stated,

> I ardently wish that the Kampuchean people
> could live in full liberty under the leadership
> of a Kampuchean revolutionary organization
> that has a clear-sighted and judicious line and

entertains close solidarity with Vietnam.[77]

The following day a refugee was reported to have said,

> I know that the Vietnamese revolution will never
> persecute the laboring people as the Kampuchean
> authorities do. The Kampuchean authorities say
> they are Communists, but in fact they are reac-
> tionaries.[78]

These broadcasts put Vietnam publicly behind attempts to
overthrow the Phnom Penh regime, and the CPK leadership
undoubtedly interpreted the broadcasts as proof that
the Vietnamese were not sincere about negotiations but
rather wanted to destroy their regime.

It was in the negative context of this escalation
of their political war against the Kampuchean regime that
the Vietnamese launched a new diplomatic initiative. On
5 February, the Vietnamese held a press conference in
Hanoi in which they outlined three proposals aimed at
an "early settlement of problems concerning relations
between Vietnam and Kampuchea." [79] The three proposals
were:

1. An immediate end shall be put to all hostile
    military activities in the border region.
    The armed forces of each side shall be stationed
    within their respective territory five kilo-
    meters from the border;
2. The two sides shall meet at once in Hanoi or
    or Phnom Penh or at a place along the
    border to discuss and conclude a treaty,
    in which they will undertake to respect
    each other's independence, sovereignty and
    territorial integrity, to refrain from
    aggression, from the use of force or the
    threat of the use of force in their relations
    with each other, from interference in each
    other's internal affairs, and from subversive
    activities against each other, to treat each
    other on an equal footing, and to live in
    peace and friendship in a good neighborly
    relationship. The two sides shall sign a
    treaty on the border question on the basis of
    respect for each other's territorial soveignty
    within the existing border;
3. The two sides shall reach an agreement on an
    appropriate form of international guarantee and
    supervision. These proposals received the
    implicit support of China.[80] They were unaccept-
    able, however, to the Kampucheans. Because
    the Vietnamese proposals had not been officially
    addressed to the Kampuchean government nor

officially transmitted to Kampuchean,[81] the
Kampucheans rejected them by ignoring them.
The Kampuchean rejection followed from their
1976 diplomatic position as well as from the
events of 1977 and early 1978. The Vietnamese
had made, and no doubt saw themselves as having
made, important concessions. These concessions,
however, did not entirely meet the minimal
package demands the Kampucheans had been making
since May 1976, nor did they erase the bitterness
engendered by the December 1977 Vietnamese
invasion and the late January 1978 Vietnamese
radio broadcasts. The Vietnamese proposal,
in point one for mutual withdrawals, was in
accordance with the Kampuchean proposals of
June 1977, but the language of point two made
it clear that the Vietnamese were still
denying the validity of Sihanouk's interpretation of their 1967 statements, and thus
were rejecting the principles of border
nonnegotiability and unique Kampuchean
rights to make rationalizing readjustments.
Rather, the Vietnamese were calling for
renegotiations to establish a new border
treaty on the basis of mutual readjustments.
Official Vietnamese commentary on the proposals
that accompanied their publication made this
explicit.[82] Vietnamese spokesmen also stated
that the Vietnamese continued to reject the
Brevie line as a border delineating territorial
waters.[83] Moreover, although the proposals
avoided the term "special relationship,"
the Vietnamese soon reiterated that their
long term goal remained the establishment of
such a relationship between Kampuchea and
Vietnam.[84] Finally, since the Kampucheans
had long expressed their opposition to any
third-party involvement in or mediation of
the conflict, the proposal for an international
guarantee was an affront to the Kampucheans
and not an attraction. In June 1977, the
Vietnamese proposals, minus the third point,
might have got talks restarted. However, in
February 1978, following division level
fighting and Vietnamese radio broadcasts
calling for the overthrow of the CPK regime,
the Vietnamese concessions were not enough.

The Vietnamese proposals therefore did not even bring
a break in the fighting, which continued at a relatively
low level. Vietnamese forces launched assaults into
Kampuchean territory in the far northeast,[85] and Kampuchean forces continued their attacks around Ha Tien and

farther north in Mekong delta frontiers zones,[86]
while both sides shelled each other's territories.
Meanwhile, on 15 February, Hanoi Radio broadcast new
support for the overthrow of the CPK regime.[87]

CHINA AND THE WIDENING INDOCHINA CONFLICT

The Kampuchean shelling, on top of its refusal to
respond to the Vietnamese proposals and new Kampuchean
ground forays, soon provoked Vietnam into what in
retrospect seems to have been a diplomatic mistake:
ever more obvious polemics against China. Beginning
on 1 February, the Chinese had begun to ship fresh
military supplies to Kampuchea. These shipments were
the fruit of Kampuchea's adamant behavior during Teng
Ying-ch'ao's visit. Although most of the supplies
consisted of ammunition needed to relieve month-old
shortages, they also included quantities of antitank
weaponry that would make the armor spearheads of any
future Vietnamese invasion much more vulnerable than they
had been in December and a number of 130-millimeter
Chinese artillery pieces that could be used either to
harass a new Vietnamese invasion force or to shell targets
on Vietnamese territory without resort to infantry
assaults. The number of 130-mm. guns was evidently not
large, and foreign intelligence analysts concluded that
they were little more than showpiece weapons with a
mainly psychological value.[88] However, it seems that
the Kampucheans quickly transported the 130-mm. guns --
and all the other arms and ammunition supplied by China --
to the frontlines. The Kampucheans evidently immediately
integrated the 130-mm. guns into artillery units that had
been relying mostly on 105-mm. and 155-mm. howitzers
captured or taken over from Lon Nol troops to shell
a number of Vietnamese provincial towns. These shellings
had been going on since the Kampucheans had gone on the
counteroffensive in early January, but now they became
more destructive and more often hit targets relatively
deep in Vietnam. This apparently infuriated the
Vietnamese.[89] Although the Chinese shipments had
actually begun before the Vietnamese had announced
their three-point proposals and although the real reasons
for their rejection were to be found in their unacceptability to Phnom Penh and not in Peking, which actually
favored the Vietnamese proposals, the Vietnamese evidently
concluded that the Chinese were objectively behind the
Kampucheans' continued intransigence and were responsible
for sealing the fate of the proposals. On 10 February,
the Vietnamese quoted a Czechoslovakian analysis of
the conflict that accused "international reactionaries" --
a codeword for China -- of "desiring to encroach upon
the Southeast Asian region and trying their best to split
the solidarity of Vietnam and Kampuchea.[90] On 20 February,

Hanoi Radio declared that "The enemy" -- apparently
China -- "has poured more fuel onto the flames of conflict, (and) backed Phnom Penh in its military attacks
as well as its slander campaign against Vietnam.[91]
Finally, on 21 February, the Vietnamese made the object
of their attacks obvious by stating that

> imperialists and international reactionaries have
> helped (the Kampucheans) build up and equip
> overnight a dozen divisions armed with long-
> range artillery and war planes which Kampuchea
> did not have before 1975. Assisted and encouraged
> by the imperialists and international reactionaries,
> the Kampucheans have turned friends into foes and
> pointed their guns at their old comrades-in-arms
> who helped them win victory.[90]

The reference was clearly to China. Although available
evidence indicates that they had not in fact supplied
the Kampucheans with any aircraft, they had equipped the
Kampuchean army after 1975 and recently supplied the
130-mm. guns.

From the Chinese point of view, these public
polemics put the Vietnamese firmly on the side of
Soviet anti-Chinese activities. China was not chastened
but provoked, and the potential for a Vietnamese use of
Chinese mediation to bring about a negotiated settlement
with Kampuchea -- should the Kampucheans ever become
amenable -- was reduced almost to zero. Instead of
creating or even maintaining diplomatic options,
Vietnam had closed them.

The Chinese did not immediately respond to the
Vietnamese polemics. The Chinese silence, however, did
not mean that Vietnam's polemics had left the Chinese
unaffected. Three months later, when conflict over the
problems of ethnic Chinese in Vietnam was added to the
picture, the full extent of Chinese anger was revealed.

In the meantime, the Chinese lent further, but still
limited support to Kampuchea. This was done by dispatch-
ing, on 4 March, a Chinese railway "survey" team --
probably composed of military engineering personnel --
to Kampuchea to work on the rail line from the Gulf of
Siam port at Kompong Som to Phnom Penh.[93] The leaders
of this team stayed in Kampuchea until 1 April.[94] Most
of the rest of the team apparently stayed behind and
remained in place along the rail line. This team helped
Kampuchea in two ways. First, the Kompong Som-Phnom
Penh rail line is a crucial logistical lifeline between
central Kampuchea and the outside world, and its smooth
functioning obviously facilitates, directly and indirectly,
the Kampuchean war effort. Second, and more importantly,
it cuts across potential Vietnamese invasion routes in
southeast Kampuchea.[95] A Chinese presence along this

rail line therefore acted as an important tripwire
deterrence mechanism against large scale Vietnamese
military action. The stationing of military engineering
personnel along major communications routes of
China's allies is a tactic that was developed by the
Chinese during the Second Indochina War to deter
escalatory foreign aggression. During that war,
this tactic involved a Chinese presence along northern
Vietnamese and northern Laotian communications lines,
and was intended to deter U.S. invasions. Deterrence
of these invasions not only benefited Vietnam and
Laos, but also China, which realized that if U.S.
invasion occurred, China would almost certainly be
drawn into direct combat with the U.S. The deterrence
was therefore designed to prevent a U.S. escalation
that would necessitate Chinese intervention.[96] Now
the Chinese were trying to deter an escalatory Vietnamese
invasion that might draw China into a combat confrontation with Vietnam. There had been much speculation,
which neither the Kampucheans nor the Chinese could
afford to ignore, that the Kampuchean rejection of the
three-point Vietnamese proposals might be followed by
another invasion, this time on a larger scale and with
more ambitious objectives.[97] Whether or not the Vietnamese had actually seriously contemplated such a move,
the Chinese presence along the Kompong Som-Phnom
Penh rail line meant that this and certain other Vietnamese military options were rendered much more dangerous.
The Vietnamese could not include plans to cut this
lifeline or make sweeps across southeast Kampuchea in
any military action without risking Chinese military
intervention. Sometime in March, the Chinese also
supplied the Kampucheans with a radar-based antiaircraft
system for Phnom Penh. This reduced the potential
effectiveness of a Vietnamese air assault on the
Kampuchean capital, or its airport, which is Kampuchea's
most important air link with the outside world.[98] Both
the rail line deterrence and the radar system were
limited aid for Kampuchea because they did much more to
prevent or reduce the effectiveness of new Vietnamese
attacks than they did to bolster Kampuchea's offensive
capabilities.

For the Vietnamese, nevertheless, the situation
seemed to be going from bad to worse. Diplomacy had
proved a deadend. While the Vietnamese still had the
capability to assault Kampuchean territory in many areas
along the frontier, the Kampucheans continued to
demonstrate their capabilities in other areas, most
notably by new Ha Tien and Mekong delta region raids in
mid-March. Finally, Chinese deterrence and strengthening
of Phnom Penh's antiaircraft defenses gave the
Vietnamese less military maneuvering room. Therefore,
starting in late March, the Vietnamese apparently decided

to escalate significantly their political war to overthrow the CPK regime. This decision had three aspects.
First, the Vietnamese began seriously to construct a
guerrilla force that was to be composed of ethnic
Khmers recruited from among Kampuchean refugees,
prisoners of war and Southern Vietnam's Khmer minority
and that was to led by Vietnamese trained Kampuchean
communist cadres. They apparently hoped that this
"Khmerized" force would be capable of fighting a
guerrilla war against the CPK regime, at least if it
received the support of Vietnamese logistics,
artillery, and air power, and regular interventions by
Vietnamese main force units.[99] Second, the Vietnamese
apparently began preparations to augment their forces
along the frontier to make such Vietnamese support
available. These reinforcements would be used to
generally wear down Kampuchean forces both by new attacks
into Kampuchean territory and by stronger counterattacks
against Kampuchean raiders. They would also be used to
make credible threats of a new massive invasion, which
would complicate Kampuchean planning and keep Kampuchean
forces tied down waiting for such an invasion. But
the main purpose of these reinforcements was to allow
the Vietnamese to concentrate their troops in certain
areas so that they could launch regular attacks to take
and hold Kampuchean territory that would serve as bases
for the Khmerized guerrilla army.[100]Third, the Vietnamese
intensified their propaganda war against the CPK regime
and their attempts to instigate uprisings and defections
inside Kampuchea that would open the way to main force
attacks and the insertion of the Khmerized force.[101]
After March, it would become increasingly clear that
Vietnamese diplomatic and military initiatives were
essentially tactical elements of a strategy aimed at
bringing about the downfall and replacement of the
CPK regime by one acceptable to Vietnam. Political
threats, too, were not merely designed to defeat the
Kampuchean Revolutionary Army in specific battlefield
situations, but became part of an orchestrated campaign
to bring about the disappearance of the CPK regime.

In early April, the Vietnamese put all three parts
of their political offensive into motion. On 3 April,
they broadcast their most explicit call for the overthrow of the CPK regime to date. It urged Kampuchean
army units to "turn their guns around" and attack the
political leaders in Phnom Penh.[102] On 7 April, they
published two long documents: one setting forth the
Vietnamese version of the border negotiations;[103] another
giving their history of the relations between the CPK
and the VCP.[104] The latter refuted the Kampuchean charge
of Vietnamese desires to establish a French style
Indochina Federation, but, together with background
briefings for foreign journalists,[105] also attempted to

portray the CPK leaders, especially Pol Pot, as
renegades who had usurped power from "true" communists
who had been associated with a Vietnamese-sponsored
and supervised anti-French united front in the 1940s and
1950s. The Vietnamese presented these earlier Kampuchean
communists, who -- as noted above -- had been almost
totally wiped out by the Sihanouk repression before
the CPK's foundation in 1960, as the true leaders of the
revolutionary struggle that had defeated Lon Nol and
the U.S. in 1975. This portrayal was designed to lay
an historical groundwork to justify the overthrow of
the CPK regime and its replacement by another communist
regime led by Kampuchean cadres drawn from the old
Indochinese Communist Party. The publication of these
documents coincided with a buildup of Vietnamese forces
along the frontier and was followed by renewed Vietnamese
attacks against Kampuchean forces into two spots
along the frontier.[106] Meanwhile, on 10 April, the
Vietnamese finally sent an official note to the Kampucheans calling for negotiations on the basis of the
5 February three-point Vietnamese proposals. The
Kampucheans refused to accept this note.[107]

In an interview broadcast over Phnom Penh Radio on
12 April, CPK Secretary Pol Pot responded to the recent
Vietnamese moves by reiterating the existing Kampuchean
position.[108] He made it clear that if -- but only if --
Vietnam accepted the Kampuchean approach to the border
question and rejected any idea of overthrowing his
regime or establishing a special relationship with it,
friendship between Kampuchea and Vietnam could be
developed on a state-to-state level. Otherwise, there
could be no talks and no end to the battlefield hostilities. Moreover, Pol Pot implicitly ruled out the
establishment of fraternal Party-to-Party relations, even
if Kampuchean negotiating conditions were met. From the
point of view of the CPK, too much had happened to
contemplate that.

Thus, as the Kampucheans once again launched attacks
against the Ha Tien area in late April and the Vietnamese
counterattacked into early May,[108] the diplomatic deadlock that had developed two years earlier at the May 1976
technical talks on the border question had deepened and
become completely solidified. Both the Kampucheans and
the Vietnamese had suffered terribly from the fighting,
but a settlement was now more unlikely than ever before,
especially in light of the emphasis the Vietnamese were
now giving to imposing a regime of their choice on
Kampuchea. The fundamental nature of the deadlock was
reconfirmed on 15 May, when the Kampucheans privately
transmitted a negotiation proposal of their own to the
Vietnamese.[110] This proposal demanded that Vietnam
meet four preconditions in order to get talks started:

1. Stop carrying out any attack of aggression, invasion, and annexation against the territory of Democratic Kampuchea; stop any act of provocation and violation against the territory, territorial waters and air-space of Democratic Kampuchea, stop machine-gunning, pounding, bombing and carrying out air-raids against the territory and territorial waters of Democratic Kampuchea;

2. Stop sending spying agents to gather intelligence in the territory, territorial waters and islands of Democratic Kampuchea; stop carrying out any act of subversion and interference in the internal affairs of Democratic Kampuchea; stop carrying out attempts of coups d'etat or other forms of activities aiming at overthrowing the government of Democratic Kampuchea;

3. Definitively abandon the strategy aiming at putting Kampuchea under the domination of Vietnam in the "Indochina Federation: following the doctrine of "one party, one country and one people" in the Indochina belonging to Vietnam;"

4. Respect the independence, sovereignty and territorial integrity of Democratic Kampuchea: respect the rights of Kampuchea's people to decide by themselves their own destiny.

This proposal essentially restated what Pol Pot had said publicly on 21 April. Like the Kampuchean proposal of June 1977, the May 1978 proposal incorporated a combined cooling off and testing period, during which the Vietnamese were supposed to demonstrate by concrete deeds their practical acceptance of Kampuchean negotiation preconditions. These preconditions were couched in rhetorical terms, but evidently boiled down to a familiar package. Vietnamese withdrawal from all zones the Kampucheans considered theirs; Vietnamese acceptance of Sihanouk's map lines as the land border and of the Brevie line as a territorial sea border; a complete halt to Vietnamese military activities; a cessation of Vietnamese propaganda against the CPK regime and Vietnamese assertions of a necessity for a Kampuchea-Vietnam special relationship; and an end to Vietnamese support for elements inside Kampuchea hostile to the CPK leadership. In the 15 May proposal, the length of the good faith period was specified as seven months. Therefore, actual talks could not begin before the end of 1978. If the Vietnamese met the Kampuchean preconditions, a de facto ceasefire would presumably develop, and if the Vietnamese continued to fulfil them until the end of 1978,

then talks could occur. No surprisingly, however, the
Vietnamese found this package unacceptable, and they did
not respond to it until its contents leaked in early
June.[111] They then publicly rejected it and responded to
it by reissuing a slightly revised version of their 5
February proposals.[112]

Meanwhile, the Kampuchea-Vietnam conflict had helped
to push Chinese Vietnamese relations to the breaking
point. The resulting open split between China and
Vietnam, in turn, further exacerbated Kampuchea-Vietnam
relations. After the late February Vietnamese polemics
against China, longstanding tensions between the two
countries, which involved both ideological differences
and rival claims to islands and territorial waters in
the South China Sea, had intensified. In March and April,
foreign reporters visiting Hanoi heard stories of hostilities along the Sino-Vietnamese border.[113] These
hostilities were supposed to have occurred both before
and after the Vietnamese broadcasts in late February.
Although some of these reports were apparently exaggerated,
they correctly reflected significantly heightened tempers
in Peking and Hanoi and along the frontier. These
tempers had been especially inflamed by an increasing
flow of ethnic Chinese across the border from their homes
in Vietnam to their Chinese motherland. The reasons for
this refugee flow were complex. It seems that both
Hanoi and Peking had taken steps between 1975 and 1977
that had prompted it, while the war between Kampuchea
and Vietnam created a panic atmosphere that helped to
greatly increase its dimensions.[114]

On 30 April, the Chinese publicly complained about
the refugee situation.[115] The Vietnamese replied by
disclaiming responsibility and the flow of bitter
refugees into China continued.[116] on 12 May Peking
stepped up the pressure on the Vietnamese by privately
informing them that China was going to begin a suspension
of some of its economic aid projects in Vietnam on
19 May, ostensibly in order to transfer funds to refugee
relief activities. On 24 May, the Chinese publicly
accused Vietnam of ostracizing, persecuting and expelling
Chinese and claimed that the number of refugees already
in China had reached 70,000.[117] On 30 May, they
privately informed Hanoi that more aid projects
were going to be suspended.[118] Meanwhile, they began
arguing in semi-official publication[119] and in talks
with foreign diplomats[120] that Vietnam was becoming
a kind of Asian Cuba -- little more than a pawn in
Soviet worldwide strategy. This, more than anything
else, showed that China now considered the breach almost
fundamental, which meant that resolution of any of the
outstanding issues was highly unlikely. This put China
more fully in alliance with Kampuchea in the latter's
conflict with what China now increasingly perceived as the

Soviet client state of Vietnam. The reduction of ambiguity in China's position was naturally Vietnam's loss and Kampuchea's gain. It did not, however, reduce the strains in the China-Kampuchea alliance in other areas or make either side forget the disagreements of the past.

As Peking-Hanoi relations were deteriorating into public polemics and both sides began to strengthen their military positions along the Sino-Vietnamese frontier, Vietnam's political war to overthrow the CPK leadership was having its first major effects. In late May fighting broke out between forces loyal to Phnom Penh and some military units in Kampuchea's 203 Military Region, which comprises the border provinces of Kompong Cham, Svay Rieng, and Prey Veng. It seems that the CPK leaders in Phnom Penh got wind of a plot against them and moved preemptively againt the plotters, but nevertheless found themselves with a military rebellion on their hands.[121] The rebels were reportedly led by a high-ranking CPK cadre, So Phim. So Phim is an ex-Indochinese Communist Party member who later jointed the CPK.[122] In 1972, Phim, then known as So Vanna, became deputy director general for military affairs of the Kampuchean armed forces. After 1975, he was identified as CPK leader in Kampuchea's Eastern Region and became a vice-chairman of the country's State Presidium.[123] Available evidence indicates that Phom believed that Kampuchea -- and especially the Eastern Region, which borders on Vietnam -- could not continue to fight against Vietnam without bringing about a collapse of economic reconstruction efforts.[124] He probably also sympathized with a more Vietnamlike revolutionary model. Phnom Penh alleged that the Vietnamese were responsible for Phim's dissidence and had even sent members of the Central Committee of the VCP into the Eastern Region to help draw up a rebellion plan.[125] The Vietnamese denied such direct involvement, but made no secret of their support for the rebellion, which they had certainly been trying to instigate, and which they portrayed as the beginning of a new -- and authentically communist -- Kampuchean national liberation war.[126] The Kampucheans claim to have smashed the rebellion in late May, when it began, but they did not make this claim until 25 June, and it seems that small scale fighting continued into the middle of June.[127] Meanwhile, the Vietnamese again bolstered their forces along the Kampuchean frontier[128] and apparently launched several new intrusions into Kampuchean territory, which gave effective support to the rebellion by tying down and diverting loyal Kampuchean troops.[129] These intrusions were accompanied by a campaign of intense and sustained Vietnamese air strikes against Kampuchean forces. This air campaign continued at the same high level until late

August, when bad weather -- and improving Kampuchean antiaircraft capabilities -- forced a temporary slackening.[130] In mid-June, the frequency and scale of the Vietnamese ground incursions increased, probably in response to setbacks dealt to So Phim's rebellion.[131] Finally, after Phnom Penh's 25 June announcement that the rebellion had been crushed, the Vietnamese launched what at first appeared to be a new large scale invasion of Kampuchea using even more forces than were employed in December 1977.[132] It turned out that this invasion was really a feint, designed to throw Kampuchean forces into confusion while concentrated Vietnamese forces moved in to rescue the remnants of So Phim's rebellion and perhaps So Phim himself, Vietnamese forces were apparently supposed to secure a zone of Kampuchean territory, which they would occupy more or less permanently, and which would be the geographical base of a Vietnamese sponsored Kampuchean resistance government.[133]

The Vietnamese might have moved even more ambitiously, if they had not had to face an increasingly hostile China. As it was, the Vietnamese had to worry more and more about troubles with China, especially after Vietnam joined the Soviet dominated Council for Mutual Economic Assistance (COMECON) on 29 June. The Chinese saw Vietnamese entry into COMECON as an open declaration of Vietnamese alliance with the USSR. They responded, on 31 July, with an announcement of an end to all remaining economic aid projects in Vietnam.[134] They also responded, on 12 July, with increased rhetorical support for Kampuchea. For the first time, in an article appearing in People's Daily, the Chinese publicly accused Vietnam of desiring to annex Kampuchea and make it a part of an Indochina Federation. The article further declared Chinas "sympathy and support" for Phnom Penh against a Vietnamese war of aggression.[135] For the Kampucheans, who had been charging the Vietnamese with annexationism and aggression for more than six months, the Chinese statements were somewhat belated. For the Vietnamese, they were highly provocative. They prompted the Vietnamese to declare that China was "the main culprit" in Kampuchea, and that the Chinese had "cheaply bought both the souls and bodies of the Phnom Penh rulers and turned them into instruments for their counter-revolutionary global strategy"[136] The Vietnamese continued their strong propaganda attacks on both China and Kampuchea at the Nonaligned Movement conference in Yugoslavia at the end of July.[137] Kampuchea, for its part, proposed that Vietnam be expelled from the movement. The Kampucheans cited not only Vietnam's attacks on Kampuchea and its backing for the overthrow of their regime, but also the presence of Vietnamese troops in Laos and the alleged presence of Soviet bases in

Vietnam as factors disqualifying Vietnam from movement membership.[138]

The increased Chinese rhetorical support for Kampuchea after mid July was apparently accompanied by an increase in material aid. Since early February, the Chinese had reportedly provided the Kampucheans with only what was necessary to replace their losses. The early February arms shipments had not been followed by others large enough to significantly increase Kampuchea's military capabilities.[139] This pattern did not change in mid July, but more substantial aid was provided. This aid, some of which may have been airlifted into Kampuchea via Laos, apparently more than compensated for Kampuchea's increased expenditures since the new Vietnamese attacks in June, but did not give the Kampucheans any new offensive capabilities.[140]

Moreover, continuing strains in the Kampuchea-China alliance were evidenced by what transpired during a visit to China by Kampuchean Defense Minister Son Sen from 19 July to 4 August. Son Sen's visit occurred at a time when the Vienamese, who had just completed a campaign to induct an additional 350,000 persons into their armed forces[141] were launching new incursions in the same areas where there had been rebellions in May and June and where the Vietnamese had attacked in the second half of June[142] and when withdrawals of Kampucheans forces from Western provinces bordering Thailand indicated that the Kampucheans were beginning to have manpower problems.[143] Despite the Vietnamese attacks, which were apparently aimed at expanding the territory under the influence of Vietnamese supported rebels, Son Sen's visit to China was not met with much fanfare. Its coverage in the Chinese media was relatively low key. Although Son Sen met with both Hua Kuo-feng and Teng Hsiao-p'ing, as well as a number of important Chinese military officers, their rhetorical support for Kampuchea's "just struggle" conspicuously avoided any firm commitments of increased aid or any guarantee of Kampuchea's defense. Privately, the Chinese reportedly voiced criticisms of the CPK's failure to form a broader united front within Kampuchea to defend the country against Vietnam, and indicated that the Kampucheans should not expect an intervention by Chinese "volunteers" even if the military situation in Kampuchea worsened dramatically.[144] Son Sen's reception showed that the Chinese were willing to help shore up the CPK regime by associating one of its top members in a limited way with China's leading officials, but not by any qualitatively new military moves that would escalate the fighting.

Vietnam, nevertheless, soon became the recipient of a large scale Soviet arms airlift.[145] This airlift, which began in early August and continued until early September,

was related not only to the fighting between Kampuchea
and Vietnam; it also resulted from Vietnam's increasingly
ominous confrontation with the PRC and the USSR's
desire to support Vietnam in that confrontation.
Vietnam's post-1975 stocks of both Soviet and captured
U.S. arms and ammunition, together with regular small
scale Soviet arms aid after 1975, had been enough to
sustain Vietnamese forces in the fighting with Kampuchea,
but could not have seemed sufficient in the face of the
possibility of large scale combat with the PRC.
Although China and Vietnam had begun negotiations on
the overseas Chinese issue on 8 August, it is likely
that neither side expected these talks to resolve this
problem, much less the more fundamental differences between them.[146] Moreover, the Soviet airlift followed
a buildup of Chinese and Vietnamese forces along their
mutual frontier which indicated that real hostilities
between China and Vietnam could not be ruled out. [147]
Fears that such fighting could occur seemed confirmed on
25 August, when Chinese frontier security forces crossed
into Vietnam and clashed with their Vietnamese counterparts,
who had apparently been scuffling with ethnic Chinese
stranded on the Vietnamese side of a border crossing
point by China's closure of the frontier in mid-july.[148]
Six persons were killed in the clash, and the Vietnamese
responded by crossing into Chinese territory to take
temporary control of high ground above the crossing
point.[149] The Chinese then withdrew their negotiators
and accused the Vietnamese of creating an "atmosphere
of war terror and panic" along the frontier.[150] Even
if the new weaponry and ammunition was intended partly
to build up Vietnam in case of fighting with China,
however, the fact that the only current and sustained
fighting was with Kampuchea meant that almost all the
Soviet military aid found its way to that battlefront.[151]
    The Kampuchean battlefront became more active at the
end of August when for the third month in a row, Vietnamese forces launched attacks into Kampuchea.[152] The
attacks followed the transfer of a reported 10,000 -
15,000 additional Vietnamese troops -- elements of two
divisions -- to the Kampuchea theatre. Although the
Vietnamese invaders met with strong Kampuchean resistance,
their new attacks, combined with gains made since June,
allowed them to occupy a strip of Kampuchean border
territory in the province of Kompong Cham and Kratie,
reportedly including the rubber plantation towns of
Krek, Snoul, and Memut.[153] This set the stage for a
Radio Hanoi claim on 2 September that a consolidated resistance movement now existing on Kampuchean soil was
engaged in a struggle against the CPK.[154] This announcement, in turn, coincided with the arrival in Peking of
another highranking Kampuchean official, Nuon Chea.
Chea, a former member of the Indochinese Communist Party
and the Deputy Secretary of the CPK, met with several

important Chinese leaders, including Hua Kuo-feng.[155]
Chea's welcome in Peking seems to have been more
enthusiastic than that of Son Sen a month earlier, perhaps because of the Soviet airlift into Vietnam and
Vietnam's escalation of both military and political
actions against Kampuchea. However, Peking apparently
continued to make it clear that China would not send
combat troops to Kampuchea and also again expressed the
opinion that the CPK should consider a more united front
approach to the Vietnamese threat.[156]

By the end of September, the Kampucheans seem to have
reached the same conclusion. On 30 September, Phnom
Penh Radio announced that Prince Sihanouk had attended
a 28 September banquet in honor of noncommunist supporters
of the CPK. Sihanouk had consistently given his support
to the CPK's struggle against Vietnam in letters reported
by Phnom Penh Radio, but his attendence at the 28 September banquet was his first publicly announced activity
since his retirement as Kampuchea's chief of state in
April 1976. His replacement in that position, Khieu
Samphan, made it clear in a speech at the banquet that
Sihanouk's reappearance was designed to further mobilize
the Kampuchean population in preparation for another
large scale Vietnamese attack.[157] The Kampucheans seem
to have decided sometime in mid September that such an
attack was a real possibility. In the beginning of
September the Kampucheans had evidently believed that
the Vietnamese troop buildup that had been taking place
along the frontier since early April was part of a
Vietnamese "protracted war" strategy of nibbling away
at Kampuchean territory and grinding down Kampuchean
border forces.[158] By the end of the month, however, as
two huge Soviet cargo ships docked at Cam Ranh Bay in
Southern Vietnam to unload more munitions for the
Vietnamese than in all of the previous year's shipments
combined[159], as Vietnamese troops moved into offensive
positions in southem Laos[160] (interview with a U.S.
State Department Official, October 1978), as still more
reinforcements moved up to the Vietnamese border[161] and
as the dry season approached, the Kampucheans concluded
that another Vietnamese invasion similar to that carried
out in late 1977 could not be ruled out.[162] Peking
wholeheartedly agreed, and its announcement on 26 September of another suspension of talks with Vietnam on the
problem of "overseas Chinese" may have been intended in
part to warn the Vietnamese against such an attack.[163]
The Chinese also let it be known that they had the option
of putting pressure on the Sino-Vietnamese border if
Vietnam again invaded Kampuchea.[164]

In early October the Kampucheans reported new
Vietnamese attacks.[165] In mid-month they put their armed
forces on alert.[166] This was followed by more border
skirmishes.[167] Vietnamese propaganda meanwhile asserted

that popular uprisings were occurring in several places in Kampuchea. These reports seemed to have little basis in fact.[168] Rather, they seemed designed to create pretexts for direct intervention by Vietnamese forces concentrated along the frontier and by their Khmerized auxiliaries.[169] The Chinese apparently responded to the intensified Vietnamese activity as they had warned they would. Although they did not mass troops along the Sino-Vietnamese frontier, as the Vietnamese insistently charged, they evidently did step up border patrolling, and this seems to have led to several incidents involving Vietnamese frontier forces.[170] In Peking, Teng Hsiao-p'ing reiterated that China would not intervene militarily in Kampuchea but warned that if Vietnam launched an invasion, the results would not be limited to what happened in Kampuchea.[171]

Faced with deterrent threats from China, the Vietnamese decided to bring Soviet deterrence to bear against China. On 3 November, after what were apparently stormy negotiations, Vietnam signed a treaty of friendship and cooperation with the USSR. Article 6 of this alliance pact provided that

> In case either party is attacked or threatened with attack, the two parties ...shall immediately consult with each other with a view to eliminating that threat and shall take appropriate and effective measures to safeguard the peace and security of the two countries.

China now had to be prepared to face Soviet military action if it attacked or threatened Vietnam in response to a Vietnamese invasion of Kampuchea.[172]

CONCLUSION

Thus, almost a year after the December 1977 Vietnamese invasion of Kampuchea, the border dispute and the political struggle between the two countries have continued. The two countries have been completely deadlocked over the border issue. But the border issue has become almost irrelevant. The dispute has been replaced by a Vietnamese campaign to destroy Kampuchea's political regime and by a Kampuchean struggle to prevent this. Kampuchea faces a massive and multiform Vietnamese threat. Another Vietnamese invasion is a distinct possibility. A Vietnamese war of attrition accompanied by an intense campaign of subversion is a certainty. Moreover, what had originally been a dispute between Kampuchea and Vietnam has become a focal point of Sino-Soviet struggle. China, which had originally tried to prevent a confrontation, then to minimize escalation and

finally to deter Vietnam from further action against
Kampuchea, saw Vietnam first join in Soviet propaganda
attacks against it and then increasingly place itself
in what finally became a military alliance with the USSR.
If the Vietnamese launch a new invasion, they would have
to be ready for a Chinese response, but China would also
have to be ready for Soviet retaliation for any Chinese
action against Vietnam. Even if the Vietnamese do no
more than continue their war of attrition and subversion
against Kampuchea, they would surely continue to face
various forms of Chinese pressure, and the Chinese would
have to worry about and perhaps respond to Soviet counter-
pressure. In either case, the potential for a major
Sino-Soviet confrontation in Southeast Asia has become
greater than ever before.

NOTES

1.   Phnom Penh Radio, December 30, 1977 (GMT).
2.   Los Angeles Times, January 10, 1978.
3.   Facts About Vietnam-Kampuchea Border Question document
issued by the Ministry of Foreign Affairs of the Socialist
Republic of Vietnam, April 7, 1978, p. 7.
4.   "A High Vietnam Government Official Discussing
Situation Vis-a-vis Cambodia," typescript translation
of an interview conducted by a member of a foreign delegation visiting Vietnam, dated May 5, 1978.
5.   Phnom Penh Radio, January 10, 1978.
6.   Vietnam-Kampuchea Border Question, pp. 7-8; Phnom
Penh Radio, December 30, 1977.
7.   Sarin Chhak, Les Frontieres du Cambodge (Paris:
Dalloz, 1966).
8.   Roger Smith, Cambodia's Foreign Policy (Ithaca:
Cornell University Press, 1965), pp. 154-155.
9.   Vietnam-Kampuchea Border Question, p. 11; Le Monde,
January 26, 1978.
10.   Vietnam-Kampuchea Border Question, p.4.
11.   "Cambodge: Carte Administrative et Toutiere Echelle
1/5000,000," (Service Geographique des F.A.R.K., 1969).
12.   Far Eastern Economic Review, (FEER), August 19, 1977,
p. 12.
13.   Kenneth Quinn, "Political Change in Wartime: The
Khmer Krahom Revolution in Southern Cambodia, 1970-74,"
Naval War College Review, Spring 1976, p.8.
14.   Los Angeles Times, January 10, 1978.
15.   FEER, October 1, 1973, pp. 13-14.
16.   New York Times, August 26, 1973.
17.   FEER, January 20, 1978, p. 13; Los Angeles Times,
June 13, 1975.
18.   Milton Osborne, "Kampuchea and Vietnam: A
Historical Perspective," Pacific Community (Vol. 9, No. 3),
April 1978, pp. 260-261.
19.   Vietnam-Kampuchea Border Question, pp. 5-6.

20. Cambodian Information Agency (AKI), September 9, 1974.
21. New York Times, September 8, 1974.
22. Interview with a U.S. State Department official, April 1978.
23. FEER, February 5, 1978, pp. 22,24.
24. Dossier Kampuchea,document issued by the SRV's Vietnam Information Office in Prague, 1978.
25. Vietnam-Kampuchea Border Question, pp. 5-6.
26. New York Times, June 14, 1975.
27. Agence France Presse, Peking, June 23, 1975.
28. Phnom Penh Radio, December 30, 1977.
29. Phnom Penh Radio, August 2, 1975.
30. Vietnam-Kampuchea Border Question, p.6.
31. FEER, February 27, 1976.
32. Vietnam-Kampuchea Border Question, p. 8; Phnom Penh Radio, December 30, 1977.
33. Ibid.
34. Ibid.
35. Larry Palmer, "Panyaha Phromdaen Thai-Khmen," in Athit (Bangkok), Vol. 1, Nos. 30, and 14, 15, 16, 20; January 27, February 3, 1978, indicates that this was the case along the Thai frontier.
36. Interview with a U.S. State Department official, April 19, 1978.
37. Vietnam-Kampuchea Border Question, p.9.
38. Washington Post, April 8, 1978.
39. Vietnam-Kampuchea Border Question, p. 9.
40. Democratic Kampuchea Foreign Ministry letter to the Non-aligned Movement, dated March 17, 1978, p.7.
41. "Decisions Concerning the Report of the Eastern Region Conference Mid-Year 1977, July 17, 1977," p. 84.
42. Reuters,Kuala Lumpur, August 6, 1977; Ban Muang (Bangkok), July 24, 1977.
43. FEER, August 19, 1977.
44. Phnom Penh Radio, December 30, 1977.
45. Department of Press and Information, Ministry of Foreign Affairs, SRV, Facts and Documents on Democratic Kampuchea's Serious Violations of the Sovereignty and Territorial Integrity of the Socialist Republic of Vietnam, January 1978, p. 25.
46. Washington Post, January 5, 1978.
47. Los Angeles Times, January 7, 1978.
48. Los Angeles Times, January 16, 1978.
49. Livre Noire: Faits et Preuves Des Actes d'Agression du Vietnam Contre le Kampuchea (Phnom Penh, September 1978), pp. 21-22.
50. Hoang Nguyen, "The Truth About the Dispute Along the Vietnam-Kampuchean Border," Tap Chi Cong San (Hanoi), No. 4, April 1978, passim.
51. Livre Noire, pp. 37-51.
52. Agence France Presse, Hanoi, September 7, 1978.
53. Livre Noire, p. 98.
54. Gareth Porter, "Asia's New Cold War," The Nation,

64

September 9, 1978, p. 211.
55. Hanoi Radio, December 31, 1977.
56. Phnom Penh Radio, January 2, 1978.
57. Christian Science Monitor, January 9, 1978.
58. Phnom Penh Radio, January 11, 1978.
59. Los Angeles Times, January 16, 1978.
60. Phnom Penh Radio, January 17, 1978.
61. Los Angeles Times, January 14, 1978.
62. New York Times, January 14, 1973; FEER, October 1, 1973, pp. 13-14.
63. Le Monde, September 13, 1975.
64. Los Angeles Times, May 31, 1978.
65. China Quarterly, No. 60, December 1975, p. 797.
66. FEER, March 26, 1976, p. 24.
67. Peking Review, No. 5, January 28, 1977.p. 29.
68. Ibid.,October 7, 1977, p. 28.
69. Ieng Sary press conference at the United Nations, October 13, 1978.
70. Le Monde, January 11, 1978.
71. Los Angeles Times, January 14, 1978.
72. Washington Post, January 19, 1978.
73. Phnom Penh Radio, January 20, 1978.
74. Los Angeles Times, January 27, 1978
75. Hanoi Radio, January 6, 1978.
76. Le Monde, January 15-16, 1978.
77. Hanoi Radio, January 26, 1978.
78. Hanoi Radio, January 27, 1978.
79. Vietnam-Kampuchea Border Question, p. 78.
80. Christian Science Monitor, February 9, 1978.
81. Le Monde, April 8, 1978.
82. Nhan Dan, February 5, 1978.
83. Le Monde, February 7, 1978.
84. Hanoi Radio, February 13, 1978.
85. Los Angeles Times, February 18, 1978.
86. Ibid., February 14, 1978.
87. Hanoi Radio, February 15, 1978.
88. Los Angeles Times, March 3, 1978.
89. Porter, in The Nation, p. 211.
90. Hanoi Radio, February 10, 1978.
91. Hanoi Radio, February 20, 1978.
92. Hanoi Radio, February 21, 1978.
93. Phnom Penh Radio, March 4, 1978.
94. Phnom Penh Radio, April 2, 1978.
95. Christian Science Monitor, March 28, 1978.
96. Allen S. Whiting, The Chinese Calculus of Deterrence
97. New York Times, February 9, 1978.
98. Los Angeles Times, April 9, 1978.
99. Ibid., March 25, 1978.
100. Washington Post, April 8, 1978.
101. Le Monde, March 31, 1978.
102. Hanoi Radio, April 3, 1978
103. Vietnam-Kampuchea Border Question.

104. "Facts on the 'Indochinese Federation' Question," document issued by the SRV Ministry of Foreign Affairs, April 7, 1978.
105. Le Monde, March 31, 1978.
106. Los Angeles Times, April 15, 1978.
107. Hanoi Radio, May 19, 1978
108. Phnom Penh Radio, April 12, 1978.
109. Hanoi Radio, May 14, 1978.
110. Note of the Ministry of Foreign Affairs, Democratic Kampuchea, dated May 15, 1978 (non-official Kampuchean translation).
111. Agence France Presse, Bangkok, June 2, 1978.
112. Hanoi Radio, June 7, 1978.
113. FEER, March 17, 1978, p. 10; Christian Science Monitor,April 1978.
114. Porter, in The Nation, p. 210.
115. Le Monde, March 3, 1978.
116. Ibid., May 6, 1978.
117. Washington Post, May 25, 1978.
118. Hanoi Radio, July 6, 1978.
119. Le Monde, May 30, 1978.
120. Porter, in The Nation, p. 211.
121. Nhan Dan, September 3, 1978; FEER, November 3, 1978, pp. 15-16.
122. Le Monde, October 15/16, 1978.
123. FEER, August 11, 1978, p. 13.
124. Phnom Penh Radio, May 10, 1978.
125. Phnom Penh Radio, June 24, 1978.
126. Hanoi Radio, June 24, 1978.
127. Phnom Penh Radio, June 24, 1978.
128. Los Angeles Times, June 12, 1978; Washington Post, June 18, 1978.
129. Phnom Penh Radio, June 3, 1978.
130. New York Times, August 2, 1978; Los Angeles Times, August 24, 1978.
131. Washington Post, August 6, 1978.
132. Le Monde, June 29, 1978.
133. Washington Post, July 2, 1978.
134. New York Times, July 4, 1978.
135. Le Monde, July 14, 1978.
136. Hanoi Radio, July 15, 1978.
137. Le Monde August 1, 1978.
138. Le Monde, July 24, 1978.
139. Washington Post,July 1, 1978.
140. FEER, July 14, 1978, p. 7; Los Angeles Times, 25 August 1978.
141. New York Times, July 28, 1978.
142. Los Angeles Times, August 1, 1978.
143. New York Times, August 4, 1978.
144. FEER, August 11, 1978.
145. Los Angeles Times, August 25, 1978.
146. Le Monde, August 9, 1978.
147. Christian Science Monitor, July 11, 1978.

148. Los Angeles Times, August 26, 1978.
149. Washington Post, August 27, 1978.
150. Christian Science Monitor, August 28, 1978.
151. Los Angeles Times, October 5, 1978.
152. Christian Science Monitor, August 29, 1978; September 1, 1978.
153. Los Angeles Times, September 9, 1978; Le Monde, September 27, 1978.
154. Le Monde, September 6, 1978.
155. Phnom Penh Radio, September 8, 1978.
156. Phnom Penh Radio, September 17, 1978.
157. Phnom Penh Radio, September 30, 1978.
158. Phnom Penh Radio, September 10, 1978.
159. Los Angeles Times, October 5, 1978.
160. Interview with a State Department official, October 1978.
161. Christian Science Monitor, October 5, 1978.
162. Kyodo, Phnom Penh, September 29, 1978.
163. Christian Science Monitor, September 29, 1978.
164. Le Monde, September 28, 1978.
165. Washington Post, October 11, 1978.
166. Le Monde, October 17, 1978.
167. Christian Science Monitor, October 24, 1978.
168. Le Monde, October 14, 1978.
169. Los Angeles Times, October 25, 1978.
170. Ibid.
171. Le Monde, October 25, 1978.
172. Washington Post, November 4 and 5, 1978.

BIBLIOGRAPHY

Chhak, Sarin. Les Frontieres du Cambodge (Paris: Dalloz, 1966).
Department of Press and Information, Ministry of Foreign Affairs, SRV, Facts and Documents on Democratic Kampuchea's Serious Violations of the Sovereignty and Territorial Integrity of the Socialist Republic of Vietnam. (January 1978).
Dossier Kampuchea, document issued by the SRV's Vietnam Information Office in Prague, 1978.
Facts About Vietnam-Kampuchea Border Question, document issued by the Ministry of Foreign Affairs of the Socialist Republic of Vietnam, April 7, 1978.
Facts on the 'Indochinese Federation' Question,"document issued by the SRV Ministry of Foreign Affairs, April 7, 1978.
Livre Noire: Faits et Preuves Des Actes d'Agression et d'Annexion du Vietnam Contre le Kampuchea (Phnom Penh, September 1978).
Osborne, Milton. Kampuchea and Vietnam: "A Historial Perspective," Pacific Community (Vol. 9, No. 3), April 1978.
Porter, Gareth, "Asia's New Cold War," The Nation,

September 9, 1978.
Quinn, Kenneth, "Political Change in Wartime: The
    Khmer Krahom Revolution in Southern Cambodia,
    1970-74," Naval War College Review, Spring 1976.
Smith, Roger. Cambodia's Foreign Policy (Ithaca:
    Cornell University Press, 1965).
Whiting, Allen S. The Chinese Calculus of Deterrence
    (Ann Arbor: University of Michigan Press, 1975).

3

Vietnamese Policy and the Indochina Crisis

Gareth Porter

    Vietnam's invasion of Kampuchea in December 1978, which overthrew the Pol Pot regime and installed a goverment dependent on continued Vietnamese military presence, was a major turning point in the international politics of Southeast Asia. It put the Vietnamese for the first time in the position of dominating the entire Indochinese peninsula, precipitated the Chinese invasion of Vietnam in February 1979, and further polarized relations between Communist Indochina and non-Communist states both in and outside the region. Its origins and dynamics, therefore, present a major challenge to the understanding of policymakers and scholars alike.

    The Vietnamese move into Kampuchea poses, above all else, the question of Vietnamese aims outside its borders. Two polar explanations for the move have arisen, one seeing it as simply the fulfillment of Vietnam's ambition to control all of Indochina, and therefore defining Vietnam as an inherently expansionist power, the other seeing it simply as a defensive response to a serious threat from Beijing on Vietnam's southwestern flank. This analysis begins from the premise that neither of these polar explanations adequately reflects the interplay of history, ideology and the perception of immediate threat which constitute the basis of Vietnamese policymaking toward its neighbors. It is true that the decades-long Vietnamese Communist view of the ideological and strategic necessity for Indochinese unity, and the continuing political links between the Vietnamese and elements within the Kampuchean Communist movement, pulled the Vietnamese toward intervention in Kampuchea. But the use of military force to topple the Kampuchean Communist regime and the occupation of the country by Vietnamese forces were not part of a plan which the Vietnamese had waited for nearly five decades to put into action, nor were they the inevitable outcome of the Vietnamese conception of Indochina. It is also clear the Vietnam perceived a threat from China, not only in the Pol Pot

regime's policy of attacking Vietnam militarily with
Chinese arms, but in the broader Chinese policy of putting pressure on Vietnam. But again, the invasion was
neither the only Victnamese response possible, nor the
inevitable one; it reflected the ideological, geopolitical and historical/cultural predispositions of the
Hanoi leadership as well as the immediate context of
events.

Underlying Vietnamese responses to the external
events of 1978 was the Marxist-Leninist ideological
framework that defined for the Party leadership both its
own role as a part of the world revolution and the nature of the regimes in Beijing and Phnom Penh. In this
ideological framework, China was not merely a major
power on Vietnam's northern border with interest conflicting with its own, but a traitor to the socialist
camp, which was using Marxism-Leninism to destroy socialism in the world. The threat from China was thus
perceived not only in traditional geopolitical, territorial terms, but as an ideological threat to every
socialist society, including Vietnam. The Soviet Union,
on the other hand, whatever its faults, remained for the
Vietnamese the most important member of the socialist
camp, which was still seen as mankind's best hope for
progress.

Vietnamese Marxism-Leninism also defined the Pol
Pot regime in Kampuchea not merely as extremely nationalistic and virulently anti-Vietnamese but as a fundamental deviation from Marxism-Leninism. Vietnam's view
of its own responsibility to the world revolution - its
concept of "proletarian internationalism" which is as
old as the Vietnamese Communist movement itself -
required that it do what it could to keep the revolutions in Laos and Kampuchea on the path of genuine
Marxism-Leninism. Thus the domestic policies of extreme
coercion, widespread violence against former urban
dwellers, and seemingly irrational economic and social
policies, represented as much of a threat to socialism
in Indochina as the restoration of the old regime. Even
more critical, however, was the suppression by the Pol
Pot group of those elements of the Party and army who
were critical of the regime's domestic and international
line. Failure to help them preserve the core of genuine
Marxism-Leninism represented, from Hanoi's perspective,
the refusal of the international duty of a Communist
Party long associated with the Kampuchean Communist
movement.

Hanoi was also responding to the crisis by applying
geopolitical concepts and calculations which any Vietnamese state in its geographical position would have
used to guide its policy. They believed Chinese policy
treated Vietnam as part of a sphere of influence - an
interpretation of Chinese foreign policy shared by many

historians. Consequently, they attempted to balance
Chinese pressures by moving closer to a faraway ally,
the Soviet Union, while trying to balance greater dependence on the Soviets with improved relations with
capitalist states, especially the U.S. And the Vietnamese considered Laos, Kampuchea and Vietnam as a
strategic unit, from both miliatary and political viewpoints, noting that control of Laos and Kampuchea has
always been used by the enemies of an independent Vietnam to weaken and isolate it.

At a much deeper, partly conscious and partly
unconscious level, Vietnamese decisions were influenced
by collective historical memories of relations with its
neighbors. In the case of China, the historical memory
goes back a millenium. The cultural and national
identity of the Vietnamese people was forged largely in
the process of resisting Chinese efforts to sinify the
Vietnamese, giving Vietnamese leaders an extreme sensitivity to any Chinese effort to force Vietnam to follow
China's lead. While the Vietnamese revolutionaries had
managed to suppress such defensive reactions during the
years when China was Vietnam's closest revolutionary
ally, Sino-Vietnamese conflict quickly brought them to
the fore. The first hint of postwar Chinese pressure on
Vietnam to conform to its international line thus provoked an almost instinctive Vietnamese determination to
resist.

Vietnamese relations with revolutionary Kampuchea
brought an entirely different set of historical memories
and emotions into play: not memories of the nineteenth
century Vietnamese occupation of Kampuchea which remain
so vivid among the Khmer, but of the Vietnamese role in
creating, nourishing and defending the Kampuchean revolution. The Vietnamese Communist Party had set up the
Kampuchean Communist movement, trained its cadres and
sent troops to fight alongside Kampucheans. This
history of Vietnamese political tutelage in regard to
Kampuchean Communism, created the implicit presumption
that a Kampuchea under a Communist regime would regard
Vietnam as its closest ally. The frustration of that
expectation by the Pol Pot leadership branded him a
traitor to the interests of the Kampuchean revoltuion.

While the Vietnamese leadership approached their
relations with Beijing and Phnom Penh with certain
ideological, geopolitical and historical-emotional
predispositions, it was a particular configuration of
external developments in 1978 that triggered the dramatic Vietnamese decisions of that year. With the same
predispositions, the Vietnamese had attempted to maintain a modus vivendi with China and tolerated an un-
friendly regime in Phnom Penh from 1975 to 1978. But
the configuration of events changed rapidly during the
first half of 1978, confronting Hanoi with harsh new

choices. The analysis that follows attempts, therefore,
to trace the historical background of the conflicts in
Sino-Vietnamese and Vietnamese-Kampuchean relations
which formed the basis of Vietnamese interpretations of
the behavior of its neighbors, and then reconstructs the
perceptions and calculations underlying the key Vietnamese policy decisions in 1978-1979.

This analysis of Vietnamese relations with Kampuchea and China shows how tightly the two problems inter-
twined. Events during the first half of 1978 brought
together crises in Vietnam's relations with both neighbors in a remarkable conjuncture that swiftly narrowed
the options previously open to Hanoi. The border war
with Kampuchea reached a critical point in January 1978
and became the central issue in Sino-Vietnamese relations for the first time and created a new political
reality for the Vietnamese: a two-front conflict with
China. The sudden exodus of the ethnic Chinese from
Vietnam and the People's Republic of China's (PRC) move
to cut economic assistance projects, denounce Vietnamese
policies and unilaterally send ships to repatriate
ethnic Chinese from Vietnam, combined to trigger Vietnamese preparations for much heavier Chinese pressures
on Vietnam in the future. At the same time, the Vietnamese strategy for dealing with the Kampuchean crisis
in such a way as to avoid a confrontation with China -
a plan for a military-political uprising/coup by
opponents of the Pol Pot regime within the Kampuchean
army and Party itself, suddenly collapsed. Hanoi then
faced the prospect of allowing an irrevocably hostile
regime in Phnom Penh, aligned militarily and politically
with China, to consolidate its power. The interplay
between the two sides of Vietnam's foreign policy crisis
of 1978 is thus the key to understanding its decisions
on military intervention in Kampuchea.

SINO-VIETNAMESE RELATIONS: FROM ALLIES TO ADVERSARIES

The irony of modern Sino-Vietnamese relations is
that the Vietnamese, with their traditional sensitivities
about Chinese claims to cultural superiority and ambitions to dominate Vietnam, looked to China for guidance
in carrying out the revolution within Vietnam far more
than it ever looked to the Soviet Union. Beginning in
the 1940's, the Vietnamese leadership had recognized
Mao's thought as "Marxism-Leninism in a semi-feudal semi-
colonial country," and applied Chinese experiences in
military, financial and economic fields during the anti-
French resistance and in the land reform period of the
mid-1950's.[1]

It was only after the errors of the land reform
were publicly criticized by the Party leadership in 1956
that there was serious debate within the Party over the

appropriateness of Chinese experiences to Vietnamese
conditions.[2] But it was Mao's Great Leap Forward that
turned the tide within the Vietnamese Party against
deference to Chinese experience and Maoist ideology.
By the time of the Third Party Congress in 1960, the
Vietnamese Party had reached a consensus that Maoism
was not applicable to Vietnam, and that the Vietnamese
revolution had to have its own independent line on
socialist construction.[3] After recapitulating Vietnam's
own experiences at the Congress, the Vietnamese leadership declared its ideological independence from the
Chinese by sharply downgrading the significance of the
Chinese revolution as a model to the same level as those
of the Korean and Vietnamese revolutions.[4]

Between 1960 and 1964, the Vietnamese Party moved
steadily closer to the Chinese view of the Soviet Union
as "revisionist," rejecting the Soviet argument that
waging armed struggle in South Vietnam could escalate
into a world war.[5] But by 1963-64, there were already
ideological differences emerging between the Chinese and
Vietnamese Parties over the Soviet Union and the socialist camp.[6] The Vietnamese refused to go along with
China's exclusion of the Soviet Union from its anti-
imperialist front insisting on maintaining "solidarity"
and normal state relations with the Soviet Union,
despite an offer by the Chinese Communist Party's (CCP)
Secretary General Deng Xiao-ping in late 1964 to pay all
the expenses of the war in South Vietnam if Vietnam
would break relations with Moscow.[7]

The divergent Chinese and Vietnamese views of the
Soviet Union chrystallized into conflicting geopolitical
interests after the U.S. intervened in Vietnam directly
in 1965. The Vietnamese subordinated their opposition to
revisionism in the Soviet Union to the need to cooperate
with the Soviets against the U.S. in Vietnam, while Mao
and his supporters put the anti-Soviet struggle ahead of
opposition to the U.S. in Vietnam.[8] The Chinese refused
discussions with the Soviets and Vietnamese on joint
action in support of the Vietnamese in March 1965.[9]
Even worse, from the Vietnamese viewpoint, was the
Chinese decision to reduce the risk of direct military
confrontation with the U.S. over Vietnam, making it clear
that the PRC would intervene in Vietnam only if China
itself were attacked, thus leaving the Democratic Republic of Vietnam (DRV) without any Chinese deterrent to
U.S. attack.[10]

The Cultural Revolution in China widened the
ideological gulf between Vietnam and China and provoked
some new doubts about Chinese intentions toward Vietnam.
The Vietnamese saw it as a power struggle within the
Chinese leadership, in which Mao used violence to destroy
the Chinese Communists and genuine Marxist-Leninist
leaders like Liu Shao-chi.[11] The Vietnamese were dis-

turbed by Red Guard attacks on trains carrying Soviet and Chinese military supplies to North Vietnam and on the Vietnamese consulate in Nanning in June 1968.[12] Even more serious, however, was the export of the Chinese cultural revolution to Vietnam. In Hanoi and Haiphong, as well as in border provinces with large ethnic Chinese populations, Maoists carried on their own cultural revolution, accusing the Vietnamese Party and government of revisionism. The Vietnamese held the PRC itself responsible for instigating these activities.[13]

The PRC was suspicious of Vietnamese interest in negotiating with the U.S., seeing Moscow's hand behind every diplomatic move on the Vietnam war. When the Vietnamese agreed to talks with the U.S. in April 1968 without consulting China, Beijing was openly critical. In October 1968, a Chinese official threatened to end PRC assistance to Vietnam if it continued to negotiate with the U.S. in cooperation with the Soviets.[14]

When the PRC revised its attitude toward Vietnam's negotiations with the U.S. in 1969, Hanoi saw it as a function of the PRC's desire for normalization of re- lations with the U.S.[15] When the first Kissinger trip to Beijing was revealed in July 1971 Hanoi publicly vowed that it would not bow to the pressure of great powers, suggesting that it assumed that the meeting involved a U.S.-China deal on Indochina at the expense of Vietnam.[16] That assumption seemed to be supported by an interview Mao gave to Edgar Snow in mid-1971 in which he indicated China's willingness to agree to a "negotiated Hano-Saigon settlement which would preserve some shell of the American-made regime at least for a decent interval."[17] Despite Zhou En-lai's efforts to reassure the Vietnamese that China would not normalize relations with the U.S. until all U.S. troops were out of Indochina, the admission that both Indochina and Taiwan would be discussed simply confirmed the Vietnamese fear that normalization would involve a trade-off between U.S. concessions on Taiwan and Chinese policy toward Indochina.[18]

The Shanghai communique's sentence that the U.S. would gradually withdraw its forces from Taiwan "as tension in the area diminishes" was read in Hanoi as meaning that China was invited to put pressure on the Vietnamese to settle the war on U.S. terms as the price for a Taiwan settlement.[19] Mao's suggestion to Pham Van Dong in November 1971 that the DRV accept a "slow solution" to the problem of Thieu, just as China was doing on Taiwan, was the basis of the Vietnamese inter- pretation of the communique.[20] When the U.S. State Department publicly aired China's interest in a "balkanized" Indochina, one in which Vietnam would be kept divided in 1972, Vietnam's conviction that China was interested in preventing the reunification of Vietnam was complete.[21]

The signing of the Paris peace agreement marked another watershed in Sino-Vietnamese relations. Following the withdrawal of U.S. troops, China began to deemphasize support for the Communist movements in Indochina and to stress the aim of blocking Soviet influence in Southeast Asia. In talks with Le Duan and Pham Van Dong after the peace agreement, Zhou En-lai urged the Vietnamese to "relax" for a period of years before completing the overthrow of Thieu, arguing that it would be difficult for the U.S. to intervene again after such a delay. He offered to continue the same level of economic assistance as in the 1973 for the next five years, but offered no further military assistance.[22] The Vietnamese believed that the U.S. and China had reached an understanding that the PRC would end military assistance to Vietnam to minimize the possibility of a major Communist offensive in South Vietnam.[23] After the Vietnamese Communist victory in April 1975, Chinese officials said privately that they had anticipated the U.S.-supported regime surviving for some years more.[24]

The ten years from the beginning of the U.S. direct military intervention in Vietnam to the end of the war thus represented a transition from close Sino-Vietnamese collaboration and a substantial degree of agreement on international questions to sharp antagonism in national interests and ideology. While the timing of shifts in the internal Vietnamese leadership's assessment of the Chinese Party leadership remains a closely-guarded secret - probably because it was linked with significant differences withing the Vietnamese Party Political Bureau - it is clear that by the end of the war, the Vietnamese Party had come to view Maoism as a deviation from Marxism-Leninism.[25]

The Vietnamese analysis retraced the history of the Chinese Party and observed that from 1935 (when the Red Army arrived at its northwest base area after the Long March), it developed ideologically away from Marxism-Leninism. They observed that there had been only a tiny working class in China, and, more importantly, that the Chinese Party had been cut off from it during two formative decades, during which it came to rely exclusively on the peasantry, thus becoming "submerged" in it. The result, according to this analysis, was that the Chinese Party became essentially a petty bourgeois, and therefore "nationalist," party.

Based on this new analysis, the Vietnamese began to view Chinese foreign policy as the product of traditional Chinese nationalism, or "Great Han Chauvinism."[26] During the first and second Indochina War, the Vietnamese now believed, China had viewed the DRV as a key link in the

buffer zone on China's frontier protecting it from great
power aggression. China's fear of the imperialist
powers explained the PRC's support for Vietnamese armed
struggle against the French and the U.S. But at the
same time, the Vietnamese believed, China saw Vietnam as
part of its traditional sphere of interest, and therefore wished Vietnam to remain weak, divided and pliant
rather than strong, united and independent of China.
This in turn explained why China had been so willing to
have a compromise settlement which kept Vietnam divided
at the Geneva Conference of 1954, why it had repeatedly
advised the Vietnamese against resuming armed struggle
in the South, even after the Vietnamese Party leadership
had authorized the use of armed forces in the South in
early 1959, and why the Chinese had supported a compromise settlement in Laos - even one based on an understanding between Krushchev and Kennedy at Vienna in
June 1961 - despite their violent objection in principle
to Soviet negotiations with the U.S.

The Vietnamese saw the Chinese advice to Vietnam to
maintain a protracted, low level military struggle in
the South and to avoid negotiations with the U.S. as
serving both sides of the Chinese strategic interest in
Vietnam; on the one hand, it would keep the Americans
bogged down and unable to think about attacking China
itself, permitting Mao to concentrate on consolidating
his power through the Cultural Revolution: on the other
hand, it would prevent the DRV from reuniting Vietnam
and becoming a strong, independent state on China's
southern border. Furthermore, the Vietnamese concluded,
China wanted the war to continue, because it would
strain U.S.-Soviet detente: the Soviets could not appear too close to the U.S. without straining its relations with Hanoi, so continuing the war would disrupt
U.S.-Soviet cooperation.

In the wake of the U.S. defeat and Vietnamese
Communist victory in April 1975, Chinese and Vietnamese
views of Southeast Asia were diametrically opposed:
while China focused on the need for a continued U.S.
military presence in Southeast Asia to block Soviet
influence in the region, the Vietnamese urged Southeast
Asians to complete the process of eliminating the U.S.
military presence in the region, force the withdrawal of
U.S. military bases and the replacement of the pro-U.S.
Association of Southeast Asian Nations (ASEAN) with
political arrangements reflecting the new distribution
of power in the region.[27]

Chinese policy toward Vietnam after the Communist
victory departed significantly from Zhou En-lai's
cautious line during the last phase of the war, when he
called for a nuanced approach to the complex situation
that would follow the Indochina war. He warned that the
Soviet Union would try to increase its influence with

Hanoi and to obstruct relations between Vietnam and China, but that the Vietnamese would try to maintain an equilibrium between the Soviet Union and China.[28] But with its new emphasis on forming an "anti-hegemony" bloc as the basis of its relations with neighboring countries, and its success in lining up support from Thailand, Malaysia and the Philippines for an "anti-Hegemony clause" in communiques on normalization of relations, PRC leaders apparently considered the idea of an equilibrium to be illusory.[29] Now China was determined to persuade Vietnam to give up its close ties with the Soviets or make it pay a price if it did not.

The PRC made it clear it believed Vietnam was too close to the Soviet Union. A People's Daily commentary on July 29, 1975 warning Southeast Asia against "letting the tiger in through the back door while repelling the wolf through the front gate" was obviously aimed primarily at Vietnam. It pointed to the replacement of American influence in India with Soviet influence, then recalled the history of Indochina and clearly suggested that the same thing was happening there.[30] Premier Chen Hsi-lien, speaking in Thai Nguyen province of North Vietnam, warned that the superpowers were trying to put other countries under their "sphere of influence."[31]

Finally, during a visit by Le Duan to China in September 1975, Deng Xiao-ping confronted his guests with a harangue about the "contention between the superpowers for world hegemony" and the "struggle against imperialism, colonialism and hegemonism."[32] And in a private meeting with Le Duan, he presented the Vietnamese leader with Mao's "three Worlds" theory, which viewed the world as divided into three groups of states: the superpowers, the weaker capitalist nations of Europe and Japan, and the developing world, including China.[33] The "Three Worlds" strategy was to ally the second and third worlds against the two superpowers, but particularly against the most dangerous superpower, the Soviet Union.

The Vietnamese viewed the "Three Worlds" theory as confirmation that China had ceased to be a socialist state and was replacing the Marxist-Leninist view that the main contradiction in the world was between capitalism and socialism with the idea that the main contradiction was between nationalism and socialism.[34] The Vietnamese response to Deng's presentation combined rejection in substance with subtle ridicule of the pretensions of Mao and China to be Vietnam's instructor on world politics. Since it had taken Mao so long to perfect his theory, Le Duan is quoted as saying to Deng, the Vietnamese leaders would need many years to study and understand it.[35] The visit ended without the usual joint communique, indicating how far apart the two sides were in their international lines.

When the Chinese side realized that the Vietnamese

would not bend on the anti-hegemony question, it informed the Vietnamese that it would not be able to continue grant at the 1973 level as Zhou had promised, citing the fact that Vietnam now had peace.[36] China later informed Vietnam that grant aid would end after 1976, and that it would only be able to contribute half of the estimated $600 million yearly that the Vietnamese had hoped to obtain for their 1976-1980 five-year plan in long-term interest free loans.[37]

The Le Duan visit to Beijing in September 1975 was thus a major turning point in Sino-Vietnamese relations. Up to that point, the Chinese had been a major source of economic assistance,[38] and the Vietnamese had maintained a careful balance in relations between the two Communist powers, despite the increasing geopolitical strains with China. But the Chinese cut-off of grant aid in apparent retaliation for Vietnamese refusal to go along with its anti-hegemony line marked a fundamental shift in their political as well as economic relations. In the future, the Socialist Republic of Vietnam (SRV - the new name for a reunified Vietnam) would have to cooperate more closely with the Soviet Union on both political and economic planes. In October, Le Duan travelled to Moscow where the two sides agreed to the "coordination of national economic development plans" and the Soviets reportedly pledged more than $3 billion to Vietnam's five-year plan, of which $1 billion would be in grants.[39]

Meanwhile, PRC diplomacy was aiming at building a counterweight to Vietnamese influence on the mainland of Southeast Asia. The key to this new strategy was Kampuchea, which had no desire to be close to Vietnam and no ties at all with the Soviet Union. China had been the primary ally of the Kampuchean Communists during the war. In the first postwar year, it emerged as the one foreign state with a significant role in Kampuchea, with the only technical assistance mission, and the only military assistance program, aimed at building up the Kampuchean army.[40] After a visit to Beijing in August 1975, Khieu Samphan, Deputy Prime Minister of Kampuchea, signed a joint communique reflecting the current Chinese international line completely, and pledging "common struggle" against "colonialism, imperialism and hegemonism."[41]

With Kampuchea as the keystone, China began to build an informal bloc of states united by their opposition to any increase in Vietnamese power and influence on the mainland of Southeast Asia. The PRC encouraged Thailand and Kampuchea to normalize relations, even flying Kampuchea's Foreign Minister Ieng Sary to Bangkok in a Chinese plane in October 1975. They then asked Secretary of State Henry Kissinger to improve relations with Kampuchea during his visit to China the same month, and offered to assist in the process.[42] (The U.S. was not

prepared to approach the revolutionary regime in Kampuchea diplomatically but let it be known that it supported the Chinese presence in Kampuchea as counter-
weight to Vietnam).[43] The Vietnamese leadership reacted
defensively to Chinese moves aimed at isolating Vietnam
politically and diplomatically in mainland Southeast
Asia and gaining influence in Indochina, by making sure
that Laos would be tied securely to Vietnam.

The Lao Communist movement which had developed
under the tutelage of the Vietnamese Communists, had
accepted Vietnamese direction of revolutionary strategy
for all of Indochina through the war.[44] But beginning
in the early 1960's, some cadres of the Lao Party and
army, including some high-ranking military figures,
looked to China to counterbalance Vietnamese influence
and embraced the Maoist view that the Soviet Union and
Vietnam were revisionist. The Antagonism between the
pro-Chinese elements within the Pathet Lao and their
Vietnamese allies in the Laotian war became so acute
that in 1971 several battalions and a special elite
company of Pathet Lao troops defected to the Vientiane
side along with their commanders in reaction to what
they believed to have been the assassination of the
"anti-revisionist" Pathet Lao (PL) commander for
Southern Laos, General Phomma, by the Vietnamese.[45]

After the 1973 Laotian ceasefire and formation of
a coalition government, these former PL constituted the
core of the resistance to the Pathet Lao regime in
Southern Laos.[46] At the same time, China had developed
extensive influence within the Lao Party, especially in
the northern provinces of Phong Saly.[47] By late 1975,
therefore, the Vietnamese were concerned not only with
the potential danger to the Pathet Lao-dominated regime
from insurgents supported by Thailand but also with the
danger from China. Although the Lao Communists clearly
controlled the entire country by September 1975 and
could have continued to do so through what remained of
the coalition, Vietnamese and Lao Communist leaders
agreed on the need to put Vietnamese-Laotian state relations on the basis of socialist solidarity.

In February 1976, just two months after the Lao
People's Democratic Republic (LPDR) was founded, Lao
Prime Minister Kaysone Phomvihan headed a high-level
Lao Party and Government delegation to Hanoi where he
discussed close cooperation with Vietnam on military,
political and economic problems, including the continued
stationing of Vietnamese troops in Laos and construction
of an all-weather road linking Laos to the port of
Haiphong (thus ending traditional Laotian dependence on
transit through Thailand for imports and exports). The
joint statement issued after the meeting used the term
"special relationship" for the first time to characterize
Lao-Vietnamese relations and promised to work together

"to increase solidarity between Laos, Cambodia, and Vietnam."[48] While symbolizing Vietnam's intention to insure that Laos would be oriented primarily toward Vietnam in the future, the use of this term may also have been a warning to China and the Pol Pot group that Hanoi would not tolerate Kampuchea aligning itself with China against Vietnam. The Vietnamese-Laotian Friendship Treaty, signed in July 1977 at a time of rising tension between Vietnam and China over the border war being waged by Kampuchea, as well as increased insurgent activities in Laos, was a logical extension of the decisions made in early 1976.[49]

Yet another factor contributing to Vietnam's shift toward closer relations with Moscow was the need for Political-diplomatic support in its conflict with China over the strategically-located Spratly and Paracel islands in the South China Sea. The territorial issue had become a source of tension after Hanoi, eager to begin exploring for offshore oil in December 1973, asked China for negotiations on the demarcation of the maritime boundary in the Gulf of Tonkin. The PRC response was to agree to negotiate but only after publicly restating its claims to the Spratly and Paracel islands in the South China Sea. Two days after agreeing to negotiate, PRC naval and air forces drove the forces of the Thieu regime from the Paracels.[50]

This sudden military move by the PRC, without consultation with Hanoi, must have suggested to the Vietnamese that the PRC would be willing to use force to resolve territorial issues with Vietnam once it was united and inheriated the claims of the former Saigon regime to the islands. Although the DRV had not asserted a claim to the islands before or during the war, in deference to its Chinese ally, it was now looking at the islands, which both Chinese and Vietnamese states had claimed since the beginning of the nineteenth century, not only in terms of the potential for oil exploration in the area of the two island groups, but also in terms of their strategic importance: control of the islands would give the owner the ability to monitor ship movement through the South China Sea and could provide bases for air and naval reconnaissance craft or even submarines.[51] Moreover, Chinese territorial waters would extend deep into the heart of Southeast Asia and give China a claim to be a Southeast Asian power - a claim the Vietnamese were particularly eager to deny.[52]

When the negotiations on the maritime boundary opened in August 1974, the Vietnamese delegation took the position that an 1887 convention between France and the Qing court on the land border and the division of the offshore islands also defined the maritime boundary between Vietnam and China. The line referred to in the text, which appeared to be for the purpose of determining ownership of the islands, nevertheless used the term "frontiere," or boundary, giving the Vietnamese the Basis for a hardline position, which could be compromised later in return for a Chinese willingness to make concessions on the Spratlys and Paracels.[53] It would have given the Vietnamese the bulk of the waters in the Gulf, drawing the line close to China's Hainan island. The Chinese refused to recognize the line as a maritime boundary, offering instead to divide the Gulf's waters "half and half."[54]

While the talks on the maritime boundary were deadlocked, the Vietnamese indicated publicly that they intended to convene a conference of all Southeast Asian nations to discuss territorial limits once the U.S. was forced to withdraw from the region. Central Committee spokesman Hoang Tung, in an interview with a Thai journalist, declared that China "was not a Southeast Asian country" and therefore "should not have such big territory as she claims" - a reference to the Chinese claims to the Spratlys and Paracels.[55] And a few days before Saigon's surrender, Drv naval forces occupied the six key islands of the Spratly groups from Thieu's forces in a move that put the Vietnamese in a position to negotiate a compromise on the islands.[56]

Vietnamese hopes for such a compromise were briefly raised when Vice-Premier Deng, in the talks with Le Duan in September 1975, said the islands belonged to China, but that the problem could be discussed at a later time, which had been the DRV position from the beginning.[57] But only a few weeks later, Beijing's media reasserted the non-negotiable nature of China's claim to the Spratlys, threatening to use force to remove the Vietnamese military presence from them. An article in Kwangming Daily, reprinted in New China News Agency, warned, "All islands belonging to China must also return to the fold of the motherland," and that China would "never allow others to invade or occupy our territory, whatever the pretext."[58]

The article, which reversed the position taken by Deng in September, convinced the Vietnamese that there were serious differences between the "moderates," led by Deng, and the Maoists who controlled PRC propaganda organs over relations with Vietnam.[59] After Deng's removal from power and the ascendance of the "Gang of Four" in April 1976, the Vietnamese expected a continued struggle for power, with a significant weakening of the cultural revolutionary left after Mao's death. But Hanoi was pessimistic about the future of relations with China as long as the factional dispute remained unsettled.[60]

China's pressure on Vietnam to join the anti-Soviet bloc, its threat to use force on the islands occupied by

Vietnamese troops, and the growing Sino-Vietnamese rivalry over Southeast Asia pushed Vietnam to consciously rely on the Soviet Union as a counterweight to China. In an extraordinary comment to a foreign journalist in July 1976, Hoang Tung, the Central Committee spokesman, revealed that the wartime requirement for support from China had now given way to a new imperative: "Both political and cultural pressure from the North must be neutralized," he said, and therefore Vietnam had to lean toward the Soviet Union, which had a "tangibly strong...interest coinciding with Vietnamese interests - to reduce Chinese influence in this part of the world."[61] (This frank formulation of Vietnamese policy toward the PRC and the U.S.S.R. in geopolitical terms, would later be cited by the PRC as a serious anti-Chinese act by Vietnam).[62]

Vietnam's new tilt toward the Soviets did not mean that it was giving up its independence in foreign policy generally or in bilateral relations with Moscow. Nor was it ready to openly join a Soviet international bloc. Le Duan returned to Moscow for the Soviet Party's 25th Congress in February 1976 and unequivocally supported the French and Italian Parties in their insistence on following political lines which were at odds with Moscow's.[63] The Vietnamese still refused to endorse the Soviet Asian collective security proposal, or to join the Soviet-oriented economic bloc, COMECON, despite reported pressures by the Soviet leadership.[64] The Vietnamese continued to remain publicly neutral in the Sino-Soviet conflict, avoiding public criticism of Chinese policy. The Soviets were also frustrated by the Vietnamese refusal to permit them to set up a consulate or even a Tass news agency bureau in Ho Chi Minh City.[65]

But the multiple tensions with China did have a significant impact on the internal politics of the Vietnamese Party, whose leadership had always included admirers of Mao's China. Despite the disillusionment of the majority of the Central Committee, a number of its members were believed to be still influenced by Maoist thinking. The most prominent of these was Political Bureau member Hoang Van Hoan, who is said to have consistently argued that Vietnam should emulate Mao's Cultural Revolution.[66] As the Fourth Party Congress scheduled for 1976 approached, the Political Bureau decided to use the opportunity to eliminate these lingering proponents of Chinese views - as well as some ethnic minority members with family ties in China - from the Central Committee.[67]

The PRC responded to the obvious purging of friends of China from the Vietnamese Party leadership during the Party Congress by cutting off all loans to Vietnam. In February 1977, it answered Pham Van Dong's letter of October 1976 listing Vietnamese needs for new loans, by

saying that it could not provide any new assistance,
citing economic disruption by the "Gang of Four" and by
earthquakes as the reasons.[68]
 The Sino-Vietnamese land border, which had not
previously been a source of serious tension, became a
new element of the conflict after 1974 as the geopolitical tensions began to cast a shadow on every aspect of
Sino-Vietnamese relations. The border problem consisted
of two distinct issues: the "borderline left by history"
and the de facto shifts of territorial control which had
occurred both before and after the two Communist states
first controlled the border region. "The borderline
left by history" was an issue because France and the
Qing court had signed conventions delineating the
boundary in 1887 and 1895 reflecting the traditional
Sino-Vietnamese boundary, but then, in 1897, France had
ceded to China a number of areas which had historically
been Vietnamese territory, in conjunction with the
negotiation of a trade treaty.[69]
 The Vietnamese had avoided raising this issue after
anti-French resistance war, both to preserve the best
possible relations with the PRC and to delay border
negotiations until Vietnam was unified and in a stronger
position to assert its interests, proposing in 1957 that
China and Vietnam maintain the status quo on the borderline, pending negotiations at the central government
level.[70] When Hanoi considered the border question
after the war, the existence of a Chinese faction committed to a hardline on territorial issues discouraged
any early negotiations.
 But meanwhile the Vietnamese saw the DRV as the
victim of gradual, piecemeal encroachments on Vietnamese territory by the PRC, continuing a process begun
under the anti-Communist Chinese regime.[71] According
to the Vietnamese, Chinese farmers who had settled on
the Vietnamese side of the historical boundary line in
dozens of places had been considered by the PRC to be
part of the adjoining Chinese province; border roads
built by the Chinese had destroyed vestiges of the
historical borderline and shifted the border up to one
kilometer inside Vietnamese territory, and border
markers moved into Vietnamese territory before 1949
were not returned to their original position, and others
were shifted as well. The Vietnamese claimed 50 territorial encroachments between 1957 and 1977.[72]
 Vietnamese efforts at the local level to demand
restoration of the historical borderline were rejected
by the PRC on the ground that all such matters could be
negotiated only at the central government level.
Beginning in 1974 Vietnamese protests against such encroachments resulted in numerous incidents between Vietnamese and Chinese personnel in the border area -
usually only arguments or small scuffles but including

one serious clash that left 51 Chinese wounded.[73] The total amount of land involved in the disputes, said by the Chinese side to be only 60 square kilometers,[74] was far less important than the impact on the perceptions of each side about the other's intentions.

Territorial issues loomed larger in Sino-Vietnamese relations in 1977. Pham Van Dong, stopping briefly in Beijing in mid-April, asked for negotiations on the islands, but the PRC refused.[75] In June, just before a visit by Vo Nguyen Giap, the Chinese People's Daily again made it clear that the PRC intended to take back the Spratlys, which were still occupied by Vietnamese naval forces. In response, Hanoi carried out a combined naval and air military exercise in the vicinity of the Paracels just before Giap's arrival.[76] During Pham Van Dong's return to Beijing in June, PRC Vice-Premier Li Xian-nian charged that the Vietnamese were stalling on negotiating the land border and interfering with the activities of Chinese border guards and inhabitants. He pressed the SRV to enter into border negotiations, while insisting again that it abandon any claim to the Paracels or Spratlys.[77]

This time Vietnam agreed to the proposal, and negotiations on the land border began in October 1977. The SRV tabled a draft boundary treaty calling for restoration of the historical Sino-Vietnamese boundary prior to the 1897 convention in which France ceded territory to the Qing Dynasty. The Chinese denied that the 1897 agreement was the result of Qing Dynasty "pressure" on France as argued by the Vietnamese and took it as part of the status quo to be ratified under a new agreement.[78] The negotiations thus confirmed the long-held Vietnamese suspicions that China would deny its rightful territorial boundary.

By 1977, Vietnam's ethnic Chinese population was also becoming a contentious issue in Sino-Vietnamese relations. The 150,000 ethnic Chinese (Hoa in Vietnamese) in North Vietnam had been the subject of verbal agreement between the two Communist Parties in 1955 that "the Hoa people in Vietnam are placed under the leadership of the Vietnam Workers' Party and will gradually become Vietnamese citizens."[79] A written agreement two years later affirmed that all work relating to the Hoa would henceforth be the responsibility of the Vietnamese Party.[80] But despite the agreement that the Hoa would gradually become Vietnamese citizens, Hanoi reached a tacit accommodation with the Hoa population under which they would be treated as Vietnamese citizens except in one important respect: they would not have to serve in the military.[81]

Beijing had no complaint about Hanoi's policy toward the Hoa in the North.[82] The conflict arose over the more than one million Hoa in South Vietnam, who had

been forced by the Ngo Dinh Diem regime in 1956 to take
Vietnamese citizenship. The only agreement between
Vietnamese and Chinese parties on the Hoa in the South
was that the issue would be discussed after liberation
of the South.[83] But in 1975, the Vietnamese leadership
considered the question of Hoa nationality in light of
its fundamental conflict with the PRC, the past evidence
of Chinese subversion of the Hoa during the Cultural
Revolution, and the necessity for nationalizing the
assets of Hoa capitalists in the socialist transormation
of South Vietnam. Under the circumstances, they were
unwilling to give the PRC a veto over the policy toward
the Hoa. Moreover, whatever the wrongs of Diem's use
of coercion to make the Hoa Vietnamese citizens, nearly
two decades had now passed, and they felt no obligation
to turn back the clock. The nationality question in the
South was considered a historical fait accompli.[84]

In preparing for the February 1976 nation-wide
election for the National Assembly, therefore, Vietnamese authorities required that all residents register
under the nationality they had acquired during the previous South Vietnamese regime, meaning that virtually
all of them had to register as Vietnamese citizens.
Those who refused to do so lost their ration privileges
and were treated as foreign residents, with higher taxes
and other discriminatory measures.[85] They were also
forbidden to engage in certain trades, including fishery,
forestry, communications, radio and television, technical professions, and printing or typewriting.[86]

The first PRC protest against this Vietnamese
policy appears to have come in Vice-Premier Li's talk
with Pham Van Dong in June 1977, when he argued that
the Vietnamese had contravened the 1955 agreement, and
emphasized that Vietnam had acted unilaterally without
consulting the PRC as it had in the past on the Hoa.[87]
Most important, however, was the indication that the PRC
would regard the Hoa in the future as Chinese nationals
and assert the PRC's responsibility to protect their
rights. Given the declared Vietnamese intention to carry
out the socialist transormation of the Hoa-dominated
capitalist trade sector in South Vietnam, this was a
warning of potentially serious conflict over the rights
of the Hoa in the South.

The suddenly renewed PRC interest in the rights of
the Hoa in the South convinced the Vietnamese that Hoa
groups demanding the restoration of Chinese nationality
were inspired by the PRC.[88] Most Hoa did apparently
want their Chinese nationality restored in order to
avoid military conscription and to be able to travel to
China more easily.[89] But those Hoa who made the demands
were considered by Vietnamese security officials to be
agents of PRC influence, regardless of the degree of
contact with Beijing.[90]

In the first days of 1978, the PRC took another step which linked the issue of the Hoa in Vietnam even more tightly with the geopolitical conflict between China and Vietnam. At a conference on Overseas Chinese to adapt PRC policy to "the motherland's new period of development and the new situation," the Director of the Overseas Chinese Affairs Office, Liao Zheng-zi, said the Overseas Chinese were part of the "international united front against hegemonism."[91] This policy, which implied strongly that the Overseas Chinese would be encouraged to actively carry out China's foreign policy line against the Soviet Union, represented a fundamental reversal of the policy adopted in the late 1950's of trying to eliminate the Overseas Chinese as a source of friction with Southeast Asian governments by encouraging them to take citizenship in the country in which they lived and stay out of political life or return to China if they could not abide by those stipulations.[92]

The Soviet Union reacted quickly to this new policy, charging that Beijing was trying to impose its anti-Soviet policy on Southeast Asia through its influence among Overseas Chinese.[93] The Vietnamese did not comment at the time, but previous experience with disturbance among the Hoa and PRC policy pronouncements left no doubt in the minds of Hanoi's leaders in early 1978 that the Hoa were part of the PRC's strategy to weaken Vietnam and bring it to heel.

The new strains which emerged in Sino-Vietnamese relations over territorial issues, and the ethnic Chinese, would have been manageable had it not been for the more fundamental geopolitical conflict over the Vietnamese-Soviet relationship and the rivalry over influence in Southeast Asia. While the Soviet factor loomed behind the crisis in 1978, it was the Vietnam-Kampuchean confrontation that propelled the conflict toward war in 1978-79.

Ostensibly, the Vietnam-Kampuchean conflict was a border war. But its historical roots and its central dynamic lay in the factional disunity within the Kampuchean Communist movement. To understand the role of Kampuchea in the Sino-Vietnamese conflict, therefore, it is necessary to trace the history of the Kampuchean Communist Party and its relationship to the Vietnamese Party.

VIETNAM AND THE INTRA-PARTY STRUGGLE IN KAMPUCHEA

From the establishment of the Indochinese Communist Party in 1930, the Vietnamese Party leadership viewed Laos and Kampuchea as secondary arenas of revolutionary struggle which would be liberated after, and as a result of, the victory of the revolution in Vietnam. From the Vietnamese perspective, the activities of Laotian and

Kampuchean revolutionaries had to contribute to the defeat of the imperialists in the primary arena of struggle, Vietnam. It is not surprising that this Vietnamese conception of the roles of the Laotian and Kampuchean Communists in relation to Vietnam antagonized a number of fiercely nationalistic Kampuchean Communists, led by Saloth Sar, later to become Pol Pot, and Ieng Sary. But many Kampuchean Communists, trained by the Vietnamese in the Indochinese Communist Party or assisted by them in the Second Indochina War, were loyal to the broader Indochina-focused revolutionary strategy, based on Vietnamese success and assistance. The contradictory responses to the Vietnam's strategy for Indochina was at the heart of the struggle for power within the Kampuchean Party from the late 1950's on and the key factor in the postwar conflict between Vietnam and Kampuchea.

The Vietnamese Communists themselves did not initially link the Vietnamese revolution with Laos and Kampuchea, probably because they had not thought of their smaller neighbors as being ready for revolution. The initiative came from Comintern, which directed the Vietnamese to change the name of the party from "Vietnamese" to "Indochinese Comunist Party" (ICP). The resolution of the October 1930 Party Congress at which the change was explained, said that excluding Laos and Kampuchea was a "mistake," because, although the three countries differed in language, customs and race, they "must be closely associated" politically and economically.[94] No further explanation was offered, but the implication was that Laos and Kampuchea were so far behind Vietnam in their political and economic development that without Vietnamese assistance and leadership of the revolutionary movements there, both during and after the struggle for independence, they would be used by the French against the Vietnamese revolution.

This purely strategic rationale for the Indochinese scope of the Party posed the problem of formulating an appropriate political program for associating the three countries once independence was achieved. The Vietnamese acknowledged that Vietnam, Laos and Kampuchea were "Three separate countries, each with its own history" and that each had been an independent country for a long time. Yet the need for "close association" suggested that a formal structure of cooperation was the object of the Party's policy. The ICP program calling for an "Indochinese Federation" to be formed by the free choice of each of the three peoples was thus a solution which preserved both the strategic interests of the Vietnamese revolution and the principle of self-determination.[95]

The danger of the "Indochinese Federation" program was that the Vietnamese would use their control over anti-French forces in Laos and Kampuchea to manipulate

such an outcome, justifying it with an idealized conception of natural harmony of interest among the three
peoples. Such a justification did appear in Vietnamese
documents during the 1930's, expressing the theme that
the French colonialists were responsible for whatever
antagonisms existed among the three peoples by practic-
ing a policy of "separating Vietnamese from Khmers and
Lao," and using one people against another.[96]

The war of resistance against the French confirmed
the importance of Indochinese unity to the success of
the Vietnamese revolution. From the beginning of the
war, the royal governments in both Laos and Kampuchea
were prepared to collaborate with the French against the
Vietnamese nationalists, for reasons of historical fear
of Vietnamese expansionism. The French used Lao and
Kampuchean troops against the Vietnamese, and used Lao
and Kampuchean territory as bases for operations in
Vietnam. In 1950, as the Vietnamese began preparations
for the counteroffensive phase of the war, General Vo
Nguyen Giap put the Vietnamese role in helping Lao and
Kampuchean liberation movements on a purely strategic
basis: "Indochina is a strategic unit, a single theater
of operations. Therefore, we have the task of helping
to liberate all of Indochina...especially for reasons of
strategic geography, we cannot conveive of a Vietnam
completely independent while Cambodia and Laos are ruled
by imperialism..."[97]

Laos and Cambodia, Giap noted, had become "secure
rear areas of the enemy and their strongest points in
the entire Indochina theater." An important part of
Vietnamese strategy in the war, therefore, was to "expand
the Lao and Cambodian battlefields." The emphasis in
Vietnamese strategy in the other two countries of Indochina was to build indigenous armed forces which could
operate in conjunction with Vietnamese forces in the
country, gradually taking on more combat functions. In
Kampuchea, combined Khmer-Vietnamese military forces had
set up "liberation zones" in a number of provinces in
the Southwest, Southeast and Northwest by 1950.[98] In
the context of the urgent military requirements of the
Vietnamese, the building of Communist movement in Kampuchea was clearly regarded as a subordinate task which
was aimed primarily at serving the military struggle.
In the Khmer Issarak front which the Vietnamese set up in
late 1946 and early 1947, there had been only a few
Khmer Communists, and Party units included Vietnamese at
every level.[99]

There is no evidence of any intention to set up a
separate Kampuchean Party structure until 1951, after
the French had negotiated "independence" for the three
governments of Indochina which were collaborating with
them. The Vietnamese leaders then tried to boost claim
of the anti-French resistance forces in Laos and Cambodia

to represent national independence by forming new
national fronts in both Laos and Kampuchea in 1950,
which were publicly linked with the Vietnamese National
Front organization, the Lien Viet, in a "Joint National
Front of Vietnam, Kampuchea and Laos" in 1951.[100]   A
related step was the break-up of the Indochinese Communist Party into three national parties, announced by
the Vietnamese Party leadership at the February 1951
National Congress, at which the Party took the name
Vietnam Workers' Party. The move was aimed at blunting
French propaganda and easing the suspicions of Laotians
and Kampucheans that Vietnam wished to control its
neighbors.[101]

It is evident that the Vietnamese did not regard
the Kampuchean Party which was to be formed as a real
Communist Party. In 1951, the Kampuchean Communists
were probably considered too few and too inexperienced,
and conditions in the country not yet ripe for an anti-
feudal revolution to establish a full-fledged Communist
Party. The Khmer People's Revolutionary Party which was
announced in September was actually a Provisional Executive Committee, made up mostly of Vietnamese Party
members.[102] By the time of the Geneva Conference, the
Party still had not achieved its goal of holding a
National Congress, and there were still as many Vietnamese and Khmers on the "Temporary Executive Committee."[103]

Moreover, the Vietnamese Party did not consider it
a party of the working class but rather the "vanguard
Party of the national gathering together of all the
patriotic and progressive elements of the Khmer population."[104] The state of the Khmer Party gave it the
task of "collaborating closely with the Vietnamese and
Lao peoples...and to carry on a firm struggle so as to
annihilate the French colonialists, the American inter-
ventionists and their puppet lackeys...," with no mention of any anti-feudal revolutionary task.[105]

The Vietnamese were not interested in activities
directed against the Sihanouk government unless they
contributed to the struggle against the main imperialist
enemy. The 1954 Geneva Conference began a new phase of
the Vietnamese Party's strategy, in which the enemy was
no longer French colonialism but the U.S. which was
threatening to intervene in Indochina. Henceforth, the
Democratic Republic of Vietnam would seek to exploit
conflicts between the French and their clients, on one
hand, and the U.S. and its clients, on the other.[106]
When it became clear that Sihanouk was both firm in control domestically and ready to remain neutral in the
cold war struggle in Southeast Asia - even while ac-
cepting military assistance from the U.S. - the Vietnamese made a strategic decision to make support for his
neutralist policies the central point of their policy

toward Kampuchea.[107]

Although the Vietnamese had reservations about Kruschev's "peaceful transition" thesis in 1956, they argued, according the the Kampuchean account, that armed struggle was not necessary to achieve a socialist Kampuchea, and that a peaceful transition could be achieved by supporting the Sihanouk regime.[108] The Kampuchean Party leadership continued to consult with the Vietnamese Party leadership after 1954, in order to maintain a common line for the three Indochinese Parties.[109] It accepted the Vietnamese line of opposing class struggle and called for peaceful political struggle in favor of a neutralist Kampuchea.[110] Meanwhile, Sihanouk carried out the arrest of Communist cadres and harrassed leftists who tried to participate in legal politics.[111]

The Vietnamese line for Kampuchea sparked an ideological debate within the Kampuchean Party, as younger members who had studied Marxism in France rather than in the ICP and owed no loyalty to the Vietnamese concept of an Indochina-wide revolution, criticized the Vietnamese line as "revisionist". According to Ieng Sary's later account, these members, including Sary himself and Pol Pot, rejected the idea of "peaceful transition to socialism" and held that armed struggle was the only possible route to a socialist Kampuchea.[112]

Some of these dissidents formed a committee in 1957, presumably without the permission of the "temporary Central Committee" whose Chairman, Sieu Heng, defected to the Phnom Penh government in 1959, enabled Sihanouk to round up 90 percent of the Party's membership. A National Congress was held in September 1960[114] which adopted the new line that Kampuchea was still under the influence of imperialism and that the enemies of the revolution were the imperialists and the feudal landowners. Revolutionary political and armed struggle were put forward as the methods of struggle to be used by the Party. The Congress also decided to move most of the newly elected Central Committee into the countryside to organize peasant bases.[115]

Although the top two position in the leadership were still help by ex-ICP members, Pol Pot now held the third position in the leadership. It was clear to the Vietnamese that those elements in the Kampuchean Party who rejected the Vietnamese line were gaining control over the Party's direction. The Vietnamese leadership considered Pol Pot and Ieng Sary as "adventurists" and "ultra-leftists,"[116] and openly opposed the Kampuchean Party's new class analysis as well as its line of armed struggle, citing the Moscow resolution of 81 Communist or workers' parties which called the defence of peace the primary task.[117] Meanwhile, other former ICP members, continued to argue against the Pol Pot line, holding to the Vietnamese thesis that the Kampuchean Revolution would triumph immediately after those in Vietnam and Laos.[118]

Following the assassination of the Vietnamese-supported Party Secretary by Sihanouk in 1963, the Pol Pot-Ieng Sary group called for a new Central Committee election, contrary to the normal procedure. The Vietnamese regarded the resulting elevation of Pol Pot to Party Secretary as a "peaceful coup" within the Party.[119] The struggle between the two political lines then intensified. During the first visit by a Kampuchean Party delegation to Vietnam under its new leadership in 1965, the Vietnamese again urged the Kampucheans to support Sihanouk, who had rejected U.S. aid, improved relations with China and the DRV, and permitted Vietnamese troops to use sanctuaries along the Kampuchean border. If the Kampuchean Party launched an armed struggle against Sihanouk, they believed it could be fatal to the Vietnamese strategy of allying with the Prince against the U.S.[120] The Vietnamese again proposed, according to Pol Pot's account, that the Kampuchean Party wait until after Vietnam had won its victory, which would then make it easy to defeat the Phnom Penh regime.[121]

Pol Pot and his allies saw the Vietnamese proposal as confirmation of their suspicion that the Vietnamese simply wanted to keep the Kampuchean revolution "under their thumb." In 1966 the Kampuchean leadership concluded in secret that there was a "fundamental contradiction" between Vietnamese and Kampuchean revolutions and vowed to have no more than formal state relations once Kampuchea was liberated.[122]

When the Kampuchean Communists launched an armed struggle against the Phnom Penh government in January 1968, the worst fears of the Vietnamese were realized: Sihanouk began to portray the armed uprisings as a Vietnamese-Chinese initiative to influence him, and to complain about the Vietnamese troop presence on Kampuchean soil.[123] The Vietnamese, who knew by then of the similarity of Chinese and Kampuchean views on Soviet-Vietnamese "revisionism" and were the objects of open Chinese hostility in the Spring of 1968, began to suspect that the Kampuchean Party was being encouraged to wage armed struggle by Mao Tse-tung.[124]

After the military coup against Sihanouk in March 1970, both sides knew that the participation of Vietnamese troops in the struggle in Kampuchea would strengthen the hand of those in the Kampuchean Party who opposed the Pol Pot leadership.[125] Vietnamese proposals for mixed military commands and for Vietnamese cadres to be integrated into administrative organs in Kampuchea were thus rejected by the Kampuchean Party leaders.[126] But in June 1970 a Central Committee meeting of the Kampuchean Party adopted the line of military cooperation with the Vietnamese while continuing to struggle against them over major political differences.[127] Apart from Vietnamese main force troops deployed in Kampuchea against the Lon Nol army, Vietnamese "Armed Action Teams" of squad size operated in certain areas, setting up local military and administrative units, which were to be turned over to the National United Front of Kampuchea.[128]

The contest for power within the Kampuchean Party continued unabated. The Vietnamese, who had several divisions in Kampuchea until the 1972 offensive, could have easily deposed Pol Pot and his group from the leadership, but while that option was considered by Hnoi it was rejected.[129] The failure to act probably reflected optimism that opposition within the Party and army would eventually prevail anyway, and that any such move at that time would have provoked a costly fight within the Kampuchean resistance. The Vietnamese probably counted on the influence of the 5,000 Kampuchean military and technical cadres who had been trained in Hanoi between 1954 and 1970, and then returned to Kampuchea at the request of the Kampuchean Party leadership to command battalions and train new recruits. They could not have known that the Pol Pot leadership group would begin to purge these cadres in late 1973.[130] The Vietnamese apparently expected as well that certain Party and military leaders in Eastern Kampuchea who had cooperated with Vietnamese forces would help tilt the balance within the Party in favor of the "Indochina-oriented" faction. The Vietnamese were telling the Soviet Union in late 1974 that they were confident the elements closer to Vietnam would prevail over what was characterized as the pro-Chinese faction.[131]

Although information on the internal politics of postwar Kampuchea is still fragmentary, it is clear that Phnom Penh lacked firm control over the political-military apparatus that had defeated the Lon Nol regime. Thousands of cadres, some of high rank, had either been members of the Indochinese Communist Party, had been trained by Hanoi or had been associated with those who had been influenced by the Vietnamese. Entire military zones were regarded by the Kampuchean leadership as having been under Vietnamese political influence during the war, including the southwestern and eastern zones.[132] Indeed the strength of the opposition was such that the Pol Pot-Ieng Sary group had to move carefully in attempting to gain control over the Party and state apparatus.

The unresolved intraparty struggle in Kampuchea was at the center of Vietnamese-Kampuchean relations after the Communist victories of April 1975. While neither side ever referred publicly to the deep divisions in the Kampuchean Party, both understood that that

segment of the Kampuchean Party that had never owed
loyalty to the Pol Pot leadership group would look to
Vietnam for support when and if there was a showdown.
And both sides knew that the Pol Pot group would have to
turn to China to strengthen its hand against its internal opponents and the Vietnamese.

At the time of its victory the Pol Pot regime in-
dulged in what might be called a millenarian view of
Kampuchea in relation to Vietnam. The Kampuchean
leadership boasted to Sihanouk that they had defeated
the U.S. in Kampuchea, taking credit for major battles
fought by Vietnamese forces during the war, and argued
both publicly and privately that they were far more
powerful than the Vietnamese, who had been unable to
defeat the U.S. without Kampuchean assistance. There
was even talk by Khmer Communist leaders, in conversations with Sihanouk, of recovering the "lost territory"
of Khmer Krom, which had been part of Vietnam's Mekong
Delta since the 19th Century.[133]

This extremely distorted notion of Khmer strength
and Vietnamese weakness, combined with anxiety about the
strength of the opposition within the Kampuchean Party
and army favoring cooperation with Vietnam, produced a
strong preference on the part of the Pol Pot group for
a posture of military confrontation with Vietnam. The
Pol Pot leadership could not accept cooperation with
Vietnam without legitimizing the opposition to its own
past line and weakening its own tenuous hold on the
Party and government machinery. A border war with Vietnam, on the other hand, would isolate those who advocated cooperation with Vietnam. According to Sihanouk,
who had several conversations with Khiew Samphan in the
1975-78 period, the Pol Pot group planned to insure that
Kampuchea be stronger than Vietnam militarily and
economically by making the population work much harder
than the Vietnamese and would "accept a large-scale,
armed confrontation with Vietnam."[134] The justification
for the armed conflict with Vietnam would be Kampuchea's
demand for a more "just" definition of the land and
maritime boundaries with Vietnam and the need to stop
"Soviet-Vietnamese expansionism" in Southeast Asia.[135]

The Kampuchean leadership initiated armed conflict
as soon as the war had ended. On May 4, 1975, Kampuchean
forces occupied the Vietnamese island of Phu Quoc, and on
May 10 they attacked Tho Chu islands, abducting more than
500 civilian inhabitants.[136] At the same time, according
to a high Vietnamese official, there were Kampuchean
land attacks across the line which the Vietnamese understood to be the border left by the French. Vietnam
protested the attacks and called on Kampuchean forces to
pull back. When the Vietnamese demand was rejected by
Phnom Penh, the Vietnamese pushed the attackers from Tho
Chu and pursued them to their base on Poulo Wai island,

which Vietnamese forces then occupied. On the land border, Kampuchean forces pulled back from some positions, and Vietnamese forces drove them back from the remaining areas.[137]

Vietnamese policy appears to have been aimed at maintaining correct relations with Phnom Penh in order to avoid giving the Pol Pot group a pretext for moving nearer to China, while watching closely the evolution of the power struggle within the Kampuchean Party and army. The Vietnamese sought to prevent territorial issues from escalating into major conflicts, while discouraging futher military initiatives by Phnom Penh. Prior to the visit of Pol Pot to Hanoi in June 1975, Deputy Foreign Minister Phan Hien met Kampuchean officials at a border town and offered to return Poulo Wai, which the Vietnamese recognized as belonging to Kampuchea, to Phnom Penh control. He also proposed that provincial committees be created to resolve local problems on the land border or, if necessary, to report the dispute to higher levels.[138] The proposal was agreed to, and the committees functioned successfully in 1975 and 1976.

Perhaps because it realized that Kampuchean forces were not yet strong enough to hold their own in fighting with the Vietnamese on the border, the Pol Pot leadership made no further effort to provoke armed conflict on the border in 1975 and 1976. But it also kept open the option by refusing to negotiate on a border treaty. Although the two parties agreed in April 1976 that negotiations would begin in June, a preparatory meeting that began in early May broke down without any agreement on the bases for negotiations.

Phan Hien, who headed the Vietnamese delegation, recalls that the Vietnamese proposed to use the last French map before 1954 as the basis for demarcating the border - the same position Hanoi had taken in its talks with Sihanouk a decade earlier. The Kampuchean delegation would agree only to use the map as the basis for discussion, demanding the right to make some amendments to the French colonial borderline. According to Hien, the Kampucheans refused to specify in advance all the changes they wished to make, offering only one or two examples.[139] The Vietnamese rejected Kampuchea's right to unilaterally change the 1954 boundary to its advantage, as it had in the negotiations with Sihanouk.[140]

On the sea border, the Vietnamese rejected the Kampuchean demand that the Brevie line, drawn in 1939 by the Indochinese Governor-General for the purposes of assigning administrative control of the islands in the Gulf of Thailand, be considered as the maritime boundary. The Vietnamese proposed that the Brevie line be used to settle the question of ownership of the offshore islands, with those north of the line belonging to Kampuchea and those south of it belonging to Vietnma, but that the maritime boundary be drawn so as to permit easier naval access from the Vietnamese mainland to the largest island in the Gulf of Thailand, Phu Quoc, in return for Vietnamese concessions on the waters lying southwest of Phu Quoc.[141] The Kampuchean delegation requested a suspension of the talks to consult with superiors, but did not come back, and despite Vietnamese proposals for convening the negotiations the Kampuchean side never agreed to negotiate on territorial problems again.

In 1976, the attention of the Phnom Penh regime shifted from the border with Vietnam to its own control over the state and Party organizations. By its own admission, the regime had no evidence of any Vietnamese plan to overthrow it during its first year in power, and was preoccupied primarily with security problems relating to personnel of the former regime, underground agents left by the U.S. and Thai-supported Khmer Serei activities in western Kampuchea.[142] But in April 1976, according to Pol Pot regime sources, Kampuchean security officials broke up an anti-government plot, and a number of arrests were made. Confessions, undoubtedly obtained under extreme duress, were said later by Kampuchean officials to reveal both Vietnamese and CIA agent networks.[143] These dubious confessions may have been the genisis of the conviction, held by the Pol Pot group ever since, that the U.S. and Vietnam were collaborating (along with the Soviet KGB) to overthrow the new regime.[144]

By late 1976 the Pol Pot group was preoccupied with insuring security and loyalty within the Party and army itself. In September 1976, Pol Pot stepped down as Prime Minister, ostensibly for health reasons, but in fact he personally supervised a sweeping purge and reorganization of Party, military and administrative organs. During the next year, he traveled to various localities, investigating the loyalty and competence of these organizations, ordering purges and personally lecturing reeducation classes.[145]

This purge, aimed at eliminating those believed to be disloyal to the Pol Pot regime and its policies, resulted in the arrest of some 250 top Party, army and administration officials in every region of the country, and of many thousands of Communist Party members.[146] In every region of the country, Party secretaries and deputy Party secretaries, members of the Party Executive Committees, Political Commissars for Divisions and Regiments were targeted for liquidation. Often the purge of entire Party organs or military units followed. The expulsion of the entire District Party Committee in provinces bordering on Vietnam was followed by the expulsion of all the Party members as well.[147] Whole battalions were disarmed in Region 21 of the Eastern

Zone; more than 90 percent of the Party members in one regiment were liquidated.[148] All of approximately 50 province officials of Siem Reap province were removed and reportedly executed as "CIA agents." [149]

The Pol Pot group saw the purge as the final defeat of those in the Party who had opposed its policies, that would permit it to consolidate its control over the country. The Party's theoretical journal, Revolutionary Flag, reporting on the implementation of the "political mission" of the Party during the first three months of 1977, boasted that the "outside enemies" of Democratic Kampuchea- the CIA, KGB and Vietnam - which had "tried to establish spy forces...to infiltrate deeply to sabotage our Party, revolution and army for the past 27 years," had been "basically destroyed by us in the first quarter of 1977."[150]

At the same time, the Pol Pot group also carried out a program to recruit new cadres at every level and in every field, to be chosen from among those with an "unbesmirched personal history which can be checked from beginning to end."[151] This dual process of purge and new cadre formation was later referred to as a "contest for state power between the revolutionary movement...and the traitors planted among us who were working as running dogs for the imperialist aggressors, the annexationist enemy, and counter-revolutionary classes of all types."[152]

This purge was accompanied by a new policy of military initiative on the border with Vietnam and a propaganda campaign in the villages to portray Vietnam as Kampuchea's enemy. In the first three weeks of January 1977, Kampuchean regular forces attacked civilian settlements in six Vietnamese border provinces, penetrating as deeply as four kilometers into Vietnam's An Giang province. In April 1977, the border offensive was further escalated, and by May, the Kampuchean side had broken off all meetings between border liaison committees.[153] The Phnom Penh regime had prepared for further armed conflict with Vietnam by carrying out a major military buildup with Chinese military assistance, increasing the Kampuchean army from six divisions when the war ended to eleven divisions by April 1977.[154]

Meanwhile, local officials, often newly installed as part of the purge and reorganization policy, were instructed to stir up anti-Vietnamese sentiments. One Kampuchean refugee from Sisophon district near the Thai border recalled that on January 6, 1977, the local cadres called a meeting at which the people were told the Vietnamese were part of the Soviet camp and wanted to rule over all Kampuchea, a sharp departure from the friendly view of Vietnam conveyed by the previous cadres who had been replaced and executed in October 1976 on a variety of charges, including being "unfaithful to Angka."[155]

The beginning of the new anti-Vietnamese line at the same time as the Pol Pot purge of the Party and army does not appear to be mere coincidence. The Pol Pot group had been opposed by high-ranking cadres in the Party and army who advocated negotiations with Vietnam to settle the border problem, as indicated by a resolution adopted by the Party Committee of the Eastern Region in July 1977 on relations with Vietnam. The resolution, declared that the conflict between Kampuchea and Vietnam "can never be resolved politically" and asserted that the Vietnamese had a "dark scheme to conquer our land and destroy the Khmer race." It concluded:

> So how can we solve this question? Do we think we can solve it in accordance with the line of our party or must we solve it in accordance with the cowardly position of a group of traitors who kneel down and work as lackeys of the (Khmer term for the Vietnamese)? We must be determined never to be lackeys of the Yuon. So we must solve it in accordance with the position of the Party to avoid being labeled the servants of the Yuon, and to have any hope for real independence.[156]

The documents reveals both the main thrust of the Pol Pot group's new political line: that anything less than long-term military struggle with Vietnam on the border meant ultimate subordination to the Vietnamese. It further suggests that the victims of the purge were in many cases those who had advocated negotiations with Hanoi. For the "group of traitors" referred to in the resolution would hardly have merited mention in the context of policy toward Vietnam unless they had been in a position to advocate a different policy line on relations with Vietnam from that of the Pol Pot group. The implication of this document is that those supporting this "cowardly position" had to be liquidated as traitors in order to carry out the policy of armed confrontation with Vietnam.

Apparently without any central direction, a series of armed insurrections were launched by military officers and Party officials who probably feared that the nationwide purge would hit them. According to Vietnamese sources there were armed uprisings in Siem Reap and Battambang provinces in January 1977, and a mutiny by troops of the 170th Division, whose mission was to defend Phnom Penh, in February. In March, there was an insurrection in two districts of northern Kompong Thom Province.[157] By mid-year a large number of cadres had either fled to Vietnam or gone underground.[158]

By that time, So Phim, the Party chief of the

strategic Eastern Zone, comprising the border provinces
of Svay Rieng, Prey Veng, and Kompong Cham, was apparently part of a secret opposition network in the
Zone.[159] A veteran of the Indochinese Communist Party
who had worked closely with Vietnamese forces during
both the first and second Indochina Wars, So Phim was
certainly suspected by the Pol Pot group as pro-Viet-
namese, but his control over military units in the zone
made him difficult to eliminate. The Pol Pot group had
apparently tried to get him to go to Phnom Penh in 1976
by promoting him to be Deputy Chairman of the Presidium - the second highest post in the government - but
he refused to leave Military Zone 203, according to
Vietnamese sources, fearing that he would be liquidated.[160]

The purge of those who might have opposed Pol Pot's
anti-Vietnamese policies, the Kampuchean border attacks,
the signs of growing resistance to the leadership in
Phnom Penh, and the pleas for help from those who had
fled to Vietnam, combined to persuade Hanoi to begin
supporting efforts to overthrow the Pol Pot leadership.
During 1977, some of the officers who had fled the purge
to Vietnam were helped to form new military units made
up of refugees from Kampuchea.[161] At the same time, the
Vietnamese may have contacted underground resistance
cadres to lay the groundwork for a coordinated effort.
The first concrete step toward an armed resistance to
Pol Pot is said to have been the establishment of food
reserves in jungle bases in November 1977.[162]

Meanwhile, a Vietnamese proposal for an end to
hostilities and private talks on the border problem in
June was rejected by the Pol Pot regime, and Kampuchean
artillery continued to hit Vietnamese villages.[163] In
September, Kampuchean forces attacked all six border
villages in Vietnam's Dong Thap province, and three
Kampuchean divisions attacked along a 240-kilometer
front, penetrating as far as 10-kilometers into Tay Ninh
province. Over 1,000 Vietnamese civilians were
killed.[164] In retaliation, Vietnamese forces counterattacked in September. After three months of continuous
fighting, in which both sides penetrated several kilometers into the other's territory, Vietnam launched a major
offensive to inflict serious damage on the Kampuchean
army.[165] A Vietnamese spokesman said it was aimed at
putting pressure on Phnom Penh to negotiate a border settlement.[166] But in late December, Kampuchea made the war
public in a bid for international support.

By early 1978, Vietnamese officials and emissaries
of So Phim and the command of Zone 203 began to discuss
plans for the overthrow of Pol Pot by a military-
political uprising, with Vietnamese support.[167] The
critical issue in these discussions was, of course, how
deeply involved the Vietnamese would become militarily.

A combined Vietnamese invasion and internal uprising to
overthrow Pol Pot would raise the possibility of a
Chinese military retaliation against Vietnam. Vietnamese decision-making during the January-February 1978
period was therefore marked by extreme caution, for the
Vietnamese were still reluctant to provoke China militarily if there was any way to maintain a modus vivendi.
Before agreeing to support an uprising in Kampuchea,
the Vietnamese tried once more for a border settlement
which would take the pressure off its southwestern
border.

CONVERGING CONFLICTS AND WAR

     In the first months of 1978, Vietnam's border war
with Kampuchea, its support for Pol Pot's opponents in
Kampuchea, the geopolitical conflict between Vietnam
and China, the conflict over the Hoa in Vietnam and the
socialist reform of capitalist trade in South Vietnam
all converged to form a new and combustible political
mixture. The intertwining of these issues, each of
which had very different origins, altered the perceptions of Beijing and Hanoi and raised Sino-Vietnamese
tensions to the point of open confrontation.
     One can discern three distinct phases in Vietnamese
policy toward Kampuchea and China in 1978, each of them
more pessimistic than the one before about Chinese aims:
in the first phase, which ended in late February, the
Vietnamese were cautiously assessing PRC intentions in
Kampuchea and still hoping that it would restrain Phnom
Penh and use its influence to bring about a border
settlement; in the second phase, from late February
until June or July, they were acting on the conclusion
that Beijing was fully supporting Kampuchea in the war
with Vietnam, and consequently they were pursuing a
strategy of overthrowing Pol Pot by means of an internal
uprising by the opposition in the Kampuchean Party and
army; in the third phase, which began in July, the Vietnamese viewed the PRC as deliberately provoking a political break with Vietnam and began preparing for the use
of Vietnamese forces to overthrow Pol Pot and for possible war with China. Each change in Vietnamese perception of Chinese aggressiveness toward Vietnam was thus
matched by a correspondingly bolder Vietnamese policy
toward Kampuchea.
     During January and early February, Vietnamese
assessment of China's role in the Kampuchean crisis was
still in flux. Hanoi had already concluded that Pol Pot
had been encouraged by the Chinese to take an anti-
Vietnamese line, and that the 1977 attacks could not
have been carried out but for Chinese military assistance. The January 1978 issue of Tap Chi Cong San
(Communist Review) carried an editorial on the border

war which linked "imperialists and reactionaries" in efforts to destroy the solidarity between Vietnam and Kampuchea - a strong hint that Vietnam was already viewing it as part of a Chinese policy to divide Indochina and weaken Vietnam.[168] But the question remained whether China intended to push an armed confrontation between Vietnam and Kampuchea to the point of risking an all-out Vietnam-Kampuchea war. Hanoi's anxiety over China's public posture was apparent in the complaint of the Vietnamese Embassy in Beijing on Chinese media coverage when the border war was first made public. Beijing had given full play to Kampuchean charges against Vietnam, while ignoring the Vietnamese charges against Kampuchea.[169] On January 10, People's Daily gave equal treatment to the viewpoints of both sides for the first time.[170]

The Vietnamese signalled to the PRC that it expected it to rein in the Pol Pot regime on the border and push it toward a negotiated settlement. Pham Van Dong, in an interview on January 4, which emphasized the need for negotiations between Vietnam and Kampuchea to settle the border conflict, appealed to "fraternal countries and friends of the Vietnamese and Cambodian people to positively contribute to consolidating the solidarity between Vietnam and Cambodia and to refrain from doing anything that may harm the traditional friendship between the peoples of the two countries."[171]

Hanoi probably perceived the Beijing leadership as torn between its desire to keep Kampuchea as a strategic ally in mainland Southeast Asia and its fear of precipitating an open conflict with Vietnam. While Chinese Vice-Premier Ji Deng-kui was supporting a truce and negotiation of a border settlement, Deng Ying-chao, Vice-Chairman of the People's Congress, was quoted as telling French Premier Raymond Barre, "In China's view Kampuchea is the victim of Vietnamese aggression."[173] Meanwhile, the Chinese airlift of ammunition to Phnom Penh continued unabated.[174] It seemed possible to Hanoi that there were high-level differences in Beijing over whether and how hard to push Pol Pot to negotiate with the Vietnamese.

The Vietnamese leadership decided to launch a major new diplomatic initiative which would both strengthen the hands of those in Beijing who wanted to avoid a confrontation with Vietnam over Kampuchea and test the PRC's willingness to help restore peace on the Vietnam-Kampuchea border. On February 5, the Vietnamese announced a new peace proposal offering a mutual pull-back of forces to lines five kilometers from the border, immediate negotiations for a non-aggression treaty, and international guarantees and supervision to be negotiated by the two sides.[175] The troop pullback proposal was in line with PRC Vice-Premier Ji Deng-kui's private suggestion in January.[176]

But the proposal was ignored by Beijing and Phnom Penh, and Chinese arms shipments increased and began to include long-range artillery pieces.[177] Later in February, the Central Committee at its Fourth Plenum, approved a decision reached by the Political Bureau: Vietnam would support the overthrow of Pol Pot's regime by dissident Kampuchean elements, with Vietnamese military forces if necessary.[178] The Vietnamese appear to have been eager to avoid a military role in Kampuchea that would provoke Beijing's military retaliation against Vietnam. There were no signs in the months that followed of the mobilization of the country for possible war with China that would come later in the year.

At about the time the Central Committee was reaching its decision on Kampuchea, Hanoi Radio was bitterly attacking "imperialists and international reactionaries" for having encouraged the Kampuchean attacks against Vietnam.[179] But the Vietnamese stopped short of an official, open condemnation of Chinese policy. Vietnamese officials later said the SRV had decided that it would not be the first to cause an open break between the PRC and Vietnam.[180] Despite the severe tensions over Kampuchea, therefore, the Vietnamese were still looking for ways to contain the conflict with China, and the momentum of escalation was not yet irreversible.

It was not Kampuchea that triggered the crisis in Sino-Vietnamese relations but the massive exodus of the Hoa from Vietnam which began in April 1978. The exodus coincided with the SRV campaign for socialist reform of capitalist trade in Ho Chi Minh City in late March but was not caused primarily by it. The vast majority of the capitalist traders in the city were Hoa, and it was the occasion for many of them to leave South Vietnam for China, but the main cause of the exodus lay elsewhere. The socialist reform of trade was carried out in early 1978 for reasons having nothing to do with the problem of the Hoa as such. The Vietnamese leadership feared that allowing the capitalist businessmen in the South to continue to operate would inevitably encourage a "spontaneous tendency toward capitalism" in agriculture, which they were determined to collectivize gradually in phases. And it believed the capitalists were the focal point for opposition to the regime. It had decided, therefore, that the capitalists had to be not only deprived of their economic power but moved out of the cities to the New Economic Zones, where they would present no danger to the socialist revolution.[181] Many of the New Economic Zones, however, had the well-established reputation of being too primitive for settlers to have a stable livelihood.[182] The strong resistance from the predominantly Hoa capitalist community, therefore, was not surprising.

The Vietnamese were aware that the campaign would probably be portrayed by Hoa capitalists as "anti-Chinese," and tried to avoid any suggestion of racial bias in the implementation of the program. As early as June 1977, alternate member of the Party Political Bureau Vo Van Kiet, emphasized that there should be no discrimination between Chinese and Vietnamese in the socialist reform of trade.[183] Hoa refugees who left in Spring of 1978 and were interviewed by U.S. embassy officials testified, with few exceptions, that the socialist transformation of trade had been carried out without discrimination against the Hoa.[184] Many of the Hoa who left the South during April and May 1978 later gave as their reason the threat of being sent to the New Economic Zones or conscripted into the Vietnamese Army - one of the consequences of Vietnamese nationality which they had been able to escape in the past.[185] An additional factor was the rumor that war was about to break out between Vietnam and China. Moreover, a large number of Hoa joined the move to the North after hearing a rumor in Ho Chi Minh City that Hoa could go from China to Hong Kong and then to the U.S.[186]

But the majority of the between 90,000 and 10,000 Hoa who crossed the border into China in April and May 1978 were from North Vietnam.[187] China and Vietnam each accused the other of having stimulated the exodus by spreading rumors among the Hoa of an impending war between Vietnam and China.[188] Refugees interviewed later confirmed that there was indeed a panic caused by such rumors, and that at least some of it was the result of a deliberate campaign, including anonymous notes slipped under the door at night warning that all Hoa should hurry home to avoid being regarded as traitors by the Chinese troops when they arrived. But refugees from Hanoi and Haiphong reported that Vietnamese authorities were making every effort to counteract the rumors, to calm the fears of the Hoa and persuade them not to leave the country. By means of soundtrucks, Chinese language newspapers and meetings with Hoa community leaders, Vietnamese cadres reassured the Hoa that the chances of war were slight and that Vietnamese and Hoa could still live in peace with one another, and to report any efforts to persuade them to leave.[189]

The Hoa were not reassured, however. By early June, more than half of Haiphong's 35,000 Hoa had fled to China. One quarter of the Hanoi's ethnic Chinese population had left by the end of July. And 60 percent of the Quang Ninh province's 120,000 Hoa had left by mid-June.[190] The rumor campaign regarding imminent Sino-Vietnamese war was not the only factor: many Hoa from Hanoi and Haiphong had resisted taking Vietnamese nationality, and some had been fired from jobs until they accepted it; others resented the closing down of

Chinese schools as part of the assimilation program of
the Hanoi governmen.[191]
Against the background of the clash between ethnic
Chinese nationalism and Vietnam's moves to reduce or
eliminate it, there was a campaign which appealed to the
patriotism and self-interest of the Hoa in the North.
Rumors circulated in the cities of the North that they
would obtain good jobs in the PRC, and that the PRC was
requesting all Hoa to return to help build the fatherland.[192] A leading member of the Hoa community in
Hanoi who had resisted Vietnamese nationality, later
said the PRC had"mobilized a number of patriotic Hoa to
return to the motherland," in spring of 1978.[193] The
combination of rumors and appeals concerning return to
China were said by a former Hoa civil servant to have
influenced tens of thousands of Hoa to leave Vietnam.[194]
The SRV later published allegations of direct
involvement by the PRC Embassy in inciting the exodus
of the Hoa, in the form of confessions by Hoa who said
they had spread rumors of a Sino-Vietnamese war.[195]
These stories were never verified by independent sources,
but the circumstantial evidence is trong that Beijing,
watching the first signs of flight by Hoa from the
socialist reform of the capitalist sector in South Vietnam, decided to create a major issue with the SRV over
the Hoa that would serve as the basis for a political
break, and helped to incite a general panic among the
Hoa, both North and South.[196]
After informing the SRV by diplomatic note on May
12 that it was diverting resources from "a number of
projects" in Vietnam to assist the Hoa refugees in
China, the PRC publicly denounced the SRV on May 24 for
"ostracizing, persecuting and expelling" the Hoa.[197]
Only two days later, the PRC unilaterally announced that
it was sending ships to bring home the Hoa remaining in
Vietnam - another move that was certain to accelerate
the exodus. A Vietnamese proposal to negotiate on the
issue was brushed aside as a "deliberate hindrance to
China in the exercize of her lawful right to repatriate
Chinese residents" and the PRC announced that the first
ships would arrive on June 8.[198] Meanwhile, PRC official
mass media began a major propaganda campaign designed
to stir up anti-Vietnamese sentiment within China.[199]
The Vietnamese leadership viewed the sequence of
Chinese actions, from the rumor campaign and the Hoa
exodus to the aid cutoff to the propaganda campaign
against Vietnam and culminating in the threat to send
ships to Vietnam unilaterally, as both an aggression
against Vietnam and a threat of further pressures from
the PRC later on. Those actions were accompanied by
other menacing signals from Beijing. According to both
diplomatic sources in Hong Kong and Vietnamese officials,
there was a buildup of Chinese troops on the border

coinciding with the exodus of the Hoa.[200] A European who passed through Nanning airport in mid-May noticed that there were then dozens of MIG jets where there had been only a few before.[201] Against the background of this buildup, PRC Vice-Premier Deng Xiao-ping suggested, in an interview with Japanese NHK television delegation on June 5, that China was retaliating for a long series of Vietnamese provocations, and that if the Vietnamese took any further anti-Chinese step, "we will take a second step."[202] Vietnamese leaders saw it as an implied threat to take military action against Vietnam.[203]

As the Vietnamese Party Political Bureau met in early June to consider its response to the crisis with China, it also had to take into account new and disturbing developments in Kampuchea: a further escalation of the war by Phnom Penh with accelerated deliveries of new weapons by China, and the unexpected repression by the Pol Pot regime of the military units in the Eastern zone which Hanoi had evidently counted on to be the main force in the plan for overthrowing the regime. Kampuchean forces were carrying out major attacks on Vietnamese civilian settlements in March and April, despite the earlier Vietnamese cross-border operation. One Kampuchean regiment, penetrated 8 to 10 kilometers inside Vietnam in March to attack two villages in Song Be province, killing 237 civilians. And on April 24, two divisions attacked Ba Chuc village, less than 2 kilometers inside Vietnam, killing more than 2,000 civilians.[204] The Phnom Penh regime, apparently assured of Beijing's support, was in no mood to negotiate with Vietnam. On May 15, two weeks after a major attack on An Giang province's Bay Nui district, the Kampuchean Foreign Minister sent a note to the SRV saying that talks could start only after seven months, during which Vietnam had to stop interferring in Kampuchean internal affairs and abandon it alleged "Indochina Federation" strategy.[205]

Meanwhile, the Pol Pot regime was moving to preempt any effort by So Phim and his allies in the Eastern Zone to overthrow it. On May 24, at a time when the plan was apparently still in the early stages of preparation, troops loyal to Phnom Penh surrounded the Zone headquarters. So Phim was forced to order the political and military forces which would participate in the uprising into action prematurely. The result was a very costly failure, as So Phim himself and hundreds of soldiers and cadres of the rebel units were captured and executed, and the Party organizations in the areas which were aligned with the uprising forces were purged of suspected disloyal elements.[206]

In June 1978, therefore, the Vietnamese leadership faced the prospect that Pol Pot's group would consolidate its power over the entire country while continuing to

carry on an aggressive border war against Vietnam with
Chinese support. Only the use of Vietnamese troops
could prevent a situation that Hanoi perceived as an
unacceptable threat to Vietnamese security. The Vietnamese had previously ruled out toppling Pol Pot by
direct military intervention in Kampuchea, fearing a
military confrontation with China. But now they were
convinced that China was preparing its own public opinion for even stronger measures against Vietnam in the
future.[207] The fear of Chinese retaliation was therefore no longer a deterrent to direct military action
against Pol Pot.

The decisions reached during June 1978 constituted
an historic turning point for the Vietnamese revolution.
They profoundly affected Vietnamese relations with all
the major powers and with their Southeast Asian neighbors as well as the organization of the domestic economy.
The decisions, as reconstructed from interviews with
authoritative Vietnamese sources and later actions were
as follows:

1. To identify China as the main and immediate
enemy of the Vietnamese revolution, reflecting the view
that U.S. power had receded from the mainland of Asia
and that China was not attempting to "fill the vacuum"
left by the U.S. withdrawal.[208]

2. To begin planning for a military offensive aimed
at overthrowing the Pol Pot regime and destroying its
army.[209]

3. To begin a major military buildup, scrap the
existing five-year plan, and reorient the economy to the
new security requirements of the country, reducing the
army's economic reconstruction role and relocating such
construction projects to security zones.[210]

4. To establish closer economic and security ties
with the Soviet Union, reversing previous policy by
joining the Soviet-sponsored economic bloc, COMECON, and
beginning to negotiate with Moscow on a Treaty of
Friendship.[211]

5. To step up the effort already begun earlier in
the spring to normalize relations with the U.S., in order
to exploit contradictions between the U.S. and Chinese
interests in East Asia and, perhaps less explicitly, to
attempt to balance the closer ties with the Soviet
Union.[212]

6. To make a new effort to seek a diplomatic accommodation with ASEAN which could serve as the basis for
more friendly relations with the non-Communist states of
the region.[213]

The decisions on diplomatic initiatives toward the
Soviet Union, the U.S. and ASEAN, and propaganda moves
anticipating the eventual overthrow of the Pol Pot regime
were implemented immediately. On June 20, Hanoi broadcast excerpts of a Nhan Dan article in Khmer and English

calling the Pol Pot regime "the most ferocious murderer in the history of mankind" and calling on the world to "stop this self-genocide."[214] It was the beginning of a series of articles condemning genocide in Kampuchea and calling on Kampuchean troops to turn their guns on the regime in Phnom Penh. On June 28, the SRV was accepted as a member of COMECON during its meeting in Bucharest.[215] On July 5, Deputy Foreign Minister Phan Hien said the U.S. was ready to normalize relations with Vietnam without the precondition of U.S. reconstruction assistance.[216] On July 6, he declared that Vietnam now regarded ASEAN as an organization for economic cooperation and was willing to begin talks with it, and in late July, he indicated that Vietnam wanted to negotiate a common formula with ASEAN for a "peace zone" in Southeast Asia.[217]

But the new line toward China and the reorientation of the economy toward defense had to be explained fully to the Central Committee and ratified by a Central Committee plenum before being fully implemented. The next full Central Committee plenum was scheduled for mid-July, and the Political Bureau normally had to prepare reports months in advance for consideration at the plenum. But after the events of May and June, the content of the plenum shifted to what was called the "new situation," a phrase used to characterize only major turning points such as the start of the U.S. bombing of North Vietnam.[218] The resolution passed by the Central Committee Plenum, as Vo Nguyen Giap described it, "clearly pointed to the new and very dangerous enemy of the Vietnamese revolution and its hostile plots against our country, and set forth the tasks of quickly increasing the economic and national defense potentials and of comprehensively preparing the country to readily defeat the Chinese aggressors.[219]

During the next several months, the SRV was preparing for war on two fronts: a lightning attack in Kampuchea which would destroy the Pol Pot regime and its army, and a war of resistance against a possible Chinese invasion. While the plans for Kampuchea proceeded in secret, the preparations for a Chinese invasion were open and public. The Party's theoretical journal set the tone for the new phase of Vietnam's relations with China, referring in a September 1978 article to the "long-range plot to subvert and annex our country by big-nation expansionism." The article warned that "we must actively prepare ourselves to successfully cope with a large-scale war of aggression if ever the enemy should recklessly launch one."[220]

Responding to the increased danger of a Chinese attack on Vietnam, the Vietnamese sought a security commitment from the Soviet Union both to deter a Chinese attack and to increase Vietnamese capabilities for

repelling it should it occur. The Soviet Union and
Vietnam had discussed the possibility of a Friendship
Treaty since 1975, but the Vietnamese had always de-
mured.[221] Now the Vietnamese wanted an agreement that
included a clause calling for the two parties to take
"appropriate and effective measures" if either were
attacked, such as the Soviet-Indian Friendship Treaty of
1971.[222] The "new situation" gave Moscow a stronger
bargaining position than before to try to wrest additional military cooperation from the Vietnamese.

The Vietnamese were aware that a Friendship Treaty
with the Soviets would be interpreted as the beginning
of alliance with the Soviet Union against China, and
they wished to soften the impact of such a move - and
to counterbalance the added Soviet influence resulting
from it - by improving relations with the U.S. and with
the non-Communist Southeast Asian countries. They
calculated that the Friendship Treaty would not appear
so much a step into the Soviet orbit if it followed
normalization of relations with the U.S. and the offer
of treaties of non-aggression and friendship with the
ASEAN states. So the SRV diplomatic strategy in September and October was to delay completing the negotiations
with the Soviets until the possibilities for new accommodations with the U.S. and the ASEAN states had been
exhausted.

During visits to Bangkok, Manila and Jakarta,
Premier Pham Van Dong proposed non-aggression treaties
in which the Vietnamese would pledge for the first time
not to support local insurgent groups. The ASEAN states
rebuffed the idea of a non-aggression pact but agreed
to put the substance of the Vietnamese proposal in joint
communiques in which they pledged to refrain from
"direct or indirect" subversion, and allusion to the
question of party-to-party relations. Despite rebuffs
to the idea of non-aggression treaties in the first
three capitals, Dong repeated the proposal in Kuala
Lumpur and Singapore, suggesting that the Vietnamese were
eager to have it on the record that they were willing to
enter into such a treaty with each of the ASEAN states
before the Vietnamese-Soviet Friendship Treaty was
signed.[224]

Meanwhile, the SRV pursued a new relationship with
the U.S. Nguyen Co Thach met with the U.S. Assistant
Secretary of State Richard Holbrooke at the United
Nations in late September to discuss normalization of
relations. The meeting resulted in agreement in principle that the two sides would sign a normalization agreement but not on when the signing could take place. Thach
wanted to complete the agreement in November, after the
U.S. congressional elections, but Holbrooke said he
could make no commitment on a date. Thach remained in
New York awaiting notification on when the next and final

meeting could take place, but weeks went by without further word from the U.S. side.[225]

Meanwhile, Hanoi was watching Kampuchea anxiously, as the Pol Pot regime, realizing its perilous situation, tried to improve its international image. The first sign of the new international face of Democratic Kampuchea was the sudden appearance at the beginning of October of Prince Norodom Sihanouk at a banquet in Phnom Penh after three years in total eclipse.[226] This was followed in mid-October by a press conference at the United Nations by Ieng Sary at which he offered to open Kampuchea's borders to Western observers including journalists to counter charges of massive human rights violations, and said U.N. Secretary General Kurt Waldheim had been invited to visit, and repeated an August 1978 offer to sign a treaty of non-aggression and friendship with Vietnam.[227]

This aggressive public relations effort by Democratic Kampuchea alarmed the Vietnamese leadership, which counted heavily on the image of the Pol Pot regime as a "genocidal" regime to offset the inevitable protests against the Vietnamese invasion. Acting Foreign Minister Thach later revealed that the Vietnamese concern with a successful effort by Phnom Penh to change its image was the reason why Hanoi felt so much urgency about the schedule for the Kampuchean operation.[228] After a month's wait in New York, Thach was ordered to leave for Moscow at the end of October for the final negotiations on the Vietnam-Soviet Friendship Treaty.

The primary issue remaining to be negotiated in the Treaty of Friendship was what types of military cooperation would be provided for in an unpublished annex. Soviet officials later revealed that the agreement involved the use of Vietnamese ports and airbases for Soviet warships and aircraft for refueling purposes (the same arrangements enjoyed by the U.S. in Thailand following the U.S. withdrawal from the airbases there). Other forms of military cooperation, such as the construction of military communications facilities, were also envisioned on a case by case basis.[229]

The Vietnamese made these concessions in the context of formal Soviet commitment to take action in response to a threat to Vietnamese security. The Vietnamese hoped it would reduce the chances of a major Chinese attack against Vietnam. At the same time, the Vietnamese went to great lengths to reassure non-Communist states that it was not a military alliance, and that its real purpose was more economic than political, seeking to avoid the impression that the SRV had moved any closer to the Soviet Union in signing the agreement.[230]

Hanoi's strategy for minimizing the possibility of a major Chinese attack included establishing a Kampuchean national front organization which could take the credit

for the overthrow of the Pol Pot regime and seizing control of the country so quickly that Beijing would not
have time to respond. On December 3, a new radio station began broadcasting in French to Kampuchea from the
Vietnamese-Kampuchean border area, announcing the formation of the Kampuchean United Front for National Salva-
tion in the "liberated zone" of Kampuchea - an area
believed by analysts in Thailand to consist of about 600
square miles of Krek, Memot and Snoul districts held by
the Vietnamese troops.[231] Following its formation, the
KNUFNS would provide a Kampuchean cover for the Vietnamese military offensive in Kampuchea.

In December, the Vietnamese began to spread the
word to certain foreign diplomats that its plans were to
gain control of Eastern Kampuchea up to the Eastern bank
of the Mekong for the KNUFNS, in the belief that the Pol
Pot regime would sooner or later fall of its own
weight.[232] But the Vietnamese military plan was apparently to seize control of as much of the country as possible and destroy the army of Pol Pot as quickly and
completely as possible. Only four days before the Vietnamese launched its final offensive in Kampuchea, Vo
Nguyen Giap declared in a speech that the Vietnamese
army faced the "historic mission" of defeating the
aggressive war of the reactionary clique in Phnom Penh
and urged the army to "firmly grasp the following
strategy: gain control in order to wipe out the enemy,
and exterminate the enemy in order to seize control."[233]

On December 25, the Vietnamese People's Army threw
more than 100,000 troops and its air force into the
Kampuchean offensive. Within fifteen days, it had
entered an empty Phnom Penh and was driving to capture
the main military base of Democratic Kampuchea, at
Kompong Chhnang, 80 kilometers northwest of Phnom Penh.
By January 12, when the Kompong Chhnang base fell, the
Vietnamese had virtually uncontested control of the
major towns and roads.[234] A spokesman for the Defense
Ministry, explaining Vietnamese strategy in the Kampuchean offensive, said later that the Chinese had calculated that only half of the country would be controlled
by anti-Pol Pot forces in the 1978-79 dry season, and
that the swiftness of the victory over Pol Pot had given
the Chinese no time to send relief or to put pressure on
Vietnam from the North.[235]

Although the SRV was braced for a possible Chinese
military counter-blow, the Vietnamese calculated that it
would not happen, because of Chinese reluctance to damage
its economic plans and fear of Soviet retaliation.[236]
So the Vietnamese were surprised when Chinese troops
crossed the border in a multi-division invasion of Vietnam's northern provinces. But after the initial shock,
the Vietnamese appeared confident that they could handle
the invasion militarily. The PRC informed foreign

governments immediately that the operation would last
only about two weeks.[237] On February 26, Deng himself
said the war might be over in 10 days or so, while the
PRC Vice-Premier gave public assurances that Chinese
troops would not move out of the border region toward
the Red River Delta and Hanoi.[238]

The invasion was costly to the SRV, because of the
destruction wrought by Chinese troops in four Vietnamese
border provinces.[239] According to Vietnamese figures,
the Chinese destroyed all four province capitals and
every one of 320 villages in the provinces were affected,
making a total of 320,000 people homeless. They also
reportedly destroyed nearly every hospital and infirmary
in the region, as well as 82 percent of the schools.
Most of the buffaloes and oxen were killed or taken back
to China. The one major industry in the region, the
apatite mine and accompanying plants for phsphate ferti-
lizers, were completely destroyed by explosives.[240]

Despite the cost, however, the Vietnamese believed
that the invasion represented a defeat for the Chinese.
They asserted that they had frustrated PRC hopes of
inflicting a serious defeat on Vietnamese main forces.[241]
The poor Chinese military performance confirmed the Vietnamese belief that its forces were superior to China's
in weaponry, mobility, coordination and training, and
that they could defeat any future Chinese attack.[242] The
Vietnamese saw the limited scope and duration of the
attack as an implicit recognition by Beijing that it did
not dare go too deep into Vietnamese territory, both
because of the prohibitive costs and uncertain outcome,
and beacuse of the fear of Soviet military reaction.[243]
Moreover the Chinese had failed to "revitalize" the Pol
Pot forces by forcing Vietnam to withdraw troops from
Kampuchea to cope with the threat from China.[244]
Finally, the Vietnamese calculated that the invasion had
created new difficulties for the PRC's "four Modernizations" program while provoking an anti-war movement in
China.[245]

The Vietnamese occupation of Kampuchea and the
Chinese invasion of Vietnam brought fundamental, long-
term changes in Vietnam's relations with the great powers
and its Southeast Asian neighbors. First, it initiated
a new level of military cooperation between Vietnam and
the Soviet Union, giving the relationship more of the
character of a strategic alliance than ever before.[246]
During the invasion, the Soviets, implementing the
November 1978 Friendship Treaty, launched a major airlift of military supplies to the Vietnamese and sailed
a naval task force on an intelligence-gathering mission
into Vietnamese waters, with some of the ships docking
at Danang and Cam Ranh Bay. In mid-April, long-range
Soviet reconnaissance aircraft began flying missions out
of Danang, and in early May, Soviet submarines entered

Cam Ranh Bay for the first time. Meanwhile, the Soviet Union constructed naval and air communications facilities in Danang.

Second, the invasion ended the Vietnamese hopes for normalization of relations with the U.S. which was henceforth linked with China's aggressive intentions toward Vietnam. From the Spring of 1978 until February, SRV leaders had clung to the hope that there would be only a "loose connection" between the U.S.-China relationship and U.S.-Vietnam relations, meaning that the U.S. would not normalize with Vietnam before China.[247] By November 1978, the Vietnamese leadership was beginning to prepare for the possibility of a "tight linkage" between U.S.-China policy and U.S. policy toward Vietnam, meaning that the U.S. would coordinate its policy toward Vietnam with the PRC.[248] But even after the breakoff of talks on normalization by the U.S. in December, Hanoi left the door ajar for normal relations with the U.S.

It was the Chinese invasion of Vietnam, coming only days after Deng's visit to Washington and Tokyo, that destroyed the idea of dividing the U.S. from China on Indochina. The Vietnamese concluded that the U.S. and China had colluded in planning the attack. Picking up a theme sounded publicly by the Soviets when the Chinese first invaded, the Vietnamese Party journal charged in an article written immediately after the war, that China's attack had the "approval, encouragement and collusion of the international imperialists and reactionaries, particularly those in the United States and Japan."[249] The Vietnamese analysis reversed the rationale for the invasion usually attributed to Deng - that he wanted to push the U.S. into taking a stronger stand against the Soviets - and asserted that the PRC had invaded "to please imperialism and thus secure more money and weapons for the 'Four Modernizations" program..."[250]

Finally, the response of the ASEAN states to the Vietnamese ouster of Pol Pot and continued military presence in Kampuchea, which was to continue recognizing Pol Pot and insist on Vietnamese military withdrawal and a compromise political regime in Phnom Penh, inevitably widened the political distance between Vietnam and non-Communist Southeast Asia. After the ASEAN states again rebuffed a Vietnamese offer to sign bilateral non-aggression pacts in early June 1979 and continued to take a strong anti-Vietnamese position on Kampuchea,[252] the Vietnamese hardened their attitude toward ASEAN. Secretary of State Thach, speaking at the non-aligned ministerial conference in Havana in early September 1979, directed his attack at "some ASEAN countries" who were joining with China and Japan to request that the U.S. maintain its military presence in Southeast Asia, even as they demanded that Vietnamese troops withdraw from Kampuchea.[253] A Nhan Dan editorial, anticipating an

effort to seat the Pol Pot representative at the United
Nations General Assembly in September, accused the ASEAN
countries of "following the Chinese expansionists and
the U.S. imperialists against the three Indochinese
people" in demanding a seat for the Pol Pot regime.[254]
    The public postures of Vietnam and China in the
negotiations on normalizing relations which began in
April 1979 illuminated the long-term strategies of the
two parties toward the conflict. The Vietnamese saw the
primary issue as being the PRC's threat to the territorial integrity and independence of Vietnam and aimed
at an agreement which would ease tensions on the border
and bind China to foreswear the use of force against the
Vietnam. The SRV's three-point proposal consisted of
the creation of a demilitarized zone 6 to 10 kilometers
wide straddling the line of actual territorial control
prior to February 17, 1979; the restoration of normal
relations based on the principles of peaceful coexist
ence, and the settlement of territorial questions on the
basis of the 1887 and 1895 Sino-French conventions - but
not the 1897 convention ceding historically Vietnamese
territory to China.[255]
    The PRC dismissed this proposal, charging that it
"evades the crucial and substantive issues in relations
between the two countries."[256] The Chinese delegation
insisted that normalization of relations could not take
place without the settlement of all issues causing
tension, including political questions which were not
bilateral issues between Vietnam and China. The PRC
couterproposal included a provision the "Neither side
should seek hegemony in Indochina, Southeast Asia or
any other part of the world, and each is opposed to
efforts by another country or group of countries to
establish such hegemonly. Neither side shall station
troops in other countries, and those already stationed
abroad must be withdrawn to their own country."[257] These
two sentences, contained in point 2 of Beijing's eight-
point proposal, demanded that Vietnam agree to the usual
anti-hegemony language used by China to symbolize opposition to the Soviet Union and at the same time, abandon
its role in propping up the fragile regimes in Laos and
Kampuchea. The PRC thus made it clear that it would
maintain pressure on the Vietnamese border so long as
Vietnam pursued policies toward the Soviet Union and
Indochina hostile to Chinese interests.
    The Chinese proposal also made peaceful coexistence
with Vietnam contingent on Vietnamese agreement to take
back those Hoa who had left Vietnam in 1978 or 1979 and
now wanted to return; the restoration of full rights for
the Hoa in Vietnam, including the restoration of "law-
fully acquired properties in that country;" the renunciation of all Vietnamese claims on the Xisha and Nansha
islands and withdrawal of all Vietnamese personnel from

the islands; and the acceptance of the French cession of Vietnamese territory to China in 1897 as the basis for the land border settlement.

The SRV objected stenuously to the introduction of Vietnam's relations with the Soviet Union and with Laos and Kampuchea into the Sino-Vietnamese negotiations. Phan Hien characterized the Chinese proposal as demanding the Vietnam "give up its present policy of independence and sovereignty and its present policy of peace, friendship and cooperation in order to follow its big-nation hegemonistic policy of colluding with imperialism." He noted that, while Vietnam protested against the PRC policy of "colluding with imperialism," it had not demanded that Beijing "renounce its relations with the United States as a precondition for normalizing Sino-Vietnamese relations."[258]

In response to the demand that Vietnam withdraw its military presence from Laos and Kampuchea, the SRV began to put even greater emphasis outside the Sino-Vietnamese talks on the concept of Indochinese unity. Hanoi argued that they had faced the same enemies in the past and were now again the "victims of the same aggressive plan."[259] It charged the PRC with attempting to "split the three peoples and to use one country against another so as to annex one country after another..."[260] As Vietnam became more isolated from its neighbors, it thus tended to see the political unity of Vietnam, Laos and Kampuchea as more vital to the survival of its security and independence than ever before.

As for the PRC demand that Vietnam repatriate the Hoa who wished to return to Vietnam, Hanoi viewed it as part of Beijing's overall plan to gain control of Vietnam. In rejecting the demand, the Vietnamese commented that China was urging Vietnam to "receive the Chinese fifth column composed of Hoa people whom it has previously incited or coerced to return to China to be trained as spies and special action agents."[261]

Vietnam's conflict with China constitutes its central dilemma as a nation. As long as it remains unresolved, Vietnam will face the constant threat of Chinese invasion and subversion of its ethnic minorities as well as support for anti-Vietnamese forces in Laos and Kampuchea. The SRV must keep itself on a war footing at home and station tens of thousands of troops and up to 200,000 in Kampuchea for an indefinite period, jeopardizing its ability to resolve its own economic crisis.

Moreover, Vietnam has been forced to give up its pre-1978 hopes of balancing relations with the Soviet Union and Eastern Europe by relations with capitalist countries, particularly the U.S. The coincidence of the crisis in Vietnamese relations with China and the shift in U.S. policy toward closer relations with China made a pronounced tilt in U.S. policy toward China and against

Vietnam inevitable. The Vietnamese move into Kampuchea strengthened that endency in U.S. policy and created a new obstacle to U.S.-Vietnam relations. Relations with Japan, which still provides substantial economic assistance, are strained by Japanese apprehensions about Vietnamese-Soviet military cooperation.

The rapprochement between Vietnam and the ASEAN states, which had gradually developed between 1976 and 1978, but abruptly reversed by the Vietnamese invasion of Kampuchea, may be resumed in time. There are significant divergences of views of Vietnam and China within ASEAN, which have strained the facade of unity behind Thailand's hardline opposition to any accommodation to Vietnamese influence in Kampuchea. But by the beginning of 1980, Vietnam found itself still isolated politically in non-Communist Southeast Asia. Facing a hostile China backed by the U.S. and an unsympathetic ASEAN, and denounced by the Western press, Hanoi feels it is the victim of a coordinated global attack. But the feeling of being beleaguered by foes simply confirms for the Vietnamese leadership the SRV's mission in world politics. In January 1980 Pham Van Dong likened Vietnam today to the Soviet Union in its first two decades: the Soviet Union was "the victim of a violent campaign and of all kinds of attacks coming from all directions," but emerged from this "bigger and stronger,..." Vietnam, he said, would also "emerge stronger, much stronger than before..."[262]

The parallel with the Soviet Union comes naturally to the Vietnamese, who have seen Vietnam during its two wars of resistance as the "focal point" of contradictions in the world.[263] The Vietnamese see China threatening not only Vietnamese independence but socialism throughout the world, and portray the SRV as once more on the frontline in the struggle against those forces in the world hostile to socialism and bent on expansion. A Vietnamese analysis at the end of 1979 suggests that the U.S. and China are determined to prevent Vietnam from becoming a model of socialism in Southeast Asia. Just as support for the Soviet Union when it was the sole socialist state was the test of a government, party or personality as "progressive or reactionary," the analysis asserts, support for Vietnam and Kampuchea is once again the litmus test of any political standpoint.[264]

The analogy with the Soviet Union in its early years breaks down, of course, in one key respect: the Vietnamese have support of a great power in the Soviet Union itself. Against a historical background of centuries of Vietnamese resistance to Chinese invasion and occupation without any major outside ally, the "strategic alliance" with the Soviet Union gives Hanoi a historically unprecedented position of strength vis a vis China. The Vietnamese-Soviet alliance is, like all others, subject

to the vicissitudes of international politics. But the
Vietnamese have an overriding interest in maintaining
it intact unless friendly relations with China are restored or some other great power or combination of states
provides sufficient material and political support to
reduce the dependence on Moscow.

Whatever the short-term costs and risks, therefore,
Hanoi can be expected to continue to pursue its objectives of a politically united bloc of Indochinese states
and close links with the Soviet Union, in defiance of
China's wishes. While the Vietnamese refusal to accommodate China seems foolhardy to the Western observer, it
is only the logical culmination of both the history of
the Vietnamese struggle for national independence and
the history of world revolution.

NOTES

1.   See King Chen, Vietnam and China, 1939-1954
(Princeton: Princeton University Press, 1969), pp. 253
and 269.

2.   An extraordinary public debate on the use of
methods patterned on the Chinese land reform took place
during 1956-58. Hoc Tap, No. 11, Nov.-Dec. 1956. Quyet
Tien Va Thanh Hoai, "May Y Kien Ve Cong Tac Cai Cach
Ruong Dat", Ibid., No. 1 1958, pp. 6-18.

3.   Interview with Foreign Ministry official, Hanoi,
November 17, 1978.

4.   Truong Chinh, "On the Party's Ideological Work,"
Third National Congress of the Vietnam Workers' Party
(Hanoi: Foreign Languages Publishing House, 1960), p. 31.

5.   For a detailed discussion of Vietnamese policy
on the international line of the camp, see Gareth Porter,
"Vietnam and the Socialist Camp: Center or Periphery?"
in William Turley, ed., Vietnamese Communism in
Comparative Perspective (Boulder: Westview Press, 1980).
pp. 225-263.

6.   Ibid. pp. 250-253.

7.   Chinese Aggression Against Vietnam: The Root of
the Problem (Hanoi: Foreign Languages Publishing House,
1979), p. 27. The allegation was also made by Vietnamese
Central Committee spokesman Hoang Tung in an interview
with Le Monde, October 14, 1978.

8.   See Porter, "Vietnam and the Socialist Camp."
See Donald S. Zagoria, Vietnam Triangle (New York:
Pegasus, 1967), pp. 63-98.

9.   "The Truth About Vietnam-China Relations Over
the Last 30 Years," SRV' Foreign Ministry's White Book on
SRV-PRC Relations, Foreign Broadcast Information Service
Daily Report, Asia and Pacific, (Hereafter cited as FBIS,
AP, DR). Supplement, October 19, 1979, pp. 17-17. The

Chinese response to the Vietnamese White Paper consisted
of an article by former Vietnamese Political Bureau
member Hoang Van Hoan, now in Beijing, published by
Xinhau, November 27, 1979, in Foreign Broadcast Information Service, People's Republic of China, DR. November
27, 1979, pp. E1-14; People's Daily and Xinhua commen-
tators' article: "Sino-Vietnamese Relations During
Vietnam's Anti-French, Anti-American Struggle - On
Vietnamese Foreign Ministry's White Book Concerning
Vietnam-China Relations," Zinhua, November 20, 1979,
FBIS, PRC, DR, November 23, 1979, pp. E5-10.

10. Peking Review, October 8, 1965, p. 14. Daniel
Tretiak, "Challenge and Control," in Far Eastern
Economic Review, October 27, 1966. The Vietnamese White
Paper suggests the existence of a secret military agreement between the PRC and the SRV under which China
pledged to provide pilots for the defense of Hanoi if requested by Vietnam. It charges that the Chinese begged
off in 1965 when the Vietnamese requested the pilots.
The Chinese refutation does not deny the specifics of the
charge. "The Truth About Vietnam-China Relations,"
p.17.

11. Interview with Xuan Thuy, member of the Party
Political Bureau, Hanoi, November 2, 1978; interview with
Secretary of State Nguyen Co Thach, Hanoi, November 16,
1978.

12. Stanley Karnow, Mao and China, From Revolution
to Revolution (New York: Viking Press, 1972), p. 439.

13. Interview with Deputy Foreign Minister Phan
Hien, Hanoi, November 2, 1978; Chinese Aggression
Against Vietnam, pp. 26-27.

14. "The Truth About Vietnam-China Relations,"
p. 19.

15. Interview with Foreign Ministry official,
Hanoi, November 17, 1978.

16. Nhan Dan, July 19, 20 and 22, 1971. Cited in
Jay Taylor, China and Southeast Asia, Peking's Relations
with Revolutionary Movements, second edition (New York:
Praeger, 1976), p. 190, footnote, 71.

17. Life, July 30, 1971, reported in New York
Times, News Service, July 28, 1971.

18. "The Truth About Vietnam-China Relations,"
p. 22.

19. Interview with Thach, October 8, 1978. This
was apparently Kissinger's intention. See Bernard Kalb
and Marvin Kalb, Kissinger (Boston: Little, Brown and
Company, 1974), p. 279.

20. "Truth About Vietnam-China Relations," p. 22.

21. Problems of War Victims in Indochina, Part IV,
North Vietnam Hearings before the Subcommittee to
Investigate Problems Connected With Refugees and

Escapees, of the Committee on the Judiciary, U.S. Senate, 2nd session, September 28, 1972, p. 33. Sullivan made similar comments and referred to China's preference for a "Balkanized" Indochina, after the agreement was signed. See the Sunday Star and Daily News, February 4, 1973, p. A8.

22. "The Truth About Vietnam-China Relations," p. 26.

23. Interview by an American delegation with Hoang Tung, November 12, 1975. See Gareth Porter, "Pressing Ford to Drop Thieu," The New Republic, February 8, 1975, pp. 19-20.

24. Robert S. Elegant, "China Looks For Neighborhood Allies," Los Angeles Times, June 30, 1975. Phan Hien, who was in China in October-November 1974, recalls having the distinct impression that Chinese officials refused to take seriously his warning that the Thieu regime was in serious trouble. Interview, Hanoi, November 2, 1978.

25. The Vietnamese Party refrained from publishing its analysis of the ideological deviation of the Chinese Party until after the Chinese invasion of 1979. This summary is based on Van Phong, "Quan he Trung-Viet va Viet-Trung" [Chinese-Vietnamese and Vietnamese-Chinese Relations], Nghien Cuu Lich Su, No. 4, July-August 1979, pp. 10-11; Chinese Aggression Against Vietnam, p. 8. This analysis parallels the Soviet analysis of Maoism, first published in Leonid Ilichev, "Revolutionary Science and Our Age. Against the Anti-Leninist Course of the Chinese Leaders," Kommunist, No. 11, July 11, 1964, pp. 12-35.

26. This summary of the Vietnamese interpretation of Chinese foreign policy is based on an interview with an official of the SRV Foreign Ministry, Hanoi, November 17, 1978, and on an interview with Minister of State Nguyen Co Thach, New York, October 8, 1978. (Thach became Foreign Minister in February 1980).

27. For the Chinese policy on East Asia immediately after the war, see Robert G. Sutter, Chinese Foreign Policy After the Cultural Revolution (Boulder: Westview Press, 1978), pp. 42-49. For Vietnam's view of Southeast Asia after the war, see "A Great Change in Southeast Asia," Quan Doi Nhan Dan, May 28, 1975, FBIS, AP, DR, May 30, 1975, p. K5. See also Nguyen Cao Hien, "Southeast Asia After Vietnam," Hoc Tap, February 1976.

28. Zhou's speech on "Current International Problems," in early March 1973 is quoted in Chao Ch'ien, "Peiping-Moscow Confrontation in Indochina," Issues and Studies (Taipei), March 1978, p. 60.

29. On China's diplomatic campaign in Southeast Asia on the "anti-hegemony" issue, see Joachim Glaubitz, "Anti-Hegemony in China's Foreign Policy," Asian Survey,

March 1976, p. 212-214.

30. People's Daily, July 29, 1975, NCNA in English, Beijing, July 29, 1975.

31. NCNA, September 3, 1975, FBIS, PRC, DR, September 12, 1975, pp. A11-15.

32. Beijing, NCNA in English, September 22, 1975. FBIS, PRC, DR, September 23, 1975, p. A14-16.

33. For the test of Deng Xiao - Ping's speech to the United Nations General Assembly on the Three Worlds theory in 1974, see China Reconstructs, Vol. 23, No. 6, June 1974.

34. The Vietnamese refrained from publishing any criticism of Chinese foreign policy until 1978, but a later critique of the Three Worlds theory is found in the "The 'Three Worlds' Theory is the Guideline of the Beijing Reactionary Clique's Foreign Policy," Hanoi International Service in Mandarin, May 25, 1979, FBIS, AP, DR, May 29, 1979, pp. K5-7.

35. Interview with a member of the Central Committee, Hanoi, November 2, 1978.

36. Interview with Thach, November 16, 1978.

37. "Note of the Government of the Socialist Republic of Vietnam to the Government of the People's Republic of China." May 18, 1978, Documents Related to the Question of the Hoa People in Vietnam (Department of Press and Information, Ministry of Foreign Affairs, Socialist Republic of Vietnam, July 1978), p. 12; Francois Nivolon, "Vietnam on the Aid Trail," Far Eastern Economic Review, December 9, 1977, p. 38.

38. From 1955 to 1961, Chinese grants and credits totaled $457 million, compared to Soviet and East European totals of $130 million and $145 million respectively. Alexander Eckstein, Communist China's Economic Growth and Foreign Trade (New York: McGraw-Hill 1966), p. 164. During the war, grant aid from China was estimated at about $1 billion, while Soviet and East European assistance, both grants and loans, totaled at $1.8 billion. Nivolon, "Vietnam on the Aid Trail," p. 38.

39. Nivolon, loc. cit.

40. The first defector from the Pol Pot regime, Pech Lim Kuon, said in May 1976 that there were "well over a thousand Chinese in Phnom Penh and cities around the country" acting as technical advisers. Washington Post, May 4, 1976.

41. Beijing NCNA in English, August 19, 1975, FBIS, PRC, DR, August 19, 1975, p. A14-17.

42. On the Thai-Kampuchean talks in 1975, see New York Times, October 29, 1975. Information on China's approach to Kissinger on improving relations with Kampuchea came from an interview with a U.S. official who had been briefed on Kissinger's trip, May 9, 1977.

43. Edith Lenart, "Indochina: Talks on the Wounds of War," *Far Eastern Economic Review*, December 19, 1975.

44. For the background on relations between Leotian and Vietnamese Communist Parties, see Paul F. Langer and Joseph J. Zasloff, *North Vietnam and the Pathet Lao, Partners in the Struggle For Laos* (Cambridge: Harvard University Press, 1970).

45. Interview with a Vietnamese specialist on Laos, November 22, 1979.

46. Joel Henri of AFP reported in 1976 that ex-Pathet Lao officers were leading resistance forces against the Communist regime "to fight against Moscow and Hanoi's takeover of Laos," *Bangkok Post*, March 23, 1976.

47. Interview with Vietnamese specialist on Laos. For confirmation of the pro-Chinese Pathet Lao influence in Phong Saly province, see AFP dispatch quoting diplomatic sources in Bangkok. Hong Kong AFP in English, May 15, 1978. FBIS, PRC, DR, May 16, 1978, p. A10.

48. On the Lao-Vietnamese discussions, see *The New York Times*, February 12, 1976. Information on the discussion of stationing Vietnamese troops came from an interview with a Vietnamese specialist on Laos. The quotation from the Joint Communique is in *Nhan Dan*, February 12, 1976. The term "special relationship" was first publicly applied to both Laos and Kampuchea at the Fourth Party Congress. See "Political Report of the Central Committee," *Communist Party of Viet Nam, 4th National Congress, Documents* (Hanoi: Foreign Languages Publishing House, 1977), p. 151.

49. For the text of the Laos-Vietnam treaty of friendship and cooperation, see Vientiane KPL in English, July 19, 1977, FBIS, AP, DR, July 19, 1977, p. I8-11. On the declining security in Laos by late 1976, see Brian Eads, "Communists Seen Losing Control in Laos Countryside," *Washington Post*, December 17, 1976.

50. "Memorandum on Chinese Provocations and Territorial Encroachments Upon Vietnamese Territory," Ministry of Foreign Affairs, SRV, March 15, 1979, *Vietnam News Bulletin* (Embassy of the SRV in Canberra, April 10, 1979), pp. 8-9.

51. See Lee Lai-To, *The People's Republic of China and the South China Sea*, Department of Political Science, University of Singapore, Occasional Paper, No. 31, 1977.

52. For a map of China's claimed territoral waters in Southeast Asia, see *Petroleum News Southeast Asia* (Hong Kong, July 1973).

53. "Memorandum on Chinese Provocations," p. 10. The text of article 2 of the convention says, "The islands which are to the east of the meridien of Paris

105 degrees, 43 minutes longitude, that is the North-South line passing through the eastern tip of the islands of Tcha-Kou or Ouanchan island (Tra Co) and forming the boundary also belong to China. The Go-tho islands and the other island to the west of this meridien belong to Annam." L. de Reinach, ed., Recueil des Traites conclus par la France en Extreme-Orient (1644-1902), pp. 300-301.

54. Speech by Han Nian-long, Vice-Minister of Foreign Affairs, May 12, 1979, FBIS, PRC, DR, May 14, 1979, p. A35; interview with Li Xian-nan by a Japanese newspaper, cited in Nayan Chanda, "End of the Battle But Not of the War," Far Eastern Economic Review, March 16, 1979, p. 11.

55. The Voice of the Nation (Bangkok)., November 23, 1974.

56. The Vietnamese move, unnoticed in the rush by Communist forces to final victory in South Vietnam, was not announced by the Provisional Revolutionary Government until May 6, 1975. "Spratlys: Quiet Volcano of the South China Seas," South China Morning Post, September 25, 1975.

57. Text of speech by Phan Hien to the Third Plenary Session of the Sino-Vietnamese negotiations, May 4, 1979. Hanoi, VNA in English, May 4, 1979. FBIS, AP, DR, May 4, 1979, p. K4. The PRC confirmed that Deng had expressed the willingness to negotiate in "The Vietnamese Authorities Are a Typical Example of Those Who Do Not Mean What They Say," Xinhua Domestic Service, August 14, 1979, FBIS, PRC, DR, August 15, 1979, p. E6.

58. Shih Ti-tsu, "The South Sea Islands Have Been China's Territory Since Ancient Times," Kwangming Daily, NCNA, November 26, 1975, FBIS, PRC, DR, November 28, 1975, pp. E7-8.

59. Thach noted that the Gang of Four not only put out propaganda contradicting Deng's approach on the issue but openly criticized him after the Tienanmen incident for having suggested that there could be negotiations with Vietnam on the islands, Interview, November 16, 1978.

60. Interview by Cora Weiss with Hoang Tung, Hanoi, August 1976.

61. "Vietnam: Editor Outlines Relationship with PRC, USSR," Defense and Foreign Affairs Daily, July 13, 1976, p. 2.

62. "Memorandum Outlining Vice-Premier Li Xian-nian's Talks With Premier Pham Van Dong on June 10, 1977," Beijing, Xinhua in English, March 22, 1979, FBIS, PRC, DR, March 22, 1979, p. E2.

63. Nayan Chanda, "United Vietnam Treads Its Own Firecely Independent Path," Washington Post, May 27, 1976.

64. "Vietnam," *Far Eastern Economic Review, Asia Yearbook*, 1978, p. 331.

65. Nayan Chanda, *Washington Post*, May 27, 1976.

66. Nayan Chanda, "A Massive Shock For Vietnam," *Far Eastern Economic Review*, August 10, 1979, p. 8.

67. Nayan Chanda, "Vietnam Prepares For the Worst," *Far Eastern Economic Review*, June 9, 1978, p. 11.

68. "Memorandum Outlining," p. E7.

69. "Memorandum on Chinese Provocations," pp. 1-2.

70. Ibid., p. 2.

71. Ibid., pp. 3-8.

72. Nayan Chanda, "End of the Battle," p. 10.

73. "Memorandum Outlining," pp. 3-4.

74. Interview with Vice Premier Li Xian-nian in Chanda, "End of the Battle," p. 10.

75. "Huang Hua's Report on the World Situation." Text of a report by PRC Foreign Minister Huang Hua to a Conference of high level cadres, July 30, 1977, obtained by Taiwanese intelligence. *Issues and Studies*, December 1977, p. 81.

76. Chao Ch'en, "Peking-Moscow Confrontation in Indochina," p. 64.

77. "Memorandum Outlining," pp. E3-5.

78. The text of the draft treaty is in "Memorandum on Chinese Provocations," pp. 12-14. For the Chinese position, see "Facts About the Sino-Vietnamese Boundary Dispute," Xinhua, May 13, 1979, FBIS, PRC, DR, May 15, 1979, P. E1.

79. Interview with Foreign Ministry official, Hanoi, November 17, 1978.

80. Ibid.

81. Charles Benoit, "Vietnam's Boat People," in this volume. Paul Quinn-Judge and Sophie Quinn-Judge, "Refugee Camps, Hong Kong, June 4-10," unpublished report on interviews with a number of refugees in June 1979, p. 15.

82. See "Memorandum Outlining," p. E6.

83. *Documents Related to the Question of the Hoa*, note of the PRC to the SRV, May 30, 1978, p. 61.

84. "Statement of the Ministry of Foreign Affairs of the Socialist Republic of Vietnam on the Issue of Hoa People in Vietnam," *Ibid.*, p. 25.

85. "Memorandum Outlining," p. E6. "Statement of the Chinese Foreign Ministry," June 9, 1978, *Documents Related to the Question of the Hoa*, p. 69.

86. "Decision of SRV Government Council on the Policy Towards Foreigners Residing and Making a Living in Vietnam," April 25, 1977. *The Hoa in Vietnam, Dossier* (Hanoi: Foreign Languages Publishing House, 1978), pp. 109-112.

87. "Memorandum Outlining," p. E6.

88. In 1976, an "Association of Autonomous Chinese"

distributed leaflets opposing the nationwide census, in which the Hoa had to register under their nationality in the previous regime; in early December 1977 the "Marxist-Leninist Youth League" passed out anti-SRV leaflets at a school in Cholon, the Chinese sector of Saigon. SRV authorities later charged that these organizations were Beijing-inspired. The author was shown security dossiers on these organizations, with the original leaflets in Vietnamese at Chi Hoa prison. Also see Ho Chi Minh City VNA in English to VNA Hanoi, September 12, 1978. FBIS, AP, DR, September 22, 1978, annex, p. 4.

89. Interview with Huynh Tung, a Hoa who fled to China and later returned to Vietnam, Ho Chi Minh City, November 8, 1978. Interview with Huyen Nghiep Tan, a Hoa under arrest at Chi Hoa prison, Ho Chi Minh City, November 10, 1978.

90. Security officials in Ho Chi Minh City arrested Hoa who were handing out leaflets opposing the con-scription of Hoa in December 1977. Interview with Le Quy Chanh, Deputy Chairman of People's Council, Ho Chi Minh City, November 6, 1978. The interview with Huyen Nghiep Tan, accused by security officials of "acting on orders of Beijing to report the situation in Vietnam" and "following the Chinese line in opposing Vietnam" revealed that he had spoken only twice to a Chinese cadre visiting Ho Chi Minh City with an artistic troupe and did not regard himself as an agent of the PRC.

91. Liao Zheng-zi, "A Critique of the Reactionary Fallacies of the 'Gang of Four" About the So-Called 'Overseas Relations'," People's Daily, January 4, 1978. Beijing NCNA in English, January 4, 1978, FBIS, PRC, DR, January 5, 1978, pp. E12, E15-16.

92. On PRC policy toward Overseas Chinese up to the Cultural Revolution, see Stephen Fitzgerald, "China and the Overseas Chinese: Perceptions and Policies," China Quarterly, No. 44, October-December, 1970, pp. 1-37.

93. "Sacrificing the Interests of Overseas Chinese," Moscow Radio Peace and Progress in Madarin to Southeast Asia, January 7, 1978, FBIS, USSR, DR, January 11, 1978, pp. C2-3. "Counting on Hua Chiao," Tass commentary, Pravda, January 13, 1978, FBIS, USSR, DR, January 15, 1978, p. C2.

94. "An nghi quyet cua Trung Uong toan the hoi nghi noi ve tinh hinh hien tai o Dong Duong va nhiem vu can kip cua Dang" (Resolution of the Central Committee Plenary Conference on the Present Situation in Indochina and the Urgent Tasks of the Party), October 1930, in Lich Su Dang Cong San Viet-Nam, trich van kien Dang, (History of the Vietnamese Communist Party, Excerpts from Party Documents). Vol. I (1930-1945) (Hanoi: Nha Xuat Ban Sach Giao Khoa Mac Le-nin, 1978), p. 60.

95. The ICP "Action Program" of 1932 demands that the Kampuchean and Lao peoples be given the "right to self-determination without mentioning the idea of an Indochinese Federation. The 1935 Party Congress was apparently the occasion for the first official mention of the Federation program. An official Vietnamese Communist source published in 1978 says that it gave each of the three states the right to join such a Federation or set up a separate state. "Facts on the "Indochinese Federation' Question" (Hanoi: Socialist Republic of Vietnam, Ministry of Foreign Affairs, 1978), p. 41. The 1939 Central Committee Resolution, repeating the necessity for the three Indochinese peoples to work closely together in winning independence, put forward the slogan "Government of the Federation of Indochinese Democratic Republics." It said that each of the three peoples "has the right to determine its fate in accordance with its own wishes, but self-determination does not necessarily mean separation from one another." "Nghi quyet cua Ban Trung Uong Dang" (Resolution of the Party Central Committee), November 6, 7, and 8, 1939, in Lich su, p. 269.

96. This theme first appears in the "Action Program" of 1932, which says, "From the time Indochina was occupied, the imperialists have continued to carry out a policy of division and maintaining hatred of this people toward that people." Lich su, p. 107. It is developed further in the 1941 Party resolution, "With regard to peoples different from one another, like Kampuchea and Laos, the French also separate them from the Vietnamese people, make them hate the Vietnamese and not have any sympathy with each other." "Hoi nghi Trung Uong lan thu VIII Dang Cong San Dong Duong," (Eighth Central Committee Conference of the Indochinese Communist Party), May 1941, Lich su, p. 333.

97. Vo Nguyen Giap, Nhiem vu quan su truoc mat chuyen sang tong phan cong (Immediate Military Tasks for Switching Over to the General Counter-Offensive (Ha Dong: Resistance and Administrative Committee of Ha Dong Province, 1950), p. 14. Original document in Vietnamese language collection, South Asia Section, Library of Congress.

98. Ibid., p. 15. In Kampuchea, combined Khmer-Vietnamese forces had set up "liberated zones" in a number of provinces in the southeast, southwest and northwest by 1950.

99. Interview with Pham Van Ba, former Indochinese Communist Party member and member of the Party Coordinating Committee in Kampuchea during the anti-French resistance war, Ho Chi Minh City, November 12, 1978.

100. This development is documented in Stephen R. Heder, "The Historical Bases of the Kampuchea-Vietnam Conflict: The Development of the Kampuchean Communist

Movements and its Relations with Vietnamese Communism,
1930-1970," unpublished manuscript, May 1978, pp. 11-16.

101. An internal study document, dated November 1,
1951 explained the division into three parties as
follows: "The nationalist elements of Laos and Cambodia
might have suspected Vietnam of wishing to control
Cambodia and Laos. The band of imperalists and puppets
would have been able to launch counter-propaganda
destined to separate Vietnam from Cambodia and Laos,
fomenting trouble among the Cambodian and Laotian
peoples." "Remarks on the Official Appearance of the
Vietnam Workers' Party," translation of a captured
document (exact origin and addressees are unknown), item
no. 2 in a collection of captured Communist Party documents compiled by the U.S. Department of State. Pham
Van Ba recalled that the decision to split the ICP into
three parties was made in response to the French
negotiation of "independence" for its client governments
in Indochina. Interview, November 12, 1978.

102. Interview with Pham Van Ba.

103. Ibid.

104. Captured document dated June 24, 1952, available
in the Wason-Echols Collection, Olin Library, Cornell
University.

105. Quoted in Bernard B. Fall, The Two Viet-Nams
(New York: Praeger, 1971), p. 181. This source gives no
reference for the quote, but the Kampuchean Party
Statute is cited by Fall as a captured document in The
Viet-Minh Regime, Government and Administration in the
Democratic Republic of Viet-Nam (New York: Institute of
Pacific Relations, 1956), p. 63 and note 69, p. 78.

106. On this shift in Vietnamese strategy, see Ho
Chi Minh, "Report to the Sixth Plenum of the Viet Nam
Workers' Party Central Committee," July 15, 1954, in Ho
Chi Minh, Selected Writings (Hanoi: Foreign Languages
Publishing House, 1977), pp. 172-183.

107. On Sihanouk's acceptance of a neutralist
policy, see Roger Smith, Cambodia's Foreign Policy
(Ithaca: Cornell University Press, 1965) pp. 79-86.
The DRV was especially pleased with Sihanouk's rejection
of apparent US pressures on him to join SEATO in early
1956. Cora Weiss, "Interview With a High Vietnamese
Official," Hanoi, May 25, 1978 (typescript).

108. Interview with Democratic Kampuchea's Deputy
Prime Minister, Ieng Sary, in April 1978, p. 9.
Despite doubts about the "peaceful transition" thesis,
the Vietnamese leadership cited it explicitly in explaining to their own cadres in South Vietnam the strategy of
"peaceful political struggle" against the Diem regime.
See Gareth Porter, "Vietnam and the Socialist Camp".

109. "Interview With a High Vietnamese Official."

110.   An internal history of the Kampuchean Party
written in 1973 recalled that Sieu Heng, the Secretary of
the party "Temporary Central Committee" from 1955 to
1959 had "taught the people that there were no social
classes in our Cambodian society. This meant that there
was no struggle between social classes; and that the
people, above all the farmers, did not wage revolution.
They had to follow the ruling class with Sihanouk at the
head, like Siv [Sieu] Heng had followed it." "Summary of
Annotated Party History," by the Eastern Region Military-
Political Service, p. 14, captured document translated by
the U.S. Central Intelligence Agency and obtained from
the U.S Embassy in Thailand, December 1978.

111.   Heder, "The Historical Bases," pp. 29-35.

112.   The Call, August 28, 1978, p. 9.

113.   Text of speech by Pol Pot; at meeting
commemorating the Kampuchean Communist Party's 17th
founding anniversary, September 27, 1977. Translated in
FBIS, AP, DR, October 4, 1977, p. H8.

114.   "Summary of Annotated Party History,"
pp. 14, 17-18.

115.   Text of Pol Pot speech, September 27, 1977,
pp. H8-9.

116.   Democratic Kampuchea, Livre Noir: Faits et
Preuves des Actes d'Aggression et d'Annexion du Vietnam
Contre le Kampuchea (Phnom Penh, September 1978), p. 37.
According to one knowledgeable Vietnamese official, Ieng
Sary, who was considered in 1960 to be the real leader of
the group which had seized control of the Kampuchean
Party was viewed by the Vietnamese leadership as "a
perfidious man" after the Kampuchean Party Congress.
Ieng Sary was even suspected of being a "Trotskyist,"
according to this source, who added that the Vietnamese
had "hoped to educate him." Interview with Vietnamese
official, November 22, 1978.

117.   Livre Noir, pp. 36-37. According to this
account, the Vietnamese asserted that there were still no
clear class divisions in either Kampuchean or Leotian
society. To my knowledge, no Vietnamese document refutes
this assertion.

118.   This was the gist of documents which were
brought back to Kampuchea by then Secretary-General Touch
Samouth from a visit to Vietnam in 1962, as paraphrased
by Prince Norodom Sihanouk. See Heder, "The Historical
Bases," p. 50. The high Vietnamese official previously
quoted states that, "The opposition in their party [were]
those with the same line as the Vietnam Communist Party."
Interview with Cora Weiss, Hanoi, May 25, 1978.

119.   Interview with Pham Van Ba.

120.   Interview with high Vietnamese official,
May 25, 1978.

121.   Livre Noir, p. 38.

122.   Ibid., p. 42.
123.   Heder, "The Historical Bases," pp. 77-78.
124.   Interview with high Vietnamese official,
May 25, 1978.
125.   Ibid.
126.   Livre Noir, pp. 61, 64-67.
127.   Unpublished notes of the interview with Ieng
Sary by Daniel Burstein, editor of The Call.
128.   The best available description of Vietnamese
Communist operations in Kampuchea at the beginning of the
war is U.S. Deptment of State, Bureau of Intelligence and
Research, "Cambodia: Can the Vietnamese Communists
Export Insurgency?" declassified Research Study,
September 25, 1970.
129.   Agence France Presse dispatch, September 7,
1978, quoting Hoang Tung. Translated in FBIS, AP, DR,
September 8, 1978, p. K2.
130.   Interview with a high Vietnames official;
Norodom Sihanouk, Chroniques de Guerre et d'Espoir
(Paris: Hachette/Stock, 1979), p. 52: Timothy Michael
Carney, Communist Party Power in Kampuchea (Cambodia):
Documents and Discussion, Cornell University Southeast
Asia Program, Data Paper No. 106, January 1977, p. 7.
131.   Interview with a soviet official, February 1979.
132.   See Ben Kiernan, "Conflict in the Kampuchean
Communist Movement," paper presented to the Tenth Anni-
versaryConference of the Journal of Contemporary Asia,
Stockholm, August 23-25, esp. pp. 35-45.
133.   Sihanouk, Chroniques, pp. 64-67, 94-96;
transcript of remarks by Norodom Sihanouk at the Asia
Society, Washington, D.C., February 25, 1979. For the
Pol Pot group's own published views suggesting Vietnamese
dependence on the Kampuchean Communists rather than
vice-versa, see Livre Noir, pp. 55, 81.
134.   Sihanouk, War and Hope: The Case For Cambodia
(New York: Pantheon, 1980), pp. 45-46.
135.   Ibid.
136.   "Facts About the Vietnam-Kampuchea Border
Question," document released by the SRV Foreign Ministry,
April 7, 1978 in Kampuchea Dossier (Hanoi: Vietnam
Courier, 1978), Vol. I, pp. 125-126.
137.   Interview with Phan Hien, November 2, 1978.
138.   Ibid.
139.   Ibid. Phan Hien's account suggests that the
Kampuchean delegation was planning to propose changes when
the negotiations opened in June. Curiously Political
Bureau member Xuan Thuy gave a contradictory account of
the preliminary conference, asserting that the Kampuchean
delegation produced a map with 11 changes from the pre-
1954 French map which was supposed to be the basis for
the border demarcation. Interview, November 2, 1978.

140.   Interview with Xuan Thuy.

141.   Interview with Phan Hien.

142.   Livre Noir, p. 95. On the Kampuchean leaders' concern with the possibility of a U.S. organized effort to overthrow the new government, see transcript of remarks by Ieng Sary in New York City, September 6, 1975, by the Indochina Resource Center.

143.   Norman Peagam, "Cambodia: Plagued by Unrest," The Asian Wall Street Journal, November 7, 1978. This article is based on interviews with Ieng Sary and other Kampuchean officials in Jakarta.

144.   Livre Noir, p. 103. Peagam quotes a Kampuchean official as arguing that the U.S. was conniving in Vietnamese attacks on Kampuchea because it hoped Vietnam would be "more amenable to U.S. interests, and more independent of the Soviet Union." The Kampuchean official claimed to have "captured documents" in support of this allegation.

145.   Interview with a U.S. intelligence official, August 1978; interview with a former U.S. intelligence official, February 1979.

146.   "Important Culprits (Arrested from 1976 to April 9, 1978)," document of Democratic Kampuchea reproduced in English by the People's Republic of Kampuchea for the "People's Revolutionary Tribunal Held in Phnom Penh For the Trial of the Genocide Crime of the Pol Pot-Ieng Sary Clique," August 1979, (18 pages)., giving the names, positions and dates of arrests of the top officials purged.

147.   Testimony of a district-level cadre of the Kampuchean Party. Thanh Tin, "Genocide in Kampuchea," Kampuchean Dossier II (Haono: Vietnam Courier, 1978), p. 48.

148.   Testimony of Hun Sen, former Deputy Regiment Commander in Region 21, Military Zone 203, quoted in Khanh Van, "Uprisings in Kampuchea," Quan Doi Nhan Dan, Hanoi Domestic Service, October 13, 1978, FBIS, AP, DR, October 16, 1978, p. K8. See also the testimony of Xat Xon, a former soldier in Military Region 23, in Vu Can, "Refugees from the Phnom Penh Regime Bear Witness," Kampuchea Dossier I, pp. 33-35.

149.   Wall Street Journal, October 19, 1977.

150.   "Continue to Consolidate and Develop More Strongly, the Great Victory at the Beginning of 1977 in Order to Pursue and Clean Out the Enemy and to Fulfill and Overfulfill the Party's 1977 Plan," Revolutionary Flag, No. 4, April 1977. This document, originally in Khmer, was made available to me in Vietnamese translation by the Foreign Ministry of the SRV.

151.   "Let Us Vigorously Contribute to Building the Ranks of Cadres Along the Class Line of the Party," Phnom Penh Domestic Service, April 20, 1978. Translated in

FBIS, AP, DR, April 24, 1978, p. H5.

152. Ibid., p. H6.

153. "Chronology, 1960-1978" Kampuchea Dossier I, pp. 69-70; Hoang Nguyen, "Peking's Shadow Over Angkor," Kampuchea Dossier II, p. 26.

154. Dispatch from AKAHATA correspondent Taro Miyamoto, in Phnom Penh, Tokyo JPS in English, June 14, 1979. FBIS, AP, DR June 15, 1979, Annex, p. 8. The dispatch is based on original Chinese-language document captured by Vietnamese forces in Kampuchea.

155. Interview with Nuon Speu, a 22-year old student from Phum Thmey village, Bangkok, December 5, 1978.

156. "Resolution of the Conference of the Eastern Zone of Kampuchea," typescript of a Vietnamese translation of a Kampuchean Party document on disply along with the Khmer language original at the Exhibition of Kampuchean War Crimes, Ho Chi Minh City, November 1978. My own translation was done on the spot. The SRV has circulated photocopies of the original document's title page and page 84, but has ignored these key passages on page 83.

157. Kampuchea Dossier II, p. 65; "Memorandum on United Nations General Assembly Discussion of So-Called 'Situation in Kampuchea'," Ministry of Foreign Affairs, Socialist Republic of Vietnam, Hanoi, Vietnam News Agency, November 10, 1979.

158. Biography of Hung Sen, SPK (Sapordamean Kampuchea, or Kampuchean News Agency), clandestine radio broadcast in French, June 1, 1978, FBIS, AP, DR, June 6, 1979, p. H1; "Uprisings in Kampuchea," loc. cit.

159. The existence of this secret oppotion in the Eastern Zone is reported in Kampuchea Dossier II, p. 63.

160. Interview with Pham Van Ba.

161. Notes of interviews by Joseph Crown, with Vice-Chairman of the Tay Ninh Province People's Committee, Huynh Van Luan, April 28, 1979; and with Col. Tran Cong Man, editor, Quan Doi Nhan Dan and spokesman for the Ministry of Defence, May 2, 1979.

162. Kampuchea Dossier II, p. 63.

163. Kampuchea Dossier I, p. 71.

164. Ibid. Jon Alpert, a documentary film maker, was taken to a cemetary where hundreds of civilians were buried, all of them with the same date on the headstone, September 24, 1977. The scene was shown on the McNeil-Lehrer Report, January 12, 1978.

165. Both sides' accounts suggest a rising tempo of continuous attack and counterattack. One Vietnamese account refers to "simultaneous attacks launched in September, October and December 1977 against many places in Tay Ninh Province." (Foreign Ministry document,

Hanoi VNA, January 6, 1978, FBIS, AP, DR, January 9,
1978, p. K1.) Vietnam also said that Kampuchea occupied
"several portions of Vietnamese territory, especially
an area 10km keep into Vietnamese territory on the bank
of the Eastern Vam Co canal." (Kampuchea Dossier I,
p. 71.) The most specific Kampuchean account is Khieu
Samphan's December 30, 1977 statement, which said,
"Since September 1977, the SRV Armed Forces have launched
a continuous large-scale aggressive offensive and aimed
at plundering the rise in the eastern region. Later in
November, the SRV Armed Forces carried out an aggression
offensive [as translated] in Svay Rieng Province,
penetrating several kilometers into Srok Romduol,
Prasot, Komong Rou and Chantrea." (Phnom Penh Domestic
Service, December 30, 1977, FBIS, AP, DR, January 3,
1978, p. H2.) His account indicates that the first
Vietnamese penetration beyond "several kilometers" came
in December 1977. Also see Livre Noir, p. 99, and
Pol Pot, "Let Us Continue to Firmly Hold Aloft the
Banner of the Victory of the Glorious Communist Party of
Kampuchea in Order to Defend Democratic Kampuchea, Carry
on Socialist Revolution and Build up Socialism," (Phnom
Penh, September 1978), p. 10.

     166.   Interview with Hoang Tung by Nayan Chanda,
Far Eastern Economic Review, April 21, 1978.

     167.   Information from a Vietnamese source in
Southeast Asia, February 1979.

     168.   "No Reactionary Power Can Destroy the
Solidarity and Friendship Between the Cambodian and
Vietnamese Peoples," Tap Chi Cong San, January 1978,
Hanoi International Service in Thai, January 23, 1978,
FBIS, AP, DR, January 24, 1978, pp. K19-20.

     169.   AFP dispatch, Beijing, December 31, 1977,
FBIS, PRC, DR, January 3, 1978, p. A11. AFP (Hong Kong)
in English, December 31, 1977.

     170.   AFP dispatch, Beijing, January 10, 1978.
AFP (Hong Kong) in English, January 10, 1978. FBIS, PRC,
DR, January 10, 1978, p. A10.

     171.   Hanoi domestic service in Vietnamese,
January 4, 1978, FBIS, AP, DR, January 4, 1978, pp.
K19-20.

     172.   Statement to Japanese Diet members, Wen Wei
Pao (Hong Kong), January 20, 1978, FBIS, PRC, DR,
January 23, 1978, p. N3.

     173.   This statement was cited by Phan Hien in
November 1978 as evidence of Chinese intentions to
support Kampuchea to the hilt. Interview, November 2,
1978. I have been unable to find any report of the
alleged remark in the French Press coverage of Barre's
trip to China. It may have reached Hanoi via the diplomatic grapevine.

174.   Marian K. Leighton, "perspectives on the Vietnam-Cambodia Border Conflict," Asian Survey, Vol. 8, No. 5, May 1978, p. 451. Leighton cites no source, suggesting that the information came from U.S. intelligence sources. The author was given similar information by a U.S. intelligence source in June 1978.

175.   "SRV Government Releases Statement on Vietnam-Kampuchea Relations," Hanoi VNA in English, February 5, 1978, FBIS, AP, DR, February 6, 1978, pp. K6-8.

176.   Wen Wei Pao, January 20, 1978.

177.   Leighton, "Perspectives," p. 451.

178.   Nayan Chanda, "The Timetable For a Takeover," Far Eastern Economic Review, February 23, 1979.

179.   "The Kampuchean Authorities Only Want War," Hanoi international service in English, February 20, 1978, FBIS, AP, DR, February 21, 1978, p. K5. "Kampuchea's Hostility Toward Vietnam," Hanoi international service in English, February 21, 1978, FBIS, AP, DR, February 22 1978, p. K2.

180.   Interview with a senior foreign affairs cadre, Ho Chi Minh City, November 8, 1978.

181.   Speech by Tran Trong Tan, member of the Standing Committee, Ho Chi Minh City Party Committee to the Nguyen Van Cu Party School, April 8, 1978, Cai tao triet de he thong thuong nghiep tu ban chu nghia o Thanh Pho Ho Chi Minh (Thoroughly Refore the Capitalist System of Trade in Ho Chi Minh City) (Ho Chi Minh City: Nha xuat ban Thanh Pho Ho Chi Minh, 1978), pp. 49, 53.

182.   The New Economic Zones were communities consisting of a few thousand people per zone, usually established on previously uncultivated land. While in theory each community was supposed to have received the requisite support to clear the land, social, medical and educational services and sufficient grain until the first harvest, the logistical failures were so serious and widespread that even the officially-sanctioned newspaper Tin Sang published a scathing criticism of the zones on March 10, 1978, pointing out that land had not been cleared of tree stumps and was in danger of becoming totally unproductive. It further pointed to medical problems, inadequate grain supplies and lack of safe drinking water.

183.   Speech by Vu Dinh Lieu, Chairman of the Ho Chi Minh City People's Committee, April 5, 1978, Cai tao triet de, pp. 24-25.

184.   "Report by an Officer of the American Embassy in Bangkok on Sino-Vietnamese Refugees, June 7, 1979, "Vietnam's Refugee Machine (Draft report by the Department of State, July 20, 1979, Document No. 2-20, pp. 1 and 9. This summary of extensive interviews with Sino-Vietnamese refugees noted, in reporting this conclusion,

"We are surprised that the refugees were so generous to the Vietnamese government and its cadres on this point." p. 15.

185. Ibid., p. 3. "Report of an Officer of the American Embassy in Bangkok on Refugee Motivations for Leaving Vietnam, May 19, 1978, "Vietnam's Refugee Machine, Document No. 2-10, pp. 1,3. "Comments by Refugees at a PRC Resettlement Farm on Reasons For and Methods of Escape of Ethnic Chinese From Vietnam, September 1978," Ibid., Document No. 1-40, p. 4.

186. "Comments by Refugees at a PRC Resettlement Farm," Ibid., p. 2. These interviews parallel my own with Huynh Tung, a 29-year old Hoa who had left Ho Chi Minh City in May-June 1978 but returned three weeks later. Interview, Ho Chi Minh City, November 8, 1978; also Larry Eichel, "A Successful Escape to a Different Kind of Purgatory," Philadelphia Enquirer (no date shown), reprinted in Congressional Record, June 12, 1979, p. S7490.

187. The figure of 89,700 was given by New China News Agency in late May. Washington Post, May 29, 1978. That the massive exodus began in early April is indicated in "Statement of the Spokesman of the Overseas Chinese Affairs Office of the State Council of the People's Republic of China," Documents Related to the Question of the Hoa, p. 55. Chinese officials told U.S. officials that the majority of the refugees in this phase of the exodus came from North Vietnam. "Comments by Refugees at the PRC Resettlement Farm," p. 3.

188. "Statement of the Spokesman of the Overseas Chinese Affairs Office," p. 55; Nguyen Yem, "Mechanism of a Campaign of Coercion," The Hoa in Vietnam, pp. 40-50.

189. "Comments by a Refugee on Ethnic Chinese Fleeing Northern Vietnam, June 1978," Vietnam's Refugee Machine, Document No. I-20, pp. 1-3; Charles Benoit, "Viet Nam's Boat People,"

190. "Comments by a Refugee," p. 1; Paul Quinn-Judge, "Le Vietnam Face a la Chine," Le Monde Diplomatique, September 1978.

191. Benoit, "Viet Nam's Boat People," Quinn-Judge and Quinn-Judge, "Refugee Camps, Hong Kong," p. 15; "Comments by Refugees at a PRC Resettlement Farm," p. 3.

192. "Statement of an Ethnic Chinese Former SRV Civil Servant on Expulsion of Chinese from Northern Vietnam, June 1978," Vietnam's Refugee Machine, Document No. I-30, p. 1.

193. Quinn-Judge and Quinn-Judge, "Refugee Camps, Hong Kong," p. 21.

194. "Statement of an Ethnic Chinese."

195. Nhan Dan, June 7, 1978, Hanoi VNA in English,

June 7, 1978, FBIS, AP, DR, June 7, 1978, pp. K2-3.

196. See the report on a cable from U.S. Ambassador Charles Whitehouse in Bangkok to the State Department, "Ambassador Sees Chance For U.S. to Influence Hanoi," _Asian Wall Street Journal_, June 1, 1979; and Arnaud de Borchgrave, "Inside Bleak Vietnam," _Newsweek_, May 28, 1979, p. 55.

197. "Note of the Foreign Ministry of the People's Republic of China to the Embassy of the Socialist Republic of Vietnam in China," May 12, 1978, _Documents Related to the Question of the Hoa_, pp. 49-53; "Statement of the Spokesman of the Overseas Chinese Affairs Office," _Ibid._, pp. 54-59.

198. "Chinese Government Decides to Send Ships to Bring Home Persecuted Chinese From Viet Nam," _Peking Review_, June 2, 1978, p. 15; "Note of the Ministry of Foreign Affairs of the Socialist Republic of Vietnam to the Ministry of Foreign Affairs of the People's Republic of China," May 28, 1978, _Documents Related to the Question of the Hoa_, pp. 22-23; "Note of the Ministry of Foreign Affairs of the People's Republic of China to the Ministry of Foreign Affairs of the Socialist Republic of Vietnam," June 2, 1978, _Ibid._, pp. 65-66.

199. Tokyo Kyodo in English, June 3, 1978, FBIS, PRC, DR, June 5, 1978, pp. N12-13. This report linked the media campaign over Vietnam's alleged mistreatment of the Hoa with the policy of forming a "United Front" with Overseas Chinese business men to resist "hegemonism" and modernize China.

200. _Washington Post_, May 26, 1978; Nguyen Co Thach alleged that China had brought 10 divisions to the border area by the beginning of June. Interview, November 16, 1978.

201. Interview with an official of an international agency, Washington, D.C., July 1979.

202. Tokyo Kyodo in English, June 5, 1978, FBIS, PRC, DR, June 5, 1978, pp. A8-9.

203. Interview with Nguyen Co Thach, November 16, 1978.

204. Information from an exhibition on Kampuchean war crimes in Ho Chi Minh City, which included numerous pictures and other details of these and other Kampuchean attacks. For an eyewitness report indicating that the Vietnamese were on the defensive on the border _before_ these attacks, see Jean Thoraval, "The Cruel War on the VN-Cambodia Frontier," _Bangkok Post_, March 7, 1978.

205. Hoang Nguyen, "Peking's Shadow Over Angkor," _Kampuchea Dossier II_, pp. 16-17. The Kampuchean government did not publish the note, but the accuracy of the Vietnamese version of it is confirmed in an AFP dispatch from Bangkok, June 2, 1978, FBIS, AP, DR, June 2, 1978, p. H1.

206.   Vu Can, "One Can't Kill a Whole People,"
Kampuchea Dossier II, pp. 63-65.
    207.   Interview with a member of the Central
Committee; interview with a senior foreign affairs cadre,
Ho Chi Minh City, November 8, 1978.
    208.   Interview with Xuan Thuy; interview with a
member of the Central Committee. For the portrayal of
China attempting to fill the vacuum left by the retreat
of American power from Indochina (the same image used by
China to portray Soviet policy in Southeast Asia), see
the speech by Hoang Tung, July 25, 1978, Hanoi domestic
service in Vietnamese, July 26, 1978, FBIS, AP, DR.
July 28, 1978, p. K12.
    209.   The military buildup on the Kampuchean
border began around mid-year. Nayan Chanda, "The
Timetable," p. 34.
    210.   Interview with Xuan Thuy; interview with a
Central Committee member.
    211.   Interview with Thach, November 16, 1978.
    212.   Interview with a Central Committee member.
On the earlier droppings of any conditions on normal
relations with the U.S., conveyed to the U.S. via India,
see Derek Davies, "Carter's Neglect, Moscow's Victory,"
Far Eastern Economic Review, February 2, 1979, p. 20.
The idea of contradictions between U.S. and China in the
Far East was suggested by Nguyen Co Thach in the inter-
view in New York, October 8, 1978.
    213.   Interview with a Central Committee member.
    214.   Hanoi international service in Cambodian,
June 20, 1978, FBIS, AP, DR, June 21, 1978, p. K-9.
Hanoi, VNA, in English, June 20, 1978, FBIS, AP, DR,
June 21, 1978, p. K13.
    215.   Washington Post, June 29, 1978; "COMECON
and Vietnam," Vietnam Courier, No. 6, 1979, p. 30.
    216.   Interview with Mainichi Shimbun, July 6,
    217.   Bangkok Post, July 7, 1978; Nation Review
(Bangkok), July 26, 1978. Phan Hien's positive statement about ASEAN represented a significant step beyond
his July 1976 acknowledgement of assurances by ASEAN
governments that it was neither a military organization
nor influenced by a foreign power. See AFP, Hong Kong,
in English, July 8, 1976, and AFP, Hong Kong, July 13,
1976, quoting Phan Hien in Kuala Lumpur and Manila,
respectively. Despite these acknowledgements, Hanoi's
suspicions of ASEAN remained. In a 1977 interview, Phan
Hien noted that the several bilateral defense agreements
among the ASEAN states constituted "the equivalent of a
multilateral agreement," and that "without the US behind
them, they couldn't do anything." Interview, Paris,
May 6, 1977.
    218.   The term "new situation" was first used in an
editorial in the Party newspaper immediately following

the plenum. Nhan Dan, July 30, 1978.

219.   SRV Government Report read by Vo Nguyen Giap at the Opening National Assembly Session, May 28, 1979, Hanoi domestic service in Vietnamese, May 29, 1979, FBIS, AP, DR, Supplement, June 5, 1979, p. 9.   Former Political Bureau member Hoang Van Hoan, who defected to the PRC in 1979, said the Fourth Central Committee Plenum of 1978 "pinpointed China as Vietnam's immediate enemy, "Xinhua in English, August 31, 1979, FBIS, PRL, DR, September 4, 1979.

220.   Le Trong Tan, "The Two Main Objectives of the Local Military Task," Tap Chi Cong San, No. 9 (September 1978), FBIS, AP, DR, October 18, 1978, p. K21-22.

221.   Interview with a Soviet official, March 28, 1980.

222.   For a discussion of friendship treaties negotiated by the Soviet Union, See David K. Willis, "Moscow Puts Great Store on Its Friendship Treaties," Christian Science Monitor, April 13, 1979, p. 3.

223.   Interview with Nguyen Co Thach, November 16, 1979; interview with Thai Foreign Ministry official, November 29, 1978, interview with Malaysian Foreign Ministry official, December 8, 1978.   Each of the Joint Communiques used similar language. For the Vietnamese-Indonesian version, see Hanoi VNA in English, September 23, 1978, FBIS, AP, DR, September 25, 1978, pp. K11-13.

224.   Interview with Malaysian Foreign Ministry official, December 8, 1978.

225.   On U.S.-Vietnam diplomatic talks on normalization, see Gareth Porter, "Discordant Overtures: U.S. and Vietnam - The Missed Chance," The Nation, October 20, 1979, pp. 366-369.

226.   Washington Post, October 2, 1978. For comment on the significance of Sihanouk's appearance, see Nayan Chanda, "The Search For Respectability," Far Eastern Economic Review, October 13, 1978, pp. 9-10.

227.   Washington Post, October 14, 1978.

228.   Notes of an interview with Thach, by an American visitor.

229.   Japanese Foreign Ministry sources attributed this information to Soviet Vice Foreign Minister Nicolai Firyubin during Soviet-Japanese consultations. UPI dispatch, Tokyo, Washington Post, May 15, 1979. Further confirmation came from Soviet sources in Bangkok, Kyodo dispatch, Bangkok, May 15, Mainichi Shimbun, May 16, 1979, FBIS, AP, DR, May 21, 1979, Annex, p. 2. The SRV Ambassador in Japan denied the existence of such an annex on military cooperation. Yomiuri Shimbun, May 19, 1979, FBIS, AP, DR, May 21, 1979, Annex, p. 3.

230.   For an account of the Vietnamese Ambassador's

briefing of the Japanese Foreign Ministry on the treaty,
see Kyodo, November 7, 1978, FBIS, AP, DR, November 7,
1978, p. K1, for Pham Van Dong's assurances in an interview with an Indonesian newspaper, see AFP, Jakarta,
December 12, FBIS, AP, DR, December 12, 1978, p. K3.
   231.   SPK, clandestine in French to Kampuchea,
December 3, 1978, FBIS, AP, DR, December 4, 1978,
pp. H1-9. On the "liberated zone," see AFP dispatch
from Bangkok, December 4, 1978, FBIS, AP, DR, December
4, 1978, p. H9.
   232.   This message which was quickly conveyed to
U.S. diplomats, formed the basis for the view in the
U.S. intelligence community that Vietnamese forces would
not try to seize the entire country. See Don Oberdorfer,
"Reds vs. Reds in Indochina: A New, Confusing Kind of
War," Washington Post, April 1, 1979, p. B1.
   233.   Hanoi domestic service in Vietnamese,
December 22, 1978, FBIS, AP, DR, December 26, 1978,
p. K11.
   234.   Nayan Chanda. "Cambodia: Fifteen Days that
shook Asia," Far Eastern Economic Review, January 19,
1979, pp. 10-13; Richard Nations, "A Frantic Drive For
Victory," Far Eastern Economic Review January 26, 1979,
pp. 11-13.
   235.   Notes of an interview by Joseph Crown with
Col. Tran Cong Man.
   236.   Nayan Chanda, "The Timetable," p. 34. In
early February 1979, Hoang Tung told a Vietnamese source
that it was "90 percent certain" that the Chinese would
not invade. Conversation with the Vietnamese source,
January 1980.
   237.   Interview with Swedish Foreign Ministry
official, February 29, 1979; interview with U.S. government source, April 1979.
   238.   International Herald-Tribune, February 26,
1979; Washington Post, February 27, 1979.
   239.   "Communique on the Crimes of the Chinese
Expansionists and Hegemonists," VNA in English, May 15,
1979, FBIS, AP, DR, May 17, 1979, pp. K8-9. For
eyewitness reports from Western journalists, see
Washington Star, August 22, 1979; AFP dispatch from
Hanoi, March 26, 1979, FBIS, AP, DR, March 26, 1979,
p. K15.
   240.   The Chinese Aggression: Why and How it
Failed (Hanoi: Foreign Language Publishing House, 1979),
pp. 33, 42.
   241.   "Bankruptcy For Beijing's Ambitious
Objectives," Quan Doi Nhan Dan, April 11, 1979, FBIS, AP,
DR, April 16, 1979, pp. K7-11.
   242.   The Chinese Aggression, pp. 14-15.
   243.   Ibid., p. 12.

244.   Quan Doi Nhan Dan, April 11, 1979.
245.   The Chinese Aggression, pp. 18-19: Quan Doi
Nhan Dan, April 11, 1979.
246.   This paragraph is based on Nayan Chanda,
"A Prophecy Self-fulfilled," Far Eastern Economic
Review, June 1, 1979; Christian Science Monitor, May 7,
1979; Yomiuri Shimbun, October 10, 1979, FBIS, AP, DR,
October 11, 1979, Annex, p. 2.
247.   Interview with Nguyen Co Thach, October 8,
1978.
248.   Interview with Nguyen Co Thach, November 16,
1978.
249.   Le. Qui, China's Invasion: Division of Role
Between the Beijing Expansionists and Imperialists,"
Tap Chi Cong San, No. 4, April 1979. Hanoi domestic
service in Vietnamese, April 23, 1979, FBIS, AP, DR,
May 1, 1979, p. K5. The Soviet charge was first made
on February 20 and repeated the next day. See
Washington Post, February 21, and 22, 1979.
250.   Nhan Dan, April 10, 1979. Hanoi VNA in
English, April 10, 1979, FBIS, AP, DR, April 10, 1979,
FBIS, AP, DR, April 10, 1979, p. Kl.
251.   The Vietnamese non-aggression pact offer was
first reported by the Hungarian news agency correspondent in Hanoi, Budapest MTI in English, May 28, 1979,
FBIS, AP, DR, May 31, 1979, p. K3-4. The Vietnamese
proposal was made by Minister of State Thach to Thai
Foreign Minister Uppadit on June 2, AFP, Hong Kong, in
English, June 2, 1979, FBIS, AP, DR, June 4, 1979.
252.   On ASEAN's policy and actions on Kampuchea,
see Rodney Tasker, "Reason, Sanity, and Stout Hearts,"
Far Eastern Economic Review, July 13, 1979, pp. 10-11.
253.   Hanoi VNA in English, September 2, 1979,
FBIS, AP, DR, September 5, 1979, p. K18.
254.   Nhan Dan, September 15, 1979, Hanoi
domestic service in Vietnamese, September 15, 1979,
FBIS, AP, DR, September 17, 1979, pp. K5-6.
255.   "Our Just Stand," Tap Chi Cong San, No. 5,
May 1979, Hanoi domestic service in Vietnamese, May 5,
1979, FBIS, AP, DR, May 15, 1979, p. K3.
256.   Text of speech by Han Niang-long, Beijing,
Xinhau in English, April 26, 1979, FBIS, PRC, DR,
April 26, 1979, p. Ell.
257.   Ibid., pp. E9-10.
258.   Hanoi domestic service in Vietnamese,
May 4, 1979, FBIS, AP, DR, May 7, 1979, p. K4.
259.   Speech by Minister of State Nguyen Co Thach
to the Colombo Ministerial Conference of the Coordinating Bureau of Non-aligned Countries, June 8, 1979,
Hanoi VNA, in English, June 9, 1979, FBIS, AP, DR,
June 11, 1979, p. K7.

260.   "The Vietnamese-Lao-Kampuchean Relations
Are Quite Legitimate," Quan Doi Nhan Dan, May 15, 1979,
Hanoi domestic service in Vietnamese, May 13, 1979,
FBIS, AP, DR, May 16, 1979, p. K2.
        261.   "Our Just Stand," p. K4.
        262.   Pham Van Dong interview with "France
Culture." Paris Domestic Service, January 5, 1980,
FBIS, AP, DR, January 7, 1980, p. K2.
        263.   For a discussion of the importance of the
"focal point" concept in Vietnamese foreign policy,
see Porter, "Vietnam and the Socialist Camp," p. 231.
        264.   "Our Commentary: The Indochina Test,"
Hanoi, VNA, December 28, FBIS, AP, DR, December 31,
1979, p. K8.

4

Vietnam's "Boat People"

Charles Benoit

Like no existing nation, Vietnam's survival as a nation state and the existence of its people as a separate race have been defined in a crucible of conflict with China. Among the nations of Southeast Asia, Vietnam alone was ruled for nearly a thousand years as a Chinese colony and, in the thousands years since it regained its independence in 939, subject to periodic invasions and harsh occupations by China. Whereas in the other nations of Southeast Asia Chinese residents pose thorny questions of assimilation or non-assimilation, for the Vietnamese it has rather been the ominous threat of being assimilated themselves which has determined their ingrained perceptions of and uncertain feelings for China. As a result, when Vietnam perceived itself threatened by China, the loyalties of unassimilated Hoa, as the Vietnamese call their ethnic Chinese minority, especially those who resided in strategic border areas, became a cause for concern. The actions the Vietnamese admit to have taken toward the Hoa, they assert, compare favorably with those the United States took with regard to Americans of Japanese descent when America considered itself threatened by far-away Japan.

Confronted with mounting evidence of responsibility for the massive outflow of refugees, officials of the Socialist Republic of Vietnam have nonetheless persisted in their public denials of any complicity in the exodus. While admitting that some unscrupulous local officials may have abetted the outflow of refugees for personal gain, they still avers that all the boat people from Vietnam departed illegally. To counter the charges levelled against Vietnam, the authorities in Hanoi have cited instead the aftermath of an old war with the United States and the continuing threat of a new one with China as the principal causes for the fact that refugee camps from Hong Kong to Jakarta are filled to overflowing with its citizens. In light of refugee testimony that the increasingly hard times they experienced contributed to their decision to leave, many aspects of which can be legitimately attributed to war-related causes, both assertions merit examination. But because of the predominance of ethnic Chinese among the refugees, at some locations surpassing 85%, Vietnam's relations with its former ally and the policies it pursued with regard to the Hoa people, warrant particular scrutiny.

Had the Vietnamese authorities not adopted policies which singled out the Hoa people, the refugee exodus would not have reached such unmanageable proportions. Simply put, there would still have been desperate boat people fleeing political and economic changes which affected them adversely, but they would have been far fewer in number. To understand the magnitude of the refugee exodus, one must seek the reasons why and the means whereby the Hoa fled in such large numbers.

If there are many on the islands of Indonesia who, given their determination to leave South Vietnam, ultimately consider themselves beneficiaries of the policy the government adopted, crowded into warehouses, former prisons and barracks and hastily constructed shelters in Hong Kong are thousands of Hoa from north Vietnam who are its decided victims. In addition, China is providing haven for 250,000 others it claims were driven across its border or expelled in boats.

"Vietnam's relations with China have always been very complex," reminisced a former major in Hanoi's army. "Though China helped Vietnam a great deal during its wars against the French and the Americans, still the Vietnamese live in great fear of China's real intentions. When the two countries are on good terms, everything is fine; but once they turn sour, the Vietnamese become alarmed and react instinctively," he added.

Major Bong, a pseudonym used here to prevent his background from adversely affecting his chances for resettlement, had been a party member for 30 years with a long record of participation in Vietnam's revolutionary struggles. Nevertheless, in late 1978 he found himself stripped of his responsibilities and, after China's invasion of Vietnam, expelled. "In 1952 I was with Ho Chi Minh in Viet Bac, in 1954 with Vo Nguyen Giap at Dien Bien Phu. But all the same, at a time when Vietnam was being threatened by China, the Vietnamese no longer dared have Hoa people in their military. After China's invasion they feared a second attack, this time with Hanoi as its objective, and so on February 18 (one day after China's invasion) began expelling us overseas."

Major Bong now derives scant solace from the 30 years he devoted to a cause he once believed in. "In the course of the war I escaped death many times," he said with the proud air one associates with high-ranking communist cadres. "Those who have seen what I have seen and know what I know, but find themselves in the free world, are few," he said with a trace of bitterness that he had otherwise concealed well.

I had located him working in a textile factory in Kowloon, where he and his family had found employment and lodging until they could be resettled in a third country.

"In 1948, when I was only 14, I carried secret messages between Viet Minh units fighting the French," recalled Le Van Ban, more recently a planning cadre at the Ministry of Supply in Hanoi. Like Major Bong, Mr. Ban was ill prepared for his presence in a Hong Kong refugee camp. "It all happened so suddenly," he said. "Just two months before, I was recommending to my Chinese friends that they best leave, assuming that because I was Vietnamese with a long record of service, I would have no trouble." Although Mr. Ban, which again is not his real name, is Vietnamese, his wife is Hoa.

Equally at home in the Chinese or Vietnamese language, he spent many years in China. "As a reward for my good showing against the French, I was sent there to study," he said proudly. "In 1953 many Vietnamese soldiers went to China to study anti-aircraft techniques, so I was assigned to stay on as an interpreter."

But he learned to his regret that a China specialist married to a Chinese at the time of a Chinese invasion was no longer trusted. "On March 22, 1979, we were officially told to sell our belongings and prepare to be temporarily relocated to the countryside. The cadres cleverly characterized our leaving Hanoi in the same terms used to describe the population dispersal out of the cities during the American bombing. The implication was that once the crisis had passed we could return. But when they tell you to turn over your apartment and sell your property, it is clear that you are never going to return," he said.

"In fact because of the effect on our family, my wife had already decided to leave; but as a cadre I still did not dare move without orders." He disclosed that as part of his responsibilities at the Ministry of Supply he knew the locations of Vietnam's underground oil storage depots. "With that kind of knowledge if I were caught trying to flee the country, I would have been dealt with as a traitor," he said.

He later learned that a new directive exempted Chinese women married to Vietnamese from the security measures, but his mind was already made up. "My family had already suffered enough, especially my children," he said.

As we spoke he began rummaging among the bags and bundles which surrounded the small open area where we sat Indian-style on straw mats covering the cement floor. In each of the giant rooms of what would have been a multi-storied factory building had refugees not moved in

first, several dozen families were housed. Their belongings demarcated the few square yards allotted to
each family. Having located what he sought, Mr. Ban
handed me a small book, the diary of his 15 year-old
daughter. Its entries bear silent witness to the racial
animosity which erupted after China's invasion of Vietnam and the anguish it caused those who where its targets.
To cite but one entry, that of March 13, 1979:

A long time has passed, at least a month, since I
last wrote in my dairy. Why? Because a terrible
sadness has invaded my soul.

During the day I concentrate on my school work.
When I return home, I try to sing and smile to
forget that sadness. At night I gather myself
together to go to sleep, but the following day it
only recurs.

What am I sad about? I shall write so my diary
knows. It is because war has broken out between
Vietnam and China, a war which becomes more intense
and violent with each day, and which upsets my
heart and soul completely.

Because my mother is Chinese, there is something
about me which is like the Chinese. As a result I
have experienced such pain and anguish in my heart.

In school my friends pick on me saying, "Since you
are Chinese, why don't you go back to China."
Though I do my duties, I am confronted with so many
difficulties and troubles, like having rocks thrown
at me.

When I return home, because of the influence of
events outside on my parents' personality and
feelings, they are impatient and harsh with me as
well. I just cannot stand it.

When the time comes for me to be admitted to the
Youth League (the Party youth group for exemplary
students), the school's party chapter will read my
background and, though I have met all the requirements for admission, I shall be rejected on account
of my background alone. And when I reach the final
exams, it will surely be the same.

I dare not think far into the future, but I just
know that right now I hate those authorities in
Beijing without end. If it proves necessary, I shall
go to the border to meet them face to face to see
what kinds of people they are who cause so much

misery to my people and especially to families
like mine. My parents are now discussing whether
they should go or stay. Though I say I am going
to stay here at all costs, if my parents leave,
then I shall have no choice but to follow.

Ironically, what weighed heaviest in her parents'
decision to leave Vietnam was the very future whose loss
she bemoaned. "As children with Chinese blood, ours
would have had no future had we stayed," said Mrs. Ban.
The crowd which gathered about us had blinded me to
the fact that it was nearly midnight and our conversation, which had taken place in the middle of that large
room, was keeping several hundred people awake. Mr. Ban,
bedding in hand, accompanied me outside, where 20 degrees
cooler and with room to stretch, he prepared to spend the
night in the street. As we parted he added one final,
self-comforting thought. "If Ho Chi Minh had lived it
would never have come to this," he said with conviction.
The final expulsion from north Vietnam of men like
Major Bong and Le Van Ban, along with thousands of others
whose only fault was their Chinese ancestry, came after
China's invasion of Vietnam in February 1979. Their
expulsion was the culmination of a series of events
that had made the Hoa the focus of the conflict between
China and Vietnam. In the context of steadily deteriorating relations, those who had been the beneficiaries
of the once close relationship between the land of their
ancestors and that of their birth suddenly became its
victim.
"Although Vietnam still hoped to have friendly relations with China and continue receiving its assistance,
in the larger sense it had to cope with China, whose intentions it suspected," continued Major Bong. This am-
bivalence in Vietnam's attitude toward its historical
enemy, but more recent ideological ally, about which
Major Bong now spoke from personal knowledge, is best
viewed as the consequence of historical experience, confirmed more than generated by recent events. According
to Major Bong, in the context of increasing confrontation
with China, Vietnam began to take precautions along its
long border with China. "In 1977 the authorities tried
to get the Hoa living on the border to adopt Vietnamese
citizenship," he said. "Those who refused were forced
to choose between returning to China or moving inland
away from the border. Many of the poor preferred to
return to China rather than become Vietnamese citizens."
The issue of citizenship, mentioned by Major Bong
and others as the impetus behind the mass exodus of Hoa
from Vietnam is of crucial importance. One might rea-
sonably ask why it was such an overriding issue for the
Vietnamese authorities and Vietnam's ethnic Chinese
minority alike. More specifically, why was Hanoi so bent

on getting the Hoa people to adopt Vietnamese nationality
and why were the Hoa, who after all had lived in Vietnam
for generations, so adamantly opposed. In part the
answers can be found in history.

Tied by custom and ethnic pride, overseas Chinese
had traditionally retained the citizenship of their
ancestors despite generations of residence overseas.
However, with the advent of independent, nationalistic
governments in Southeast Asia after World War II, as a
prerequisite for continued residence and the right to
practice their livelihoods, overseas Chinese had been
forced to forego the concept of dual citizenship and
adopt the nationality of their new homelands. In separate agreements with several of these governments the
authorities in Beijing (Peking) had likewise set aside
its traditional posture of extraterritoriality, by which
it had asserted the right to intervene to protect the
interests of its overseas citizens.

By the mid-1950's the issue of nationality had thus
been resolved, if not solved, in the other countries of
Southeast Asia. But the peculiarities of Vietnam, a
divided nation at war, led to a different set of circumstances. In the south the government of Ngo Dinh Diem
conformed with the prevailing trend. In 1956, by restricting access to crucial occupations to citizens, it
compelled the Chinese residents of the south to adopt
Vietnamese nationality. At the time both Beijing and
Hanoi had objected. Though certainly no less nationalistic than their counterparts in Saigon, nor for that
matter the other governments of Southeast Asia, the
authorities in Hanoi did not force such a choice upon
the Chinese in the north. According to an agreement
reached in 1955 between the Central Committees of the
Vietnamese and Chinese Parties, the Chinese residents of
north Vietnam were allowed to retain their Chinese
citizenship while "enjoying the same rights as the Vietnamese people." Born of the then close relationship
between Vietnam and China, this anomalous policy created
in Vietnamese eyes a privileged ethnic minority, which
as long as the two countries enjoyed good relations, had
no adverse implications.

"We had the best of both worlds," stated Ke Xuan,
the 71 year-old patriarch of a large, once wealthy, Hoa
family from Hanoi. "The Hoa in the north had all the
rights and privileges of Vietnamese citizenship and none
of its disadvantages. From about 1970 the Vietnamese
had been trying to get us to become citizens, but few of
us regarded it to be in our best interests. We could
even vote in their elections. We were regarded as Vietnamese in all respects, except that we were not subject
to the military draft," he said. This latter prerogative,
needless to say, was of inestimable consequence in a
nation interminably at war.

According to Ke Chuong, Mr. Xuan's younger brother, in the context of Vietnam's conflict with China, the Vietnamese government's first mention of what were assumed to be its future intentions, created a furor among the Hoa in Hanoi and Haiphong. "In early May 1978, Xuan Thuy (who had represented Hanoi at the peace negotiations in Paris) replied to a Radio Beijing broadcast accusing Vietnam of persecuting the Hoa," said Ke Chuong. "In his reply he noted that China and Vietnam had agreed after 1954 that the Hoa people would all gradually become Vietnamese citizens. This announcement, which the Vietnamese radio repeated over and over again, came as a shock to us. It had never before been made public. What worried us the most was the draft, which we regarded as a sure road to death. It also meant that those Hoa with relatives in China would no longer be able to visit them. This was important for economic as well as sentimental reasons. According to practice Hoa were able to visit China once every three years. Those who went could bring Vietnamese goods to China and Chinese goods back to Vietnam for sale on the black market, so it meant an economic loss as well."

Dr. Chuong, who had been a T.B. specialist at a Hanoi hospital before his departure, attributed to the implied, impending loss of Chinese citizenship and its privileges the main reason for the mass exodus of Hoa back to China. "For more than 20 years we had been treated well and now suddenly everything began to change. Some of the Hoa who lived along the border had already begun to flee in response to the government's measures to force them to move inland away from the border. In May the Hoa from the cities began to go as well, along with increasing numbers of those in the border regions."

If the feared loss of nationality was to some the prime issue motivating the flight of Hoa to China, it was not the only cause. In May 1978, at the same time the Vietnamese government made mention of its assumption that the Hoa living in north Vietnam would eventually all become Vietnamese citizens, on the economic front other measures were taken. Although not specifically directed at the Hoa, these measures did add to their concerns about the future. "The government announced a campaign against ill-gotten property," said Dang Kien Hoa, a forty-three year old artisan from Hanoi. "Any possessions that could not be justified by one's official salary were theoretically subject to confiscation. The campaign was to be carried out in three stages, the first involving only about ten of the most wealthy families. In fact it was a crackdown on corruption among cadres, but we weren't sure how the later stages might be used against us to confiscate what we had worked so hard over the years to acquire. It was a little like being told, 'you fatten the pig, but I shall slaughter it whenever I want.' Many wealthy Hoa fled as a result," he said.

The concerns of the Hoa regarding their future economic position were based in part in their stellar success at running what amounted to an alternative economic system. Nearly every conversation with Hoa from North Vietnam confirmed the existence of a thriving black market operated by them for their own profit, but, as they repeatedly stressed, for Vietnamese convenience. They took great pride in the various ways they were able to distinguish themselves as bastions of free enterprise in an otherwise socialist economy. And they viewed with disdain the socialist regime's impoverished cadres, some of whom, they said, were willing to look the other way for periodic gratuities.

"For the Vietnamese it is an honor to be a cadre," said Dang Kien Hoa. "But our nature is to trade. Their standard of living therefore couldn't compare with ours. If you want to eat well, you must find ways to be 're-sourceful'", he said, employing a code word the Hoa use to refer to wheeling and dealing on the black market. "In our neighborhood the families of Vietnamese cadres who lived on their government salaries alone ate only rice and vegetables without meat. You figure it out. They make 50 dong a month, and a chicken costs 30 dong. To tell you the truth, my family ate a chicken every couple of days." "Sure they were jealous," added his wife, "and because of jealousy, some Vietnamese hated us. But we had money because we worked hard, and so we had meat to eat. I couldn't stand eating just spinach and rice the way they do."

In his official employment, by way of compromise with the system, Dang Kien Hoa crafted plaster figurines. "I used to make scenic pictures, but after the communists took over I made statues of Ho Chi Minh, for which there was an unlimited demand," he said. "We bought gypsum from the government, baked it, ground it into powder and cast the statuettes. Every three months I signed a contract which determined the amount we were allowed for our labor. It was a family operation, and together we made about 200 dong each month."

Unofficially, he bought contraband tobacco from Hoa who lived on the border, which was then smuggled to Hanoi. "Some I sold wholesale; the rest I rolled into the best cigarettes in Hanoi," he said with satisfaction. From this he earned about 300 dong more, which nonetheless was only "enough to live."

La Thiet Quang, a skilled factory worker from the port city of Hai Phong is another example. Although he was, by Vietnamese standards, well paid for his work in a government machine tool factory, after work he operated a factory of his own at home. "From a mold fashioned on the job and rubber bought on the black market, I produced bicycle inner tubes for sale back on the black market. If I just lived on my government salary, my family would starve. At the factory, including over-time, I earned about 120 dong. With a kilogram of pork costing 20 dong and a bowl of noodle soup 2 dong, how could I feed my family. If I just had one bowl of soup each morning, half my salary would be gone." For his "extra work," as the Hoa termed their extralegal pur-suits, he earned as much as one thousand dong each month. The average Vietnamese cadre makes in comparison at most 60 dong a month, a skilled factory worker 80 or 90.

Hoa who played out their economic destinies in a world apart from socialist endeavor were not limited to the cities. Hoa in the border areas included of course many who, alongside the Vietnamese, eked out meager livelihoods as laborers, farmers and fishermen. But others derived specific advantages as Chinese nationals living on the Vietnamese side of the Sino-Vietnamese border. Like most other borders in Southeast Asia it apparently also constituted no major obstacle to deter-mined individual enterprise.

When asked his profession Cam Chan Tong paused, then smiled broadly. "Smuggler," he replied. On a regular basis twice a week he plied the dirt paths over the hills to China and back, transporting whatever would bring a higher price on the other side. Perfume, powder, liquor and Chinese herbs were in particular demand in Vietnam. What he brought back his wife sold at the local market. "If the police came, I would hide everything until they left," she said. As the border was patrolled on both sides, not all his journeys were successful. "The cadres are as poor as beggars," he said. "Whenever they caught me, they would confiscate my goods to divide amongst themselves. I know, I was arrested often." For having lived nearly all his adult life on the border between two socialist countries, Mr. Tong was unrepentant about his preference for free enterprise. "The French never took from the people. It is just the communists who try to make us poor. They hate it if the people are rich. If we have no rice to eat or clothes to wear, they are happy", he said.

According to Mr. Tong, his extralegal pursuits and anti-socialist attitudes were not unique. "All Chinese in Lang Son engage in this sort of activity. How else could we survive? If we were to work for the governments we would make just 30 or 40 dong a month." He estimated the monthly income from the combined labors of both his wife and himself to be on the average 500 dong, an amount again considered only "enough to live."

It was in the border areas where Vietnamese pressure on the Hoa to assimilate had brought to a head the sim-mering conflict with China. But, according to Mr. Tong, expressing the same defiant attitude he had voiced re-garding economic systems, many Hoa, especially those for

whom a life in China offered no acceptable alternative,
simply stayed put. "In the past we had withstood how
many bombs?," asked the 56 year-old trader rhetorically.
"We never moved anywhere. And if it were not for the
border war, we would never have left," he added with conviction. Mr. Tong's family had lived in Lang Son 13
kilometers from China for 5 generations. Located astride
the rail line to China, Lang Son had been the frequent
target of American bombers. But on February 16 on the
eve of the Chinese invasion, he finally left, this time
never to return. "We still wanted to," he said, "but
the Vietnamese would have accused us of being Chinese
agents so we didn't dare."

The envy aroused among Vietnamese by the special
privileges the Hoa enjoyed as perpetual foreign residents
and by the better life they led by dint of their black
market activities was the subject of a conversation with
Nguyen Van Hung, an ethnic Vietnamese whose business
deals, he said, involved largely Hoa. "They enjoyed
many privileges which we Vietnamese did not have. As
ong as Vietnam and China enjoyed good relations, they
were better off in all respects than Vietnamese who
were forced to participate in socialist labor. They had
educational opportunities denied us and more freedom to
buy and sell. The government wanted the Hoa to become
citizens to join in socialist production just like the
Vietnamese, but they refused in order to have more freedom to trade and avoid the draft," he said.

Nguyen Van Hung, again a necessary pseudonym, was a
self-declared dissident who, like the Hoa, had refused
the meager lot the socialist system reserved for him.
According to his own description, he was forced to find
other ways to support himself. "Few Vietnamese were
involved in private (illicit) trading. In that respect
I guess I was more like the Hoa than my own people."

He described the circumstances which had led him to
reject socialist labor for private enterprise. In the
refugee camps on the Indonesian islands I was later to
meet many other Vietnamese and Hoa from the south who,
faced with an identical predicament, chose rather to
leave Vietnam. Nguyen Van Hung also made this choice
just as soon as it became available. "My father was a
soldier in the French army, a Catholic and a capitalist.
In 1964, when I was eleven, he was sent to a labor camp
for nine years. I still remember the date they took him
away and when he was released. Because of my family
background I received no education, and without an education all that was left for me to do was to become a
manual laborer. Not that I was afraid of working with
my hands. If I could have made a decent living, I would
have, but as a laborer you don't make enough money to
smoke even the cheapest cigarettes. One of my brothers
is a ditch digger, another a pedi-cab driver in Hanoi,

so I know. They live on rice and vegetables alone.
Once out of frustration I volunteered to join the army,
but even for that I was refused. I guess they thought
I might turn my gun against them."

"The children of cadres all go to the universities
and become engineers," he continued. "Our sweat just
results in their enjoyment. So the more they tried to
make me suffer, the more determined I became to enjoy
the good life they denied me. In spite of them I lived
well," he declared with great satisfaction.

Forced into a corner without an acceptable future,
Nguyen Van Hung became what in his own mind was a kind
of economic insurgent. "I opposed their restrictions
with all my will. Whatever the government forbid, as
long as I could make money at it, I did," he said.

In 1969 he was sentenced to three years at hard
labor for trafficking in gold, foreign exchange and
opium. "When I was released, I continued as before,
only with more experience," he added smugly. As he
spoke his eyes betrayed the glazed look of one who had
spent all his life in defiant rebellion. He proudly
displayed mementos of his prison experience, three large
tatoos on his arms and thigh. That on his thigh was
particularly noteworthy - a clenched fist in chains.

He continued regarding his relationship with the
Hoa. "In my business I depended on them a great deal.
Most of the smuggling and black market activities were
in their hands. In 1978 the government began enforcing
restrictions which precluded non-citizens from certain
sensitive occupations, including those who drove for a
living. Mostly it affected the Hoa, and afterwards it
became difficult to find ways to bring opium from Lao
Cai on the border to Hanoi."

In his desire to leave Vietnam, Nguyen Van Hung's
envy of the Hoa persisted even after their expulsion.
"After the war began with China, the Hoa were given a
choice of leaving or being relocated out of the cities
in the north to secure areas in the countryside. Most
chose to leave. But they got to leave with family and
friends. I had to leave alone without my seven brothers
and sisters. All the Hoa have to pay is 1,000 dong to
the boat organizer who bought the boat. But he charged
me 6,000 dong. Few Vietnamese dared to leave. For
Vietnamese to leave the country is to be declared a
traitor. If I had been captured, I would have been im-
prisoned for who knows how long," he said.

Without doubt, as Nguyen Van Hung asserted, the Hoa
obtained somewhat more latitude to buy and sell on the
open market by virtue of their status as foreign residents. But their relative prosperity was certainly as
much a tribute to their industry and enterprise as the
simple result of prerogatives as non-citizens. Many,
such as La Thiet Quang and Dang Kien Hoa, participated in

socialist, state-sanctioned labor in addition to their
extralegal activities. However, by their own admission
the better life they led as the fruit of their labors
tended to set them apart from the Vietnamese, who were
either less inclined or more restricted in their range
of economic activities. As a privileged minority enjoying what appeared to some ill-gotten gains then, the
Hoa in the north were extremely vulnerable when the
political climate which had sustained them suddenly
vanished.

In the summer of 1978, when China took up their
defense, the Hoa were also subject to a carefully con-
ceived rumor campaign of suspicious origins. Most cited
these rumors as the single most disruptive influence on
their lives, and in conjunction with the turmoil over
the nationality issue and possible economic sanctions,
the basic cause for the mass exodus to China.

"For several months that summer when we got up in
the morning we would find notes had been slipped under
our door," said Ke Xuan. "One said that war was coming
with China, and that all Hoa should hurry home. Those
who did not, the note said, would be regarded as traitors
and killed when the Chinese troops arrived. Another said
the (Chinese) government requested all Hoa to return to
build up the fatherland. At the time the Vietnamese
tried to reassure us. Local cadres instructed us to
report anyone who incited us to leave. They told us to
relax, that Hoa and Vietnamese could live in peace with
each other. But still people left in droves."

Views varied among the Hoa affected as to who was
stirring up trouble and for what reasons. In line with
China's charges against Vietnam some saw a cleverly
orchestrated attempt by Vietnam to induce their departure
by raising the nationality issue, conducting a campaign
against ill-gotten property and finally spreading vicious
rumors. Others were less sure. At first Hanoi charged
"bad elements among the Hoa" with sowing dissension.
But by mid-June, as the conflict between China and Vietnam escalated, Vietnam accused China by name. The
available evidence is largely circumstantial and incon-
clusive.

Ke Xuan, who made no attempt to conceal his dis-
taste for either the regime in Hanoi or that in Beijing,
was among those who suspected China. "It was a big
secret, but the Vietnamese were not behind it. They had
much to lose if we left. China had much to gain and were
the likely instigators."

Le Van Ban was less certain. "No one really knows
who spread the rumors, but the effect was tremendous.
One thing became clear. Relations between Vietnam and
China were deteriorating rapidly, war was fast becoming
a real possibility and the Hoa knew they would be the
first to suffer. In the summer of 1978 the Hoa were not

expelled. They fled in a panic."

Whether in its self-professed benign role as protector of its overseas citizens or, as the Vietnamese
have charged, malicious instigator of the exodus, China
did take certain measures during this period which
facilitated the flight of the Hoa. "It used to be difficult to get permission to visit relatives in China,"
said Dang Kien Hoa. "First you needed Vietnamese approval and the Chinese embassy made you wait for up to two
years. But then it became much easier. The Chinese no
longer required prior Vietnamese approval and the waiting
period for a visa was reduced to one week. In the past
the form to be filled out had stated 'overseas Chinese
requests permission to visit China,' but later this was
changed to 'Chinese national'." By regarding all Hoa
in Vietnam as its nationals, including those in the south
who had reluctantly become Vietnamese citizens back in
1956, China could avail itself of its implied right as
their protector. The Vietnamese regarded this arrogated
right as an egregious violation of their sovereignty.
According to Mr. Hoa a banner was placed on the Chinese
side of the border to "welcome home" returning Chinese.

The motives of those who fled from the north were
then fear of their fate in the increasingly likely event
of war between China and Vietnam, sentimental attachment
to their nationality, which they feared losing, concern
regarding their ability to maintain what they considered
an acceptable standard of living and in general an increasing perception of the erosion of privileges they
had enjoyed as perpetual foreign residents. Except on
the border, where the Vietnamese had begun to implement
security measures, their exodus was not yet, as China
charged in May, 1978, the result of "ostracizing, persecuting and expelling" the Hoa.

"As of May, 1978, the conflict was still in essence
one between the leaders of China and Vietnam," asserted
La Thiet Quang. "Public opinion was gradually turning
against us, but our lives, though sometimes uncomfortable,
were still tolerable. What China charged came later,"
he said.

In May and June, 1978, in response to the exodus of
Hoa, China curtailed, then cut off aid to Vietnam. Given
Vietnam's economic difficulties, the loss of much needed
aid was a serious development. Noting that China had
never uttered a word in defense of its suffering expa-
triates in Kampuchea (Cambodia), tens of thousands of
whom had taken refuge in Vietnam, the Vietnamese charged
China with using the Hoa question as a pretext to create
difficulties for Vietnam. But from the Vietnamese standpoint far more serious and with regard to the subsequent
exodus far more consequential was China's unilateral
despatch in June of ships to Haiphong and Ho Chi Minh
City (formerly Saigon) to "repatriate victimized Chinese

residents."

China's defense of Hoa interests in Vietnam had served only to heighten Vietnamese suspicions, some would say their paranoia, of the potential role the Hoa might play in the event of a full-fledged confrontation with China. By thus making the Hoa the focus of its conflict with Vietnam, China ensured in effect that its charges would ultimately become justified by subsequent events. According to La Thiet Quang it was not until several months later that the steadily deteriorating situation began to impinge in a way that made their lives difficult. "I used to go from Haiphong to Hanoi every week to visit my wife, but suddenly in September I had to request permission from the local authorities. Afterwards our movements were restricted by the day and hour," he said.

These restrictions, understood by some of the Hoa as necessary security measures, but by the majority as unwarranted harassment, were followed toward the end of 1978 by even harsher ones: police raids at night in search of illegal residents, gradual demotion and then dismissal for those Hoa in important or sensitive jobs and finally after China's invasion in February, 1979, the bitter choice of leaving their adopted homelands, where most had been born, or leaving the cities, said to be the potential objective of another attack, for designated sites in the countryside. For the Hoa who lived in the cities of the north at least, China's charges had become self-fulfilling.

"In March and April, 1979, local cadres called meetings with representatives from each Hoa family in Hanoi," said Dang Kien Hoa, describing the circumstances which led to his decision to leave. "We were never expelled outright. We spoke of it rather as being 'cleverly chased away.' The cadre gave us two choices. We could remain in Vietnam and be relocated to the mountains, or we could leave."

He continued regarding the perilous predicament that the Chinese invasion had created for Hoa in the north. "At these meetings the cadres analyzed the situation for us. They said China might attack again and as Chinese, when asked which road went where or where Vietnamese troops were located, we would have to tell them. If we refused to cooperate, the cadres said the Chinese would kill us. But if we did cooperate, the Vietnamese would kill us. Besides Vietnamese youths were being killed by Chinese, and they would hate us anyway. So they advised us for our own safety to leave Hanoi and live elsewhere. Under these conditions most Hoa chose to leave the country," he concluded.

If the panicky flight and later expulsion of Hoa from North Vietnam, where they had lived under socialism for 25 years, can be attributed to complications arising

from Vietnam's tortuous relations with China, in the
south, where the rigors of the socialist system were
just taking hold, a different set of circumstances
applied. There the economic policies the communist
authorities implemented against a once prosperous middle
class had already left many Hoa and Vietnamese alike
desperate to seek a better life elsewhere. For the Hoa
in the south, China's intervention was to provide not
the cause for persecution and expulsion as in the north,
but rather the opportunity to leave.

In response to China's declaration in June, 1979,
Vietnam announced that it was sending ships to repatriate victimized Hoa, while steadfastly denying that
they had been persecuted. For the first time Hanoi
stated its readiness to allow all Hoa desirous of being
repatriated to depart abord the Chinese ships. Thirty
thousand Hoa were reported to have registered in Ho Chi
Minh City in the first week alone. However, when Sino-
Vietnamese negotiations regarding necessary modalities
broke down, largely over Chinese insistence to class
all those who wanted to leave as "persecuted Chinese
residents," the boatlift which might have spared the Hoa
from their subsequent travails, was aborted. The thousands who in their desire to leave Vietnam had registered
to repatriate to China had in Vietnam's eye sided with
the enemy.

One month later in July, 1979, the Vietnamese
authorities responded with a plan of their own. The
Hoa in the south began to hear guarded mention of the
possibility of arranging through intermediaries a semi-
official departure in exchange for varying sums of
money. Some of the boat people suggested that the
security-conscious Vietnamese had misread the tremendous
response to China's call to repatriate as an affirmation
of pro-Chinese political loyalties and became alarmed.
But others took a more hard-headed view of Vietnamese
actions. "The communists decided that they couldn't
change our attitudes," said Thai Van Nhon, a once wealthy
entepreneur who had had a wide range of business interests in Saigon. "Since we refused to go to the countryside to produce as farmers and sooner or later would
have fled anyway, the government decided it might as
well collect our gold and let us go." Whatever its
genesis, this policy, never publicly admitted by the
Vietnamese government, enabled the Hoa, along with ethnic
Vietnamese who posed as Hoa, to leave in unprecedented
numbers.

Unlike some Hoa, who in the period prior to the
nationalization of all remaining private businesses in
March, 1978, had made futile attempts to accommodate
with the new system, Thai Van Nhon was never given an
opportunity. As the managing director of several enter-
prises, including an insecticide company and a plastic

factory, in September, 1975, he was declared a "compra-
dore capitalist" and placed under house arrest. "In
actuality all the communists did was to single out the
richest, those in the highest positions, as members of
the exploiter class," he said. "In the middle of the
night 50 armed soldiers surrounded my villa. For three
months the seven members of my family with two servants
were confined to one room. A soldier sat at the door
with a gun. They searched everywhere for gold, in walls
and above the ceiling, and confiscated whatever they
could find. It hurts to talk of the past, and so now
we try to concentrate on the future."

The past was an equally painful subject for Mrs.
Nhon, who had been born and brought up in Kampuchea.
"All my family died there," she said as tears rolled down
her cheeks. "My mother died on the way, and I have never
heard anything more from my family." To spare his family
from the cramped and sultry conditions at the refugee
camp, Mr. Nhon had rented a small, wooden house on stilts
in a neighboring Indonesian village. At the camp several
thousand refugees were crowded into a cavernous warehouse
provided by the Indonesian government for their temporary
shelter.

Obsessed by the recent past, Mrs. Nhon described the
effect the new government had had on the once fashionable
street where they had lived in Saigon. "Everyone is
gone," she said. "Either drafted, sent to the New
Economic Zones in the countryside, fled overseas or missing. Nothing remains, but at least our family arrived
here safely," she said, again in tears. At each mention
of the past her voice cracked with emotion. As she
spoke, her husband wrote 12 Chinese characters on a
scrap of paper which he said expressed the experiences
of Hoa in the south over the past 5 years. Translated,
they read: "a tragedy among mankind; family ruined and
property disposed; wife parted and children dispersed."

"We never thought the Americans would give up," said
Mr. Nhon, who had been caught unexpectedly in Saigon when
the war ended abruptly in 1975. "I had great faith in
the United States and believed in the domino theory.
Besides Phnom Penh had held out for six months, so I
thought why not Saigon." As an indication of the level
of his confidence, after the Paris Peace Accords were
signed in 1973, he had joined with Taiwanese and local
Hoa investors to establish the largest plastics factory
in the south.

Mr. Nhon had been born in China, lived in Malaysia
as a teenager and then moved to Saigon, where he had
prospered. Having lived most of his life in countries
where assimilation was a prerequisite for continued
residence and the opportunity to make a living, Thai Van
Nhon expressed views on the nationality question which
differed from those of Hoa in the north. "For our

forebears Chinese citizenship meant a great deal, but now practically speaking, overseas Chinese have no interest in a Taiwanese or Chinese passport. I used to go abroad often. To have had to travel on either passport would have been an impediment. So we assimilated to realize our main aim -- the pursuit of our livelihoods." On this point, making the necessary accommodations to ensure one's living, there appeared to be little disagreement with Hoa in the north. "As guests in someone else's country, since we couldn't succeed in politics, we concentrated on business. We tended to our own affairs and accepted our lot. As long as we could make money, the rest did not matter," he said.

But by March, 1978, when, in the course of the relentless socialist transformation of southern society, all remaining private businesses were nationalized, the rest was all that mattered. The Hoa, who had dominated economic life in the south, were left without any livelihood to sustain themselves. "They made us unemployed without a means to make a living," was the statement I heard time and time again in conversations with dispossessed Hoa. The authorities' subsequent attempts to get the Hoa to move to the countryside to produce food, although Vietnamese reduced to similar straits had long before been subject to the same efforts, were regarded as additional harassment. "We had no choice but to leave," said Thai Van Nhon. "They sent you to a place without houses, farming implements or amenities of any kind. Few Hoa could tolerate that kind of life and so found ways (i.e., through bribes) to sneak back to the cities. Our houses had been confiscated. All we could do was to live with friends and relatives until we could arrange our departure," he said.

For Tran Vy Hien, a soft-spoken, personable, former merchant from the central Vietnamese coastal city of Nhatrang , the years since 1975 witnesses the gradual demise of everything he had worked for in the previous twenty. From a modest beginning in 1955 as a book seller, by 1975 he owned one of the largest book stores in Nhatrang with numerous other profitable business interests and investments. When he finally left Vietnam in July, 1979, he had to borrow money to pay for his passage.

"In the beginning the cadres urged all merchants to relax and continue selling as before, but I knew that they would not allow private commerce indefinitely. After 1975 I shifted my efforts to production," said Mr. Hien, exhibiting the same spirit of accommodation and ingenuity which had enabled many Hoa in the north to prosper. He spent the next three years attempting to forestall what proved despite his best efforts to be inevitable - the order to leave the cities to become food producers in the countryside. "With the same salary as a worker I became the director of a handicraft cooperative, I organized a collective which produced starch from manioc. My mind was already made up to flee just as soon as I had the opportunity, but in the meantime I had to find a way to keep my family from being sent to the New Economic Zones to become farmers. For our factory we therefore chose a site in the countryside in the hope that our families would be allowed to remain in Nhatrang," he said.

Meanwhile the bookstore, which had been his main source of income, was forced to close. "In September, 1976, the authorities had levied confiscatory taxes in the form of what they called an excess profits tax. Those who refused to pay were jailed as an example to others. Then in early 1977 my entire inventory was appropriated, in return for which I received only a promissory note which could be redeemed for pressing personal needs, marriages and funerals were mentioned as examples, or for use in production," he said.

Increasingly convinced of no future under socialism, in late 1977, Tran Vy Hien and his family made their first attempt to flee. Though carefully organized, it failed when the beach from which they were to depart was patrolled. "It was a cooperative effort among three groups," said Mr. Hien. "A Vietnamese fisherman and his family provided the boat, another a house on the beach in which to hide. We contributed the fuel and supplies. Although we lost several thousand dollars, fortunately no one was captured."

Their next attempt came in August, 1978, two months after Tran Vy Hien had been ordered to turn over his house in Nhatrang and leave for the countryside. "A Vietnamese friend from Saigon, a former Captain in the Air Force, organized everything. All that was necessary was to share expenses. But the boat owner turned out to be a communist agent, and we were all arrested. My wife and the younger children were released after a few weeks, the older children four months later. But they kept me in jail for ten months right up until we left."

For Mr. Hien the government's policy of allowing Hoa to leave Vietnam meant not just the opportunity to leave, but also the chance to get out of jail. "Hoa jailed for attempting to flee could be released to join families going overseas. Forty per cent of those on my boat were released from jail to leave. Still it cost my wife over one thousand dollars in bribes to get me out in time."

His son-in-law, who was captured with him, remained in jail. "We had to leave without him," said Mr. Hien, pointing sadly to his eldest daughter coddling his first grandson. His Vietnamese son-in-law had made a total of six unsuccessful attempts to flee before he was finally captured. Another missing family member was his 16 year old son, thought to be somewhere in the Philippines, the only member of the family to make a successful illegal escape.

The night he and his family were caught escaping, all his wealth had been confiscated. The progressive impoverishment of Tran Vy Hien was nearly complete. All that remained was some $6,000 in gold which he had entrusted to two Chinese and four Vietnamese friends prior to his attempted escape. "I told them that if I were successful, they could keep the money as a souvenir of our friendship, but that if I failed I would need it back," he said. When the government made it possible to leave legally for a price, he needed it and much more.

Perhaps because the decision to allow Hoa to leave was implemented in Nhatrang much later than in provinces farther south, it was less clandestine in nature. In January and February, 1979, the Hoa were told informally by neighborhood cadre that they no longer needed to flee, that the government would make it possible for them to leave safely. "They told us we would be allowed to buy a seaworthy boat, fix its hull and motor and bring along a mechanic and a helmsman. We could also take along sufficient food, water, fuel and medicine. These were big advantages over trying to flee illegally," said 33 year-old Ngo Ba Thanh, who organized the boat on which Tran Vy Hien and his family left.

In March, 1979, 24 Hoa in Nhatrang filed petitions for permission to buy boats to leave. Two months later in a meeting of boat organizers at the semi-official government office at 22 Phan Chau Trinh Street the government announced its conditions. Everyone between the ages of 17 and 60 was to pay 4 taels of gold (worth approximately $300 apiece at the time). Children over 8 were charged 2 taels with no charge for adults over 60, children under 8, the blind, crippled or mentally ill. These fees, which the government termed "duty money", were paid directly to the local branch of the provincial bank, where the gold was weighed and assayed. The boat organizer collected an additional 3 taels per adult and 2 taels per child to pay for puchasing and repairing the boat, buying supplies, and conferring necessary gratuities on avaricious officials. To pay such large sums (about $2,000 per adult and $1,200 per child) the poor and the impoverished borrowed from the still wealthy among them to be repaid overseas.

"For us it was a good opportunity to get out of hell," said Tran Vy Hien, when asked how he regarded the government's apparent change of heart. "For my children it was a chance to have a better future," he continues. "As children of capitalists, already caught once trying to escape, they would have received no further education. All they had to look forward to was the life of a water buffalo, working in fields for the rest of their days.

Under communism the state reaps all the benefits. You become its slaves," he said.

As he spoke, I recalled the conversations I had had with Nguyen Van Hung, who faced with a similar prospect had been driven to selling opium to make a living.

The Sino-Vietnamese conflict was not without its repercussions in the south and provided an additional impetus to those who wanted to leave. "We were not only capitalists, but also Chinese," said Mr. Hien. "To be Chinese at the time of conflict between China and Vietnam had ominous implications. When China demanded to repatriate victimized Chinese residents, the situation became very tense. We knew that if war were to come, we would surely be suspected as a potential fifth column. At the starch factory I was ordered to make a list of all Chinese employees. My name was first on the list," he said.

Ironically, the identification of largely assimilated Hoa in the south as potential Chinese partisans came in part as the result of their own actions. Although most had become Vietnamese citizens two decades earlier and had few remaining ties with China, in the hope that as foreign nationals they might be able to fare better under communist rule, many had demanded the return of their former nationality. Some sought to avoid the draft, which became a real concern after the conflict between Vietnam and Kampuchea escalated. Others took comfort in the fact that French and Indian nationals were being allowed to leave Vietnam and hoped that Chinese nationality might afford them, as it ultimately did, a similar opportunity. As a result, for reasons which had little to do with ethnic loyalty, many were heartened when China defended their right to revert to Chinese citizenship.

The privileges the government accorded Hoa which enabled them to leave legally contrast sharpest when compared with the circumstances of ethnic Vietnamese determined to flee regardless of the chances of survival. Frequently in barely seaworthy vessels, at times even without enough fuel to reach the nearest foreign shore, they put out to sea, hoping only to leave, without the slightest assurance that they would arrive safely. Their desperate attempts to flee often left family and friends stranded or captured on the beach. They stoically set out, as the successful frequently referred to their journey to freedom, "to find one life among ninety-nine deaths."

Because the government in the delta provinces from which most of the refugees departed tried to maintain as low a profile as possible, only the boat organizers dealt directly with the public security forces who organized the exodus of the Hoa. Passengers made all their arrangements either with the boat organizers themselves or with their intermediaries who took advantage of the clandestine nature of the operation to squeeze handsome profits from those who wanted to leave, but lacked connections.

Between July, 1978, when the government began allowing the Hoa to leave, and June 15, 1979, when it called a halt to their semi-official departures, the refugee outflow was big business in South Vietnam. The government's share, its "duty money" averaged between 4 and 6 taels of gold per adult, depending on location, but the total fee the Hoa charged Vietnamese, for whom it was still illegal to leave, reached 12 and in some cases even 15 taels of gold ($4,500). The difference was someone's profit.

Tran Quoc Tuan, a fearless 24 year-old Vietnamese, spoke from bitter experience about the dangers of overloaded boats. "The boat organizer's greed is one thousand times worse than the cruelty of the communists," he said. "In November 1978, I paid ten taels to a boat organizer for my passage and Chinese papers. Three hundred and sixty people were squeezed onto a boat that was originally supposed to carry only 170. Two days out an exhaust fan down below broke and two people suffocated. We tried to return to shore, but at nine in the evening hit a sand dune and capsized. Only 110 people survived."

"I found a girl who had drowned embracing an empty water can," he continued. Becuase she died, I lived and was able to save 4 others. Two hours later we made it to a raft with 19 people aboard. It seemed each time a wave struck, someone was washed overboard. At dawn the next morning there were only 8 of us left. I swore to myself that I wouldn't go again until there was a steel boat to leave in, but when the time came, I left just like before."

Mr. Tuan showed surprisingly little pity for the plight of the Chinese with whom he had twice shared adversity, who, he said, left Vietnam for economic reasons alone. "They came here (Indonesia) not because their lives were threatened like us Vietnamese, but because their livelihoods were restricted. They suffer truly, but only from a piece of chicken to a bowl of rice. Vietnamese began going to New Economic Zones right away in 1975. No Chinese went before 1978 and even then few stayed. My father was jailed in 1975 and spent 4 months with 30 other former officials in a windowless cell with his hands and legs in chains. He still hasn't returned. We know the true value of freedom, not they, and yet we have to pay more than they."

The prospects for the future of those refugees already in Southeast Asian camps are for a long and painful wait until resettlement can be arranged overseas. The outlook for those who remain in Vietnam, but still desire to leave, is less clear. Indications are that

large numbers of would-be refugees have already committed themselves to departing by ship if allowed by the
authorities and if no other opportunity presents itself
in the meantime. According to refugee accounts, hundreds of boats were stuck in ports throughout the southern
delta on June 15, 1979, when the government called a
temporary halt to the semi-official exodus.

Whether and how those already registered depart
will depend on many factors, of which in the short term
Vietnam controls only one - the possibility of resuming
the semi-official departures. Small boats would then
once again take to the seas with the same disastrous
results.

Conditions within Vietnam are not likely to improve
quickly. And until they do, there are still going to be
potentially large numbers of refugees, desperate to seek
a better life elsewhere. Faced with acute food shortages, the government appears committed to the policy of
forcing unemployed urban dwellers to leave the cities to
become food producers. Although assuredly not without
political implications as well, this necessary economic
policy has in the past accounted for more refugees than
any other one fact. In light of the severe loss of
skilled people this short-sighted policy has caused, the
authorities in Hanoi have apparently reconsidered some
aspects and made provision for the exemption of those
with advanced degrees. But many thousands of others
remain affected. Although supported by the United
Nations, conditions in the New Economic Zones are nonetheless exceedingly bleak. Were they less so, perhaps
more would be willing to stay. But for those who refuse
to be reconciled to such a harsh fate, there is only one
other option.

Vietnam has twice halted the semi-official exodus
since it made its fateful decision in July, 1978, to
allow the Hoa to leave. In November, 1978, permission
was withheld for a period of three months. During this
time refugees continued to leave, but on large international freighters. Whether taken in response to the
international outcry against the smaller boats, as some
refugees seemed to think, or for reasons of mere convenience, passage on these larger boats was decidely
safer for those who left. But like many of the smaller
boats, they nonetheless went from port to port, denied
permission to land. Without an international guarantee
that the refugees aboard would be accepted for resettlement elsewhere, Vietnam's neighbors steadfastly refused
to allow Vietnam to shift its burdens to their shoulders.
Vietnam resumed the semi-official departures the following February.

The magnitude of the refugee exodus and the abiding
reluctance on the part of receiving nations to accept
such large numbers had combined to place concerned

officials on the horns of a dilemma. At the United
Nations conference on refugees held in Geneva in July,
1979, the Vietnamese publicly pledged to stem "illegal"
departures for a "reasonable time," something it had in
fact already done a month earlier by halting for the
second time the exodus of the Hoa. Refugees who arrived
on foreign shores after this date either fled illegally
or departed from intermediate ports in China, where many
of the Hoa have found life on state farms as unappealing
as the life from which they had fled in Vietnam.

But there is a clear conflict between international
efforts to stop refugees from leaving Vietnam and the
United Nationals Charter of Human Rights, which explicitly affirms the right of citizens to leave their
country. The United States has repeatedly pressured the
Soviet Union to permit the emigration of refugees, but
at one point American efforts included entreaties to
the same Soviet leaders to pressure Vietnam to do the
opposite. The agreement reached at Geneva thus gave
precedence to the unfortunate already in overseas camps
and to the plight of Vietnam's neighbors, who could no
longer cope with a continued influx of refugees. An
immediate solution to the refugee problem was found at
its source, but at the expense of those still in Vietnam
desiring to leave.

Although not recognized as such, Vietnam also finds
itself caught on the horns of a dilemma of sorts.
Pressured to stop the exodus, it has been simultaneously
accused of human rights violations. On January 12, 1979,
it agreed to permit the orderly departure of persons who
wished to leave Vietnam for countries of new residence.
The following June a seven-point agreement was reached
with the United Nations High Commissioner for Refugees
which in effect provided for the legal departure of all
those who wished to leave. Although admittedly unproven
and fraught with uncertainty, this agreement offers
those determined to leave the only alternative to hazar-
dous sea voyages.

Despite the high hopes of U.N. officials, this
agreement has failed to be implemented largely because,
although the right to emigrate is recognized, there is
no concomitant right to immigrate. Unless those who
register to leave are accepted by a receiving country,
there is no place for them to go. Most would likely
desire to come to the United States, but the American
government's current definition of refugees, or U.N.'s
for that matter, does not include those still in their
own country. Although an exception was made in the case
of Cuba, under existing regulations only immediate family
members of either American citizens or permanent residents of the United States qualify for the U.N. program.
And because they would be admitted as immigrants, not
refugees, relatives are required to pay all transportation

costs.   Under these conditions the U.N. program offers
relatively little hope of bringing relief.

The Chinese residents of Vietnam came over the
centuries as traders, settlers and political refugees.
Most came by boat.   Although known throughout the world
in recent months as "boat people," in Vietnamese
vernacular they have ironically been called somewhat
pejoratively by the Vietnamese after their means of con-
veyance, nguoi tau, or "boat people" for centuries.
Unless a solution to the longer-term problem is found,
it is likely that this linguistic convention will once
more be transformed into bitter reality.

5 | China's Strategy Toward Vietnam and Its Implications for the United States

Robert G. Sutter

The outpouring of Western and Asian criticism of Hanoi's treatment of ethnic minorities in Vietnam and its territorial, political and other ambitions in Southeast Asia has obscured the poor showing of China in its policy toward Vietnam during the past two years. Chinese leaders have been in the forefront of those spokesmen who have strongly condemned the Vietnamese for their systematic expulsion of the "boat people" and other refugees and for their expansion into other parts of Indochina. Peking has also actively encouraged the non-communist countries of Southeast Asia -- especially the five members of the Association for Southeast Asian Nations (ASEAN) -- to cooperate more closely in military as well as in political and economic matters against the "threat" posed by Vietnam backed by the Soviet Union; and prominent Chinese leaders have pledged support for these countries if they come under Vietnamese attack. Peking has maintained large military forces along the Sino-Vietnamese frontier, while Chinese leaders have promised that "if necessary" they will not hesitate to launch another armed attack on Vietnam.

These Chinese actions in many respects represent an attempt to make the best of what has emerged as a bad situation for China in Southeast Asia. Over the past few years, Peking has seen its interests in the region suffer several serious setbacks:

1. Most notably, Soviet influence and military presence in Vietnam and elsewhere in Indochina has been markedly increased.
2. China has been forced to care for over a quarter of a million of refugees from Vietnam and faces the prospect of having to accept many more.
3. Vietnamese military forces have reduced the pro-Chinese Cambodian government of Pol Pot to a guerrilla movement.
4. Official Chinese influence in Laos has been all

but destroyed.
5. Chinese forces reportedly suffered 20,000 casualties in the border war with Vietnam during February-March 1979, and Peking has been compelled to divert scarce resources from needed economic development in order to increase defense spending by 20 percent and thereby make up for the losses suffered in fighting with Vietnam.

Some observers judge that these setbacks were inevitable given Hanoi's stubborn determination to become the dominant regional power in Southeast Asia in opposition to China. But others make the case that China's policy toward Vietnam over the past two years had a lot to do with bringing about the current problems Peking faces in Southeast Asia. This article makes the latter case. It notes how many of Peking's problems in the region stem in large measure from a shift in China's strategy toward Vietnam begun in May 1978. Up to that point, Peking's policy had been governed considerably by a strategic Chinese concern to promote a balance of influence in Indochina and throughout Asia that was favorable to China and would prevent or upset what Peking saw as Soviet efforts to "contain" the spread of Chinese influence. Until the middle of 1978, China had relied on a carefully calibrated use of diplomatic, economic, and propaganda initiatives designed to improve China's relations with Asian states and to offset the U.S.S.R. Vietnam, which developed and maintained close ties with Moscow, remained a troublespot; but the Chinese were generally successful in containing Soviet influence in Southeast Asia while enhancing Chinese interests elsewhere along China's periphery. They did this in part by maintaining correct party and state relations with the Vietnamese and by avoiding raising Sino-Vietnamese disputes or publicly pressuring Vietnam into aligning more closely with Moscow.

This policy changed abruptly in May 1978. Under the leadership of the newly rehabilitated Vice-Premier Teng Hsiao-ping, Peking began a series of foreign policy initiatives demonstrating a more assertive Chinese policy against the Soviet Union and alleged pro-Soviet forces abroad. Vietnam was now seen as a pro-Soviet state and therefore came under increasingly heavy Chinese pressure. Peking's newly assertive anti-Soviet efforts produced some striking successes in several areas of foreign affairs, but they failed to achieve good results vis-a-vis Vietnam and Indochina. Rather, they steeled Vietnam's resistance to China, accelerated Hanoi's movement toward and deepened its relationship with the U.S.S.R., and ultimately resulted in a Sino-Vietnamese border war that in many respects was as costly to China as it was to Vietnam.

This article examines how Peking's harder policy toward Vietnam failed to secure Chinese interests in Southeast Asia and resulted in an overall serious setback for those Chinese leaders closely associated with the policy, especially Vice-Premier Teng. It also reviews how U.S. leaders -- particularly U.S. Presidential adviser Brzezinski -- publicly associated the United States with China's harder line toward Vietnam and assesses the possible implications such an association might have for the future development of Sino-American relations.

BACKGROUND - CHINESE POLICY PRIOR TO 1978

Peking's behavior in Asia over the past decade has shown that China's policy in the region has been influenced in large measure by a strategic concern to promote a balance of influence in the region that is favorable to China and to block what Peking sees as Soviet efforts to "contain" the spread of Chinese influence.[1] Peking's relations with individual neighboring countries have been influenced substantially by how China sees those nations as either helping or hindering China's anti-Soviet policy in Asia. Thus, for example, if an Asian state appears to be aligning closely with the U.S.S.R. (as in the case of Vietnam in recent years), Peking has adopted a suspicious and sometimes hostile attitude toward it and has been inclined to exert military, political, or economic pressure in an effort to move the country away from the Soviet Union and closer to China. Conversely, if an Asian country has shown signs of pulling back from close ties with the U.S.S.R. (as in the case of India during the period when Indira Gandhi was out of power), the Chinese have become more accommodating toward it and have used political, military, and economic gestures in an effort to encourage the country to move further from the U.S.S.R. and closer to the PRC.

Peking has viewed the Sino-Soviet rivalry for influence in Asia over the past decade as a zero-sum game, in which a gain for Soviet influence is seen as a loss for that of China, and vise versa. As a result, Peking has tended to view favorably not only those neighboring states that have adopted a pro-China orientation, but also those states that have refused to cooperate closely with the U.S.S.R. At the same time, Peking has also voiced support for a Western military presence in the Asian region and for political, military, and economic pacts which it sees as buffers against the expansion of Soviet influence there.

Thus, for example, the Chinese have made abundantly clear in recent years that they support the continued presence in East and South Asia of strong U.S. naval and

air forces -- and the bases for those forces -- as an
effective deterrent to the spread of Soviet military
power along China's eastern and southern periphery.
Peking leaders have warned that a precipitous American
withdrawal could result in the creation of a power
vacuum which would be likely to be filled by the Soviet
Union. At the same time, Chinese spokesmen have encouraged the United States to remain politically, economically, and strategically involved in Japan, the
Philippines, Thailand, and other non-communist states.

Peking has put aside its past fears of Japanese
militarism and has become the most vocal among the Asian
powers in urging Japan to strengthen ties with the
United States and to expand its defense capabilities,
in or der to defend better against the so-called threat
from the north. At the same time, the Chinese have
supported the Indonesian government's close ties with
the United States and Indonesia's cool response to
various Soviet blandishments, while they have ignored
the fact that the Jakarta administration has remained in
the forefront of Asian countries suspicious of Chinese
intentions.

Concerning regional groupings in Asia, Chinese
spokesmen have been increasingly supportive of the
Association of Southeast Asian Nations (ASEAN), which
they have seen as an effective means to preclude the
expansion of Soviet influence in Southeast Asia. In
contrast, they have reacted negatively to Hanoi's efforts
to broaden Southeast Asian regional cooperation to include a prominent role for Vietnam, because they have
seen Hanoi as a Soviet surrogate and thus have regarded
the Vietnamese proposal as a thinly disguised effort to
expand Soviet influence in the region. In South Asia,
Peking was suspicious of Indian proposals for regional
cooperation during the early 1970s, when it judged that
New Delhi was assisting the expansion of Soviet influence
in the region. By contrast, as India showed greater
independence vis-a-vis the U.S.S.R. later in the decade,
the Chinese responded with a positive view of New Delhi's
calls for South Asian regional cooperation.

Of course, concern over Sino-Soviet rivalry has not
been the sole factor influencing Chinese behavior toward
neighboring states. Chinese domestic politics, Maoist
ideology, Chinese territorial claims, and Chinese support
for Overseas Chinese, for Communist claims in Korea, and
for insurgencies in Southeast Asia have all served to
complicate Peking's policy from time to time. Thus, for
example, even though the PRC supports a continued strong
American military presence in Asia in order to offset
the Soviet Union, the Chinese continue to demand the
withdrawal of American forces from South Korea. At the
same time, Chinese interest in developing good relations
with Japan and the non-Communist governments of Southeast

Asia has not prevented the PRC from claiming territory
also claimed by those governments, from backing PRC
interest in the welfare of Overseas Chinese there, and
from supporting insurgent movements directed against the
Southeast Asian administrations. During the past decade,
however, these kinds of concerns have remained generally
in the background as Peking has devoted primary attention to fostering an Asian balance of power favorable to
China and unfavorable to the Soviet Union.

POLICY TOWARD VIETNAM, 1975-1978

China's recent relations with Vietnam have in many
respects underlined the anti-Soviet direction in Chinese
policy in Asia. China's approach was highlighted particularly during 1975, when Peking's general foreign
policy in Asia was dominated by Chinese worry over what
it saw as a major shift in the balance of power there.
The rapid collapse of the U.S. position in Indochina
in the spring of 1975 prompted stepped up Chinese efforts
in pragmatic, conventional diplomacy designed to stabi-
lize the East Asian balance of power to prevent further
Soviet expansion.[2]

The Sino-American relationship had remained the
centerpiece of PRC strategy in the region since the
issuing of the February 1972 Shanghai communique. In
accord with Peking's interests, Washington continued to
implement the Nixon doctrine, gradually withdrawing
from forward positions in Southeast Asia, Korea, Taiwan,
and Japan. At the same time, the United States repeatedly made clear that its withdrawal should not be interpreted as a sign of U.S. weakness, and that Washington
remained firmly opposed to any other power's attempts to
gain a dominant position in East Asia -- this applied
especially to the Soviet Union. The Nixon administration
kept sufficient force on hand to back up its stance,
thereby reassuring Peking that the Shanghai communique's
provisions against any one power's establishing "hegemony" in East Asia would be fulfilled.

Events surrounding the rapid collapse of U.S.-backed
governments in Cambodia and South Vietnam in the spring
of 1975 upset the steady development of an East Asian
balance favorable to Chinese interests. From Peking's
perspective, the stability of the newly emerging East
Asian order had met with a significant setback. While
Peking had expected the United States to withdraw eventually from Indochina, the precipitous U.S. pullback
held serious implications for China's interests. The
United States had suffered a serious defeat at a time
when U.S. leadership and resolve abroad, particularly in
East Asia, had already been called into question as a
result of the Watergate affair and the 1974-1975 economic
recession. (Peking media had noted the debilitating

impact of the economic "crisis" on U.S. internal and international strength from the very outset of the recession. The Chinese leaders were also reported by the Western press to have been seriously concerned over the fall of the Nixon administration, though Peking media discreetly remained virtually silent on the matter.)

Against this backdrop, the U.S. defeats in Indochina cast some doubt on a key premise in Peking's plan for a new East Asian order. In particular, was the United States now strong enough, and more important, was it resolute enough to continue to serve as the main strategic block against Soviet encroachment and advances in East Asia? An analysis of Chinese media behavior demonstrated that Peking judged that the United States had indeed been weakened by the Indochina events, and that U.S. strength and resolve in East Asia had been significantly affected. Shifts in Chinese media treatment reflected an altered Chinese perception of the balance of forces in the area: Peking saw the United States as less influential in Asia than before and thus viewed Washington's utility as a bulwark against future Soviet expansion as somewhat compromised.

The Chinese responded to their perception of an altered East Asian situation in several ways:

1. Peking demonstrated that it continued to adhere to the Sino-U.S. plan for a new East Asian order as articulated in the antihegemony clause of the Shanghai communique. But, whereas in the past Peking had relied mainly on U.S. strength to sustain the favorable balance, the Chinese now began to take on greater responsibility in their own right for shoring up East Asian positions against Soviet expansion. In particular, Peking moved adroitly to solidify China's relations with, and to cement anti-Soviet feelings in, the two non-Communist countries in East Asia most affected by the collapse of the U.S. position in Indochina -- the Philippines and Thailand. Peking's establishment of diplomatic relations with these states -- employing in each instance a joint communique testifying to both sides' opposition to international "hegemony" -- was intended to reassure Manila and Bangkok of their security and stability in the wake of the U.S. defeat. In particular, China's reassurances to both governments had precluded the possibility that Manila and Bangkok, in a hasty search for big power support in the new Southeast Asian situation, might have moved into a one-sided relationship with the U.S.S.R. (China, of course, had long wished to normalize relations

with these states, if possible on the basis of principles inimical to the U.S.S.R. But the speed with which Peking exploited these governments' new interest in relations with China after the Indochina events and the unusually blunt Chinese stress on anti-Soviet invective during negotiations showed heightened PRC concern to offset what was seen as growing possibilities for Soviet expansion in the face of the U.S. withdrawal.)

2. Peking acknowledged that the United States had been "beaten black and blue" in Indochina and noted that the Asian people, especially those in Southeast Asia, were increasingly successful in efforts to drive the "wolf -- the United States -- from the "front gate." But the Chinese made plain that they were opposed to any unilateral, rapid U.S. withdrawal from international involvement as a result of this setback. They clearly indicated that they wished the United States to remain heavily involved abroad, and strategically vigilant against the U.S.S.R. in Europe, the Middle East, and Asia. Peking went so far as to stress a propaganda line that the U.S. defeats in Indochina had actually presented the United States with an "opportunity" to pull back from "secondary" areas where it had been overextended, in order to serve more effectively as a strategic bulwark against Soviet expansion into more "vital" areas abroad. In this vein, Peking reduced past criticism of U.S. military presence and political influence in Asia, and gave unusually favorable play to U.S. statements of resolve to retain strong ties with Japan and selected non-Communist Asian states and to maintain a strong naval presence in the western Pacific and the Indian Ocean.

3. Peking viewed the U.S.S.R. as a more immediate and serious threat to China's aspirations in East and Southeast Asia than it had in the early 1970s. Accordingly, the Chinese adopted a more active policy against the U.S.S.R., focused on blocking Moscow's attempts to advance along China's flanks as the United States withdrew. In particular, the Chinese launched a major propaganda campaign to warn Asian states of the danger posed by the ravenous "tiger" -- the U.S.S.R. -- lurking at the rear door as the Asians pushed the "wolf" through the front gate. Peking also laid special stress on criticizing Moscow's plan for a collective security system in Asia as a thinly veiled Soviet effort to

achieve political "hegemony" in Asia, por-
traying it as the direct antithesis of the
"antihegemony front" fostered by China and its
friends.

Peking's higher profile against the U.S.S.R. caused
the Chinese to view with increased suspicion Asian states
which maintained cordial relations with Moscow, notably
Communist Vietnam. The Chinese began to show undisguised
apprehension that the Vietnamese Communists, now free
from the U.S. threat and less solicitous of China's
views, might choose to pursue policies less consonant
with PRC interest in Southeast Asia. Peking was especially concerned that Hanoi might develop closer ties
with the U.S.S.R. in the postwar situation, using relations with Moscow as a source of leverage to block the
expansion of Chinese influence in Southeast Asia as the
United States withdrew.

Peking's strategy to counter suspected Soviet encroachments in Indochina was to encourage Indochinese
states to be self-reliant and to establish closer relations with China in order to block the intervention of
both "superpowers" in the area. The new Cambodian
government, which had never received significant Soviet
support during its war against Lon Nol, was willing to
go along with Peking. Deputy Prime Minister Khieu
Samphan of Cambodia, during an August 1975 visit to
China, signed a joint communique with Chinese leaders
in which the two sides condemned the international policies of both "superpowers" and in which China was singled
out for praise as a "steel bulwark" of the world
"socialist movement."

By contrast, Hanoi's leadership continued to cultivate close relations with the Soviet Union. Peking
demonstrated its dissatisfaction by publicly stressing
before Vietnamese audiences -- for the first time in
years -- sensitive issues of the Sino-Soviet polemic and
by withholding past routine expressions of Sino-Vietnamese solidarity. Such Chinese behavior was seen most
vividly in Chinese commemoration of the DRV's thirtieth
anniversary celebrations and in Peking's treatment of a
visiting top-level Vietnamese delegation later that
month.

Celebrations in Peking in early September 1975
marking the thirtieth DRV National Day were at a lower
level than Chinese commemorations of the DRV's quin-
quennial anniversaries of 1965 and 1970, and the Chinese
expressions of friendship and solidarity were also more
reserved than in the past. Peking's treatment of the
anniversary included the customary congratulatory message from Mao Tse-tung, Chu Te, and Chou En-lai on
September 1 and a People's Daily editorial on September
2. There was also the usual September 2 DRV envoy's

reception in Peking, attended that year by CCP Politburo
members Teng Hsiao-ping, Yao Wen-yuan, and Wu Te (the
latter addressed the gathering).

Peking clebrations for the last decennial anniversary, the twentieth in 1965, had been considerably
higher in level. The DRV envoy's reception in Peking
that year had occasioned a larger PRC turnout, including
six Politburo members, and had been addressed by Chou
En-lai. Peking had also held a large rally attended by
five Politburo members and addressed by Peking Mayor
Peng Chen. Similarly, the less important twenty-fifth
anniversary in 1970 had occasioned a slightly higher
level treatment in Peking than was the case in 1975;
there had been a rally, attended by three CCP Politburo
members and addressed by Vice Premier Li Hsien-nien, and
the DRV envoy's reception had drawn three Politburo members and had been again addressed by Chou En-lai.

Peking's expressions of Sino-Vietnamese solidarity
and support were even more reserved in comparison with
those employed in marking the DRV's twenty-ninth anniversary in 1974. In the leaders' message in 1974, Mao,
Chu, and Chou had expressed their "warmest greetings,"
while this time they extended "warm congratulations."
Their 1975 message hailed the "militant unity and revolutionary friendship" between the two peoples; the message in 1974 had praised their "deep revolutionary
friendship and militant solidarity based on Marxist-
Leninist principles and proleatrian internationalism"
and had included a pledge to continue to perform "internationalist duties" in supporting the Vietnamese people's
"just cause." The September 2 People's Daily editorial
in 1974 had included in the long-standard expressions of
Sino-Vietnamese solidarity, as "nourished personally by
Chairman Mao and President Ho on the basis of Marxism-
Leninism and proletarian internationalism" and had reiterated the leaders' message pledge to perform "proletarian internationalist duties." By contrast, the
editorial this time characterized the two countries as
"friendly socialist neighbors" and "close comrades-in-
arms" and only expressed hope that the "militant friendship" between them would be continuously consolidated
and developed.

Marking the anniversary in a September 3, 1975,
speech at a steel mill in Vietnam, Vice Premier Chen
Hsi-lien of the PRC took the occasion polemically to
admonish the Vietnamese on the sensitive issue of the
danger in Southeast Asia and the world of the intensified
competition of "both" superpowers. Chen assured his
Vietnamese audience that the consolidation of the "fra-
ernal friendship and militant solidarity" between the
two nations on the basis of Marxism-Leninism and proletarian internationalism conformed to the "fundamental
interests" and constituted the "common desire" of the

two peoples. He also recalled that, in the past struggle against "U.S. imperialist aggression," the Chinese
had supported Vietnam "to the best of our ability" as
"an international obligation incumbent upon us," and he
affirmed that China would do its "utmost" to consolidate
relations in the future. At the same time, the vice
premier said that "we must take notice" of superpower
rivalry as "the root cause" of world unrest and the
source of "a new world war." While noting that superpower contention was focused in the West, Chen affirmed
that the superpowers were "doing their utmost to place
other countries under their sphere of influence" in Asia
as well, and he added specific praise for Southeast
Asian countries' continuing struggle against "superpower
intervention."

Chinese handling of the September 22-28, 1975,
visit to China by a Vietnamese Party-government delegation led by First Secretary Le Duan of the Vietnamese
Workers Party (VWP) was noticeably less effusive than it
had been for Le Duan's last visit as head of an official
delegation in June 1973. Peking comment moderated previous expressions of unity and friendship and gave more
attention to assessments (potentially offensive to
Vietnamese sensitivities) of the world situation and of
the superpowers than it had during the 1973 stay.

Expressions of Sino-Vietnamese friendship and solidarity in Vice-Premier Teng Hsiao-ping's September 22
banquet speech for the DRV guests were less elaborate
than those in the speech by Premier Chou En-lai welcoming
Le Duan in 1973. While Chou had characterized the two
nations as "close comrades-in-arms and brothers" who
"shared weal and woe" and had gone through "thick and
thin" together, Teng now called the PRC and Vietnam
"fraternal socialist neighbors" sharing a "longstanding
traditional friendship." In his speech Chou had noted
that a "profound revolutionary friendship, nurtured
personally by Mao Tse-tung and Ho Chi Minh and based on
the principles of Marxism-Leninism and proletarian internationalism," had been forged between the two nations
and that the "great friendship and militant unity"
between them had been "further enhanced and consolidated." Chou had pledged that China would continue to
perform its internationalist duty to resolutely support
Vietnam's "just struggle." This time Teng merely noted
that the Chinese people have "always treasured their
revolutionary friendship" with Vietnam, that the pre-
servation and development of their friendship on the
basis of Marxism-Leninism and proletarian internationalism was in keeping with the "common desire" and the
"fundamental interests" of the two peoples, and that the
Chinese people would "spare no effort" to do so.

The People's Daily editorial greeting Le Duan's
arrival in 1975 similarly dropped most of the expressions

of friendship that had been recited in the editorial
greeting his 1973 visit. It pledged only that the
Chinese "will, as always, actively contribute their
share" to strengthening Sino-Vietnamese friendship.
Atmospherics in the NCNA reports on the delegation's
arrival and its reception by the Chinese leadership
were also moderated. While the Sino-Vietnamese talks in
1973 had been opened in a "warm atmosphere overflowing
with revolutionary friendship and militant unity," talks
this time were characterized simply as "fraternal,
cordial, and friendly."

Similar to Chen Hsi-lien's emphasis on September 3,
Teng's speech on the 22nd stressed, without specifically
mentioning the United States and the Soviet Union, that
the hegemonism of the "superpowers" was the primary
cause of world tensions today. He warned his Vietnamese
listeners that the superpowers were subjecting the third
world to "aggression, subversion, interference, control,
and plunder," and pledged that China would "stand
unswervingly" at the side of the third world countries
as the "main force" of resistance to imperialism,
colonialism, and hegemonism. During Le Duan's 1973
visit, by contrast, Chou En-lai did not comment on the
world situation, discussing only the "completely new
situation" in Indochina in the wake of the Paris peace
agreements.

The Vietnamese left China without hosting the usual
reciprocal banquet in Peking, and there was no joint
Sino-Vietnamese communique, a protocol custom followed
with Le Duan's last official visit to China in 1973. The
only announced results of the visit were an agreement on
an interest-free Chinese loan to Vietnam and a protocol
on the supply of general goods to Vietnam.

Despite its continued cool relationship with Vietnam and concern over the cordial Vietnamese-Soviet relationship, Peking by late 1975 had begun to see the
situation in East Asia in a generally more optimistic
light. Even though U.S. power and influence in the
region had been weakened, the United States continued to
demonstrate an active interest and involvement in maintaining an East Asian balance of power that would preclude heavy Soviet penetration into the region. This
was underlined by President Ford in late 1975 when he
announced the so-called Pacific Doctrine. This strategic
policy in East Asia following defeat in Indochina was
based on U.S. air and naval power in the region and on
close U.S. ties with its traditional allies, such as
Japan, and with the PRC. It significantly avoided mentioning any major role that the Soviet Union might play
in the area.

Meanwhile, Peking had achieved considerable success
over the past few months in broadening its influence
among non-Communist Southeast Asian states. The Chinese

propaganda line warning against the danger of Soviet
expansion as the United States withdrew also was winning
new adherents in Southeast Asia. At the end of 1975, the
only areas in East Asia where the Soviet Union maintained
considerable influence were Vietnam and Laos.

Over the next two or three years, Peking persisted
with its active efforts to foster influence and reduce
the likeliehood of Soviet penetration in East and Southeast Asia.[3] Starting early in 1976, Peking entertained
top-level official delegations from all the Indochinese
countries, Singapore, Burma, Thailand, Australia, New
Zealand, Western Samoa, and Papua New Guinea. At the
same time, the Chinese attempted to solidify relations
with these states by signing new trade, aid, and scientific accords with them and Chinese leaders began their most
active period of travel in the region since before the
Cultural Revolution. They also broadened the scope of
this conventional effort to include South Asia, leading to
a marked improvement in China's position in that area;
and they continued to encourage an active U.S. naval and
air presence in the region, especially, in Japan, the
Western Pacific, and the Indian Ocean.

Vietnam's clost relations with the U.S.S.R., and
its persisting conflict with Chinese interests in Cambodia
and over the Sino-Vietnamese border, continued to represent the most serious problem for China's strategy in Asia,
but Peking maintained its past practice of sustaining
correct party and state ties with the Vietnamese leaders
and restricting signs of disagreement with the Vietnamese
largely to oblique signs in Chinese media. Even after the
Vietnamese engaged in a reportedly large-scale military
action against China's ally Cambodia in late 1977, Chinese
leaders carefully avoided criticizing Vietnamese actions.
The Chinese followed a low-keyed public posture designed
to keep channels of communication open to Vietnam and to
encourage the Vietnamese to disassociate themselves from
the U.S.S.R., while the Chinese tried to contain the
possible spread of pro-Soviet influence from Vietnam to
other parts of Southeast Asia.

China's restrained approach toward Vietnam at this
time was seen in Chinese treatment of high-level Vietnamese visitors during the latter half of 1977. Chinese
leaders gave a "cordial and friendly" welcome to SRV
Defence Minister Giap on his arrival in early June,[4]
offered standard celebrations in Peking marking Vietnam's
national day in September,[5] and provided "cordial and
Friendly" greetings for Le Duan on his visit to China
during November.[6] The latter visit demonstrated a continuation of strains between China and Vietnam, but it
produced no evidence of a deterioration in relations
between the two sides.

The cordial Chinese welcome for the Vietnamese was
particularly remarkable inasmuch as the visits came at a

time when these same Vietnamese leaders were actively
involved in solidifying Vietnam's relations with the
U.S.S.R. and were consolidating Vietnam's strategic
power at home and in Laos in apparent preparation for an
attack on Cambodia. (Cambodia later reported a major
Vietnamese assault against it during September 1977.)
Thus, for example, both Giap and Le Duan traveled to
China after extensive visits and negotiations in the
Soviet Union. Giap followed his trip to China by touring
several Vietnamese provinces bordering Cambodia, pre-
sumably in preparation for the Vietnamese assault in
September. Meanwhile, Le Duan had consolidated Viet-
namese power in Laos during his landmark visit there in
July 1977.[7]

In the wake of the Vietnamese attack on Cambodia
during September (which was not made public until Cambodia broke relations with Vietnam in early 1978), Peking
gave an extremely warm welcome to the Cambodian Comminist
Party leader Pol Pot during a visit to China in October
1977, and the Chinese media at that time announced to the
world the development of the previously clandestine Cambodian Communist Party.[8] Peking subsequently sent High-
level delegates to Cambodia in December 1977 and January
1978, led respectively by Vice-Premier Chen Yung-kuei and
by Chou En-lai's widow, Teng Ying-chao.

Although these steps clearly underlined strong
Chinese support for Cambodia, the Chinese officials
carefully eschewed criticism of Vietnam. Thus,
for example, Teng Ying-chao's January 19, 1978, speech
in Phnom Penh avoided specifically mentioning the
Cambodian-Vietnamese border problem, instead merely expressing the conviction that the Cambodians "will win
more brilliant victories in the sacred cause of defending the motherland." And while NCNA carried most of
the text of Teng's speech, it omitted the portion of the
speech of her Cambodian host which referred to the border conflict.[9] Also, two weeks earlier, Peking had
appeared to show continued good will toward Vietnam when
it announced, only a few days after Cambodia's public
break with Vietnam, that the agreement with Vietnam on
mutual supply of goods and payments for 1978 had just
been signed in Peking. The Chinese could have delayed
the agreement if they had wished to demonstrate displeasure with Hanoi. The SRV trade delegation had been
in Peking only eighteen days; the previous year's
negotiations on the annual trade agreement had kept the
Vietnamese in Peking for almost six weeks.[10]

RECENT CHINESE POLICY

China's policy of restraint toward Vietnam changed
in mid-1978, beginning in late May. At that time,
Peking began a series of diplomatic, propaganda, eco-

nomic, and military moves which appeared designed to exert much stronger pressure on Vietnam over such long-standing Sino-Vietnamese disputes as the treatment of Overseas Chinese in Vietnam, Vietnamese relations with Cambodia, the Sino-Vietnamese boundary disagreement and close Vietnamese-Soviet relations. The Vietnamese were following policies on these and other issues which had served to exacerbate Sino-Vietnamese friction. They rebuffed each of the new Chinese pressure tactics, and they tried to counter the Chinese "threat" by moving closer toward the Soviet Union.

China's precise motives in changing its policy toward Vietnam are still far from clear. It does seem evident that the overall Chinese objective in the region remained the development of a favorable balance of influence that would reduce, or preclude the expansion of, Soviet power and the power of countries seen by China as Soviet surrogates. In this regard, it appeared that the overall situation in Asia was generally good for China in mid-1978, with only Vietnam, Laos, and Afghanistan representing significant troublespots. Nevertheless, the Chinese apparently judged that their past policy of restraint toward Vietnam and their reliance on low-keyed conventional diplomatic and economic initiatives in Southeast Asia did not represent a satisfactory approach.

In any event, the new, more forceful approach toward Vietnam was closely associated with Vice-Premier Teng Hsiao-ping, whose influence grew tremendously in Chinese leadership councils during 1978. Teng was especially outspoken in his criticism of Vietnam and of Vietnamese-Soviet relations during conversations with Western visitors to China in mid-1978.[11] He charged among other things that Vietnam was already a de facto ally of the Soviet Union and had allowed the Soviet Union to establish military bases in Vietnam. (Teng was able to offer little proof of these charges, and Western intelligence sources at the time were unable to detect any solid indication that Soviet forces were in fact establishing bases in Vietnam.)

The new Chinese attitude toward Vietnam also coincided with a generally more assertive Chinese foreign policy against suspected Soviet "expansion" abroad. Thus, for example, the Chinese, beginning in mid-1978, sent several high-level envoys to areas of Africa subjected to Soviet-backed pressure,[12] began taking a markedly more active role against Soviet programs in international disarmament negotiations,[13] demonstrated unprecedented Chinese interest in Eastern Europe by sending CCP Chairman Hua Kuo-feng to Romania and Yugoslavia, and signed a peace treaty with Japan, and established normal diplomatic relations with the United States -- in the latter two cases -- on the basis of

opposition to international "hegemony" -- i.e., the
U.S.S.R.
    Peking's newly assertive policy -- under the gui-
dance of Teng Hsiao-ping -- was a considerable success
in all these areas except Vietnam and Southeast Asia.
China's altered approach toward Vietnam seriously complicated Peking's interests in Indochina and in Southeast Asia as a whole. Thus, for example, Chinese pressure tactics were at least in part responsible for the
rapid growth of Soviet influence in Vietnam, resulting
notably in the signing of a Soviet-Vietnamese friendship
treaty in November 1978. They also alarmed several of
the non-Communist countries of Southeast Asia, which
Peking in recent years had managed to reassure regarding
Chinese intentions. Now, several of these countries --
notably Indonesia and Malaysia -- saw pointed implications for them in Peking's strong defense of the interests of Overseas Chinese in Vietnam and in Chinese territorial claims against Vietnam. They also saw China
as responsible in large measure for the most serious
escalation of great power tension in the region since
the United States had pulled back from Vietnam in 1975.[14]
And, China's use of massive military force inside Vietnam almost certainly alarmed some of the non-Communist
Southeast Asian states, as well as others of China's
neighbors, regarding Peking's repeatedly expressed commitment to the establishment of a peaceful environment
in Asia. Peking's attack also substantially reduced
China's ability to meet its ambitious economic goals at
a time when it was diverting scarce resources to military action against Vietnam; and Peking's action prompted
Soviet countermoves that increased the danger of the outbreak of a broader international conflict that would
destroy the fragile stability in Asia.[15]
    In short, it seems fair to say that Peking's change
in policy toward Vietnam since mid-1978 has on balance
led to a setback for Chinese interests in the area. This
change in policy presumably is also seen in China as a
problem for those Chinese leaders who were most closely
associated with it; in this regard Teng Hsiao-ping is
outstanding. An added feature of this policy is that it
began very soon after U.S. Presidential National Security
Advisor Brzezinski visited China in May 1978. (Mr.
Brzezinski notably used his inaugural address in China
to condemn "regional hegemonism" -- a codeword used by
China to denote Vietnam.)[16] This policy's development
also   coincided with a number of unprecedented U.S.
actions, favorable to Peking and directly or indirectly
unfavorable to Vietnam, which served to leave a vivid
impression in some quarters that the United States was
China's silent partner in its new tough policy toward
Vietnam.
    Peking's new pressure tactics against Vietnam began

with a May 24, 1978, NCNA interview with a spokesman of
the Overseas Chinese Affairs Office of the PRC State
Council who accused the Vietnamese of instituting a
massive program to persecute and depoart Chinese residents in Vietnam. The initial protest was buttressed
with a carefully orchestrated propaganda campaign, using
national and provincial radios, television, press, and
newsreels to dramatize that Vietnam was brutally mis-
treating Overseas Chinese. On May 26, Peking unilaterally escalated the conflict by announcing that the
Chinese government had decided to send ships to Vietnam
to "bring home the persecuted Chinese residents."17
     Reflecting the implications of these moves for
broader Sino-Vietnamese relations, the May 24 interview
failed to note that Vietnam was a socialist country.
In repeating an otherwise standard Chinese litany, the
spokesman left out the word "socialist" in noting that
"China and Vietnam are neighboring (socialist) countries
linked by common mountains and rivers." At the same
time, articles in the Hong Kong Communist press signaled
Peking's fundamental concern with Vietnam's close relationship with the U.S.S.R., charging that Vietnam, as
a tool of Moscow, was seeking to dominate Indochina and
Southeast Asia. Thus, several Hong Kong articles in the
week after the May 24 statement portrayed Hanoi as
carrying out Moscow's designs, referring to Vietnam as a
"second Cuba." They warned also that Hanoi may turn over
naval facilities in Vietnam to the Soviet Union.
     Although Vietnam announced grudging acceptance of
Peking's plan to send ships to evacuate Vietnam's
Chinese and called for negotiations over the problem,
the polemics between China and Vietnam escalated during
the second week in June. Peking charged in its own name
that Vietnam was adopting anti-Chinese actions at the
behest of the Soviet Union, and Hanoi responded by
directly identifying Peking as Cambodia's patron. Peking
began this round of polemics with a PRC Foreign Ministry
statement of June 9 which repeated criticism of SRV
policies toward Overseas Chinese, rejected Hanoi's request for negotiations, announced that the burden of
caring for refugees from Vietnam necessitated a cut in
PRC aid to Vietnam, and implied that Hanoi was acting in
response to a foreign backer. On June 10, 1978, the
People's Daily Commentator (usually a high Party figure)
spelled out the charge that the Soviet Union was "the
behind-the-scene provocateur and supporter of Vietnamese
authorities in ostracizing Chinese residents and attacking China." The Foreign Ministry statement urged a
change in Hanoi's policies without threatening any consequences, but, by turning down the Vietnamese request
for negotiations, failing to mention Hanoi's offer to
accommodate the Chinese ships, and raising the Soviet
connection, Peking appeared to have deliberately mapped

out a collision course with Hanoi.[18]

Added Chinese pressure against Vietnam was seen in a sharply worded People's Daily Commentator article of June 17 along with the announced closing of Vietnamese consulates in China the day before. Vietnam responded by refusing to allow Overseas Chinese to exit in Chinese ships under terms set by Peking, and on June 28, five weeks after the start of the Chinese pressure, Hanoi announced that it had asked to join the Soviet bloc's economic organization, the Council for Mutual Economic Assistance (CMEA).[19]

Peking subsequently took several steps against Vietnam. On July 3, the Chinese declared an end to all Chinese economic and technical assistance to Vietnam; on July 11, Peking closed its borders to the thousands of Overseas Chinese trying to flee across the land frontier with China; and, on July 12, Peking for the first time directly condemned Hanoi's policies toward Cambodia. Vietnam rebuffed the Chinese pressure and escalated charges against China for allegedly threatening Vietnam along the Sino-Vietnamese frontier and through Chinese support for Cambodian attacks against Vietnam.

It was clear by mid-summer that Peking's moves had yet to prompt any softening of Vietnamese opposition to Chinese interests in Southeast Asia. The Chinese at this time began to show sensitivity over, and to alter, some of their recent actions. Thus, for example, a July 3 People's Daily editorial exhibited considerable concern that the dispute over Chinese residents in Vietnam might have a negative impact on PRC relations with other Southeast Asian countries that have large Overseas Chinese populations. The editorial strongly condemned alleged Soviet attempts to create anxiety in Southeast Asian countries about Chinese policies toward the Overseas Chinese. The editorial stressed that the problem with Vietnam was unique, growing out of Vietnam's "persecution" of Chinese nationals, and the China was concerned only with protecting the "justifiable rights and interests" of its citizens abroad.[20]

At the same time, Peking probably had mixed feelings over two steps that it had taken in the face of Vietnamese intransigence. Thus, the closing of the Chinese border with Vietnam on July 11 had put pressure on the Vietnamese side of the frontier for a change in policy toward Overseas Chinese there. But it had also portrayed the Chinese leaders as unfeeling in regard to the plight of the Overseas Chinese in Vietnam -- Peking had first encouraged these people to return to China and then abruptly halted their return, even though they had already left their homes in Vietnam but had yet to cross the Chinese border. Moreover, Vietnam refused to allow the Chinese ships -- sent in late spring -- to land in Vietnam, resulting in an embarrassing situation in which the Chinese were forced to order the ships to return empty to China.

In mid-July, Peking briefly tried a new, more conciliatory approach in an effort to break its deadlock with Hanoi. A July 19 PRC Foreign Ministry note offered to start talks with Vietnam on the vice foreign minister level, and an accompanying NCNA commentary called the proposal "an important step in defense of traditional Sino-Vietnamese friendship" and predicted that both sides could reach a settlement and achieve "unity and friendship." This element of conciliation was not carried over into other Chinese commentary, however, and even though the talks began in Hanoi in August, they quickly became bogged down in polemics.[21] The talks broke off in September, amid heated Sino-Vietnamese charges of mounting tension along the Sino-Vietnamese frontier and Chinese accusations that Hanoi was using its dispute with China to direct international attention from the Vietnamese military preparations against Cambodia.

In the fall, the Vietnamese took a long step forward in relations with the U.S.S.R. and successfully outmaneuvered China's power -- at least for a time -- by signing a friendship treaty with the Soviet Union, during a visit to Moscow in early November by an SRV delegation led by Le Duan. The treaty implicitly reassured the Vietnamese against Chinese pressure and allowed Hanoi to focus attention on preparing for a military attack against Cambodia. Peking's initial response did little to offset Hanoi's advantage. The Chinese dispatched a delegation led by CCP Vice Chairman Wang Tung-hsing to Phnom Penh, but Chinese leaders remained restrained in their expressions of support for the Cambodian government and avoided reference to possible Chinese assistance to the Cambodians. Teng Hsiao-ping tried but failed to elicit strong statements from Southeast Asian leaders against Vietnam during his tour of several nations there in November.

Chinese leadership considerations over what steps should be taken in the face of the new Soviet-Vietnamese treaty and in anticipation of Hanoi's apparent intention to launch a major military assault on China's ally, Cambodia, coincided with the most important Chinese leadership meetings since the death of Mao Tse-tung and the arrest of the "gang of four" in late 1976. The leadership meetings during November and December 1978 culminated in the Third Plenum of the Eleventh CCP Central Committee. According to a variety of news sources and reports in the Hong Kong Communist media, the meetings were marked by strong debate at the highest levels of the Chinese leadership over a wide variety of sensitive domestic political and economic issues.[22]

Although there were no reports of Chinese leaders

sharply disagreeing over foreign policy at this time, an analysis of Chinese media pronouncements strongly suggests that the Chinese leaders were not in agreement over how to handle their relations with Soviet-backed Vietnam and the related issue of Chinese support for Cambodia against Vietnam. Some leaders, notably Vice Premier Li Hsien-nien, pointedly associated themselves with the argument that Vietnam, backed by the Soviet Union, represented a direct threat to China and that China should adopt strong measures to deal with the threat. Other leaders, including, curiously, Teng Hsiao-ping, associated themselves with a different argument, stressing that the threat of aggression against China came from the 'north' and implicitly playing down the threat to China emanating from Vietnam in the south.

There also appeared to be differences in the Chinese leadership at this time over how far China should go in backing Pol Pot's government in Cambodia after it came under heavy attack from Vietnam in December 1978. Some leaders, notably Teng Hsiao-ping, appeared reluctant to go beyond expressions of general Chinese support for the Cambodian "people" in their resistance against the Vietnamese, whereas others, nota bly Hua Kuo-feng, pointedly associated China with strong support for the Pol Pot administration.

Perhaps the most striking feature of these seemingly contradictory points of leadership emphasis, seen in Chinese media output at this time, concerned statements of Teng Hsiao-ping in December and January. Teng, of course, had been in the forefront of Chinese leaders promoting a tough line toward Vietnam in mid-1978. He had pointedly told foreign visitors to China of the alleged threat posed by Vietnam, The "Cuba of Asia," and the alleged Soviet design to use pro-Soviet developments in places like South Yemen, Afghanistan, and Vietnam for Moscow's design of global expansion and the encirclement of China.[23] In late 1978, however, Teng's statements seemed to reflect less concern about the strategic threat to China posed by a Vietnam, even though Vietnam was now formally aligned with the U.S.S.R. and prepared to attack China's Indochina ally. He did not echo other Chinese leaders who were warning Vietnam of possible Chinese military countermeasures against it, and he was more reserved than other Chinese leaders in his pledges of support for Cambodia against Vietnam.

One can only speculate about the possible reasons for this change in Teng's approach to Vietnam, although the Vice Premier almost certainly saw that China's earlier policy of pressure had not worked well and that China might be forced to resort to greater pressure, including the use of armed attack, in order to compel Hanoi to change its policy. Teng doubtless was aware that such an attack would divert Chinese resources that were needed for the development of the Chinese economy, and would thereby complicate the chances of success in the ambitious modernization program which was the centerpiece of Teng's plan for China's future.

Teng's address to a New Year's Day meeting of the Chinese People's Political Consultative Conference was unusually emphatic in claiming that the threat to China came from the "north". Teng said: "At present, the threat to peace comes from the north, the source of instability and war in the world lies in the north, and should there be foreign agression against our country, it would also come from the north."[24]

Teng's argument may have been so strong because it implicitly contradicted the authoritative communique issued on December 23, 1978, at the end of the Third Plenum. That communique had clearly implied that the threat of aggression to China could come from the south -- or any other direction -- and had given no special stress to the threat from the north. It said: "The grave danger of war still exists. We must strengthen our national defence, and be prepared to repulse at any moment aggressors from any direction."[25]

Teng's line that China should focus attention on defence of the north received apparent support at this time from an article appearing in the Kwangming Daily on December 19, 1978. That article offered, without explanation, a detailed defence of the policy of the nineteenth century Chinese leader Tso Tsung-tang, who had stressed the importance of directing China's defense against the northern threat at the expense of, and in opposition to, others in the Chinese leadership at that time who urged that China build a stronger defence in eastern and southern regions. The Kwangming Daily article offered no explanation as to why it was recalling this historical issue -- the most important strategic debate in nineteenth century China -- except to claim that Tso had been misinterpreted by Chinese historians in recent years. In view of the face that historical allegory has long been used in modern Chinese leadership debates over foreign and domestic policy, it seems fair to conclude that the appearance of this unusual article is likely to have reflected Chinese disagreement over foreign policy strategy at this crucial time. The article suggested that the differences may have been strong, inasmuch as it used politically forceful language to defend Tso against his nineteenth century opponents, noting that "the difference (between Tso and his opponents) was a struggle between patriotism and national betrayal."[26]

People's Daily also seemed to be reflecting differences within the Chinese leadership over the nature of the threat China faced in Asia at this time. Thus, a

December 30, 1978, People's Daily Commentator article
devoted to Soviet strategy in Asia in general and in
Vietnam in particular disagreed with unnamed individuals,
who it said had judged erroneously that Vietnam's
alliance with the U.S.S.R. and other recent Soviet moves
were of primary concern to China. It disagreed with
those "people" who judged that Moscow's primary objective in the region was to threaten and encircle China.
The article argued that the danger to China was not that
important, and it also implied that general Asian and
world resistance would be sufficient to deal with the
new Vietnamese-Soviet relationship. The article said:

> Some people point out that this (Soviet activity
> in Asia) is intended to encircle China. Of course,
> the Kremlin has China in mind in pushing expan-
> sionism in Asia. But its more important objective
> is to expand its sphere of influence and rid the
> continent of the influence of the United States,
> its chief opponent, thereby threatening peace and
> security of Japan and other Asian nations in par-
> ticular. It is indeed short-sighted and dangerous
> to overlook this.
>
> The Soviet Union's Asian strategy is an important
> part of its global counter-revolutionary strategy.
> It thinks that it has scored a major gain in having
> Vietnam as its stooge for the pursuit of hegemony
> in Asia. But, contrary to its wish, this actually
> serves to show the atrocious features of the Soviet
> and Vietnamese expansionists and arouse resistance
> and opposition among the countries and people in
> Asia. Asia belongs to the Asian people. All ef-
> forts in quest of hegemony, worldwide or regional,
> are destined to fail in the end.[27]

Despite the argument seen in pronouncements of
Teng Hsiao-ping, Kwangming Daily, and People's Daily,
some high-level Chinese leaders at this time closely
associated themselves with the view that Vietnam, backed
by the U.S.S.R., was indeed a serious threat to China
and that China should take more forceful action, including the use of military counterattack, in order to deal
with Vietnam. Most notable in this regard was Vice-
Premier Li Hsien-nien. Li had not been particularly
prominent in the more assertive Chinese policy toward
Vietnam earlier in 1978, but beginning in December he
issued a series of unusually strong statements on the
issue. He implied that Vietnam was directly threatening
China and that China might resort to strong measures to
deal with Vietnam. As early as December 13, 1978, for
instance, Li warned the Vietnamese that "China's fore-
bearance has its limit and the Vietnamese authorities

are deluding themselves by thinking that we are weak
and can be bullied."[28] On December 28, Li pointed to
the Vietnam-Soviet alliance as a direct threat, first to
China and then to Southeast Asia, and he strongly warned
the Vietnamese to stop their "anti-China acts." He said:

> The Soviet social-imperialists have not given up
> their ambition to subjugate China. And the Viet-
> namese authorities, backed by the Soviet global
> hegemonists, are working overtime at their regional
> hegemonism, opposing China, ostracizing and cruelly
> persecuting Chinese nationals residing in Vietnam.
> Not long ago, the Soviet Union and Vietnam con-
> cluded a so-called treaty of friendship and cooper-
> ation which is in substance a military alliance.
> They aim their attack at China and Southeast Asian
> countries and have launched a frenzied armed
> aggression and subversive activities against Kam-
> puchea.
>
> The Vietnamese authorities must stop at once their
> criminal anti-Chinese and anti-China acts or else
> they will bear all the consequences.[29]

In the days after the Vietnamese had overrun Cambodia, Li was more outspoken than any other Chinese
leader in warning against Vietnam's "repeated provocations" against China. He said on January 8, 1979, that,
"We would like to warn Vietnam that the patience of the
Chinese people has a limit and no one should turn a deaf
ear to what they say. Our principle is: We will not
attack unless we are attacked; and if we are attacked,
we will certainly counter-attack."[30]
    Meanwhile, Teng Hsiao-ping and other Chinese leaders
seemed to show signs of disagreement over how much support China should provide the Cambodian administration
of Pol Pot in the wake of Vietnam's assault of late
December and early January. At that time, Teng Hsiao-
ping did not go beyond bland expressions of support for
the Cambodian "people" in their struggle to resist the
Vietnamese, while other Chinese leaders, notably Hua
Kuo-feng, were much more emphatic in associating themselves with strong support for the Pol Pot administration.
Thus, for example, when Teng Hsiao-ping met in Peking
with Cambodian Deputy Prime Minister Ieng Sary on January 13, he merely expressed "firm support for the Kampuchean people" in their struggle to resist Vietnamese
aggression.[31] On the same day, Hua Kuo-feng met with
Ieng Sary and offered China's strongest statement in
support of Cambodia in several months. He said, "The
Kampuchean people's struggle is our struggle. We supported you in the past, we are supporting you now, and
we will continue to support you in the future." Hua went

on to associate himself closely with Pol Pot as NCNA
reported that "Chairman Hua paid high tribute and regards
to Comrade Pol Pot and other party and state leaders of
Kampuchea and to the Kampuchean armymen and civilians
fighting on the frontline."[32]

In short, it appeared that, as the Chinese deliber-
ated over what sort of action to take against Vietnam in
the wake of Vietnam's alliance with the Soviet Union and
its attack on Cambodia, Peking's policy was at an impasse. For one thing, the assertive Chinese policy toward Vietnam, begun in May 1978, had met with at least
temporary failure. Vietnam now was aligned with the
U.S.S.R. and was successfully invading China's ally,
Cambodia; other states in Southeast Asia remained suspicious of Chinese intentions. Some observers in the
region and elsewhere saw China's failure as stemming
from its pressure tactics against Vietnam, which they
saw as speeding Vietnam's alignment with the U.S.S.R.
and prompting the Vietnamese to judge that they had
little to lose in regard to relations with China if they
went ahead and attacked Cambodia. These observers also
began to wonder whether Peking was capable of following
similar, seemingly misguided policies in other areas.[33]

Not only had China's policy toward Vietnam appeared
to have failed at this point, but Chinese leaders appeared to be divided over what to do about the failure.
Teng Hsiao-ping's comments at this juncture argued for
Chinese caution, both in assessing the nature of the
threat to China posed by Vietnam and in increasing
Chinese support for Cambodia. This represented a remarkable -- and perhaps embarrassing -- turnabout for Teng,
inasmuch as he was most closely associated with the
tough Chinese policy toward Vietnam in 1978. Meanwhile,
Li Hsien-nien and Hua Kuo-feng seemed to argue for a
continuation and increase in China's assertive policy
toward Vietnam, stressing the threat China faced from the
Vietnamese, the need for China to be ready to "counter-
attack," and stronger support for Cambodia and Pol Pot.

Thus, as the Chinese decided to launch a military
attack against Vietnam (the decision appears to have been
made by January 21, 1979, when Chinese media disclosed
the transfer of a more experienced military commander to
the Vietnamese front,)[34] they apparently did so with
divided counsel and against the background of an eight-
month policy of repeated setbacks toward Vietnam. In
view of Teng Hsiao-ping's comments advocating caution in
December and January and his close association with the
past policy toward Vietnam, it seems fair to conjecture
that policy toward Vietnam during 1978-1979 represented
the most serious international setback for the vice
Premier since his rehabilitation in mid-1977.

IMPLICATIONS FOR SINO-AMERICAN RELATIONS

Peking's tougher policy toward Vietnam coincided with progress in Sino-American normalization, culminating in the December 15, 1978, announcement of the establishment of Sino-American diplomatic relations and Vice-Premier Teng Hsiao-ping's visit to the United States in late January 1979. The United States has claimed that it did not side with China in its dispute with Vietnam, but the record shows that, beginning at least with Brzezinski's visit to China in May 1978, U.S. leaders took steps which gave an impression to the Vietnamese and other international observers that the United States was siding with China against Vietnam.

During a banquet in Peking welcoming Brzezinski to China on May 20, 1978 -- only four days before the start of China's pressure campaign against Vietnam, the U.S. leader implicitly but clearly identified the United States with Chinese opposition to Soviet-backed Vietnam. He said that the United States "recognizes -- and shares -- China's resolve to resist the efforts of any nation which seeks to establish global or regional hegemony."[35] The last two words, of course, represent code words widely used by China to denote Vietnam.

In late May, as the Chinese began their new policy toward Vietnam and unilaterally sent ships to evacuate Overseas Chinese from Vietnam, the Soviet Union conducted naval exercises in the South China Sea as an apparent show of force for Vietnam. In what may have been more than a coincidence, U.S. leaders ordered one of the two U.S. aircraft carriers of the Seventh Fleet to call at this time at Hong Kong, where the officers on board feted Chinese Communitst officials from the British colony. NCNA promptly reported this "friendly" meeting between Chinese leaders and American officers on a U.S. warship docked in what the PRC sees as Chinese territory -- this marked the first time that Peking media have been known to report such a demonstration of Chinese support for the continued U.S. military presence along their frontier. The carrier soon left Hong Kong for duty in the South China Sea, in what analysts saw as an American show of force for China in the face of the Soviet maneuvers.[36]

In mid-July, Vietnam tried to breathe new life into the dormant U.S.-Vietnamese negotiations on the normalization of diplomatic relations by telling foreign diplomats and newsmen that Hanoi no longer would require the United States to pay reparations in order to establish diplomatic and trade relations. Peking was quick to show its disapproval of the new Vietnamese stance;[37] the United States took no significant step forward in trying to normalize diplomatic or economic relations with Vietnam; and some American observers argued that the delicate process of normalizing U.S. diplomatic relations with China should have priority over improved U.S.

relations with Hanoi, even though the Vietnamese had dropped their previous preconditions and appeared very anxious to improve relations.[38]

The United States in the latter part of 1978 took several other steps which served indirectly to strengthen China's position against Vietnam. The visits of two American cabinet members and the president's adviser on science resulted in unprecedented Sino-American agreements on the transfer of U.S. technology and knowhow to China, while in November the United States indicated that, contrary to past practice, the United States would not oppose the sale of military arms to China by West European powers. These American moves were warmly welcomed by Chinese leaders, who bluntly portrayed the establishment of closer U.S.-PRC cooperation as the best way to offset the spread of Soviet influence through alleged Soviet surrogates in Vietnam and elsewhere.[39] U.S. leaders did not disassociate themselves from this Chinese view.

Several weeks before the Vietnamese invasion of Cambodia began on December 25, 1978, the United States altered its heretofore noncommital position on the Vietnamese-Cambodian dispute and came down on the side of Cambodia, China's ally. Thus, for example, the State Department announced on December 3 that the United States supported the territorial integrity of Kampuchea and it admonished that Hanoi's actions in the Vietnamese-Cambodian dispute would affect the pace of U.S.-Vietnamese normalization of relations.[40]

The December 15 communique on the establishment of U.S.-PRC diplomatic relations duly reaffirmed both sides' opposition to international "hegemony," but Hua Kuo-feng publicly stated that the normalization would be useful against "regional" as well as global hegemonism[41] -- a statement which clearly associated the United States with China's stance against Vietnam and which was not countered by any public U.S. statement. Subsequently, as is well known, the United States served as a sounding board for Teng Hsiao-ping to express China's case against Vietnam and to advise the world that reports of Chinese military buildup along the Vietnamese border meant that China intended to attack Vietnam if the latter did not change its policies. The United States waited until well after Teng had returned to China from the United States and Japan before advising that it did not share the Chinese view regarding attack against Vietnam. Meanwhile, the United States allowed Cambodian Prince Sihanouk (an official representative of a country not recognized by the United States) to meet with Teng in Washington, after which Sihanouk confirmed news reports that China was supplying Pol Pot forces with military and other supplies via Thailand. Less than a week later, President Carter issued his strongest statement of support for Thailand against possible attack from Vietnam, warning that the United States remained "intensely interested and deeply committed" to the inviolability of Thailand's borders.[42]

U.S. policy appeared to undergo a change after China invaded Vietnamese border provinces and the Soviet Union issued strong warnings of possible countermeasures. The United States provided some political backing for a Chinese-supported proposition calling for a withdrawal of Vietnam from Cambodia along with a Chinese withdrawal from Vietnam, and it once indirectly warned the Soviet Union that "steps which would extend the conflict would have serious consequences" on world peace.[43] The United States also announced that it would not allow the Chinese invasion to upset forward movement in the Sino-American normalization of relations.

But the United States avoided reaffirming strategic support for China as Peking faced increased Soviet military pressure in the wakr of its attack on Vietnam. Thus, U.S. naval forces were not reported being used -- as they had been in mid-1978 -- to counter the Soviet naval presence in the South China Sea during the Vietnamese-Chinese confrontation. U.S. officials also avoided comment in support of China as it faced unprecedented Soviet military exercises along the Sino-Soviet frontier in March 1979.[44] Some prominent news reports even noted that U.S. officials were preparing to pull back further from involvement in Asia and to adopt a new "quarantine doctrine" which would isolate the United States from the intra-communist conflicts that there expected to dominate the East Asian mainland over the next several years.[45]

This kind of American behavior raised several questions regarding American policy in Asia and future Sino-American relations. For one thing, it could have been argued that the United States was unwise during 1978 in allowing its interest in better relations with China to influence so strongly U.S. policy in Indochina, resulting in what appeared to many as a decided American "tilt" against Vietnam and in favor of China. And, it could have been viewed as misguided for American leaders to have identified the United States so closely with the tough Chinese policy toward Vietnam -- especially since that policy proved quickly to be far from successful in securing Chinese interests in the region and was subject to less than uniform Chinese leadership support. Also, the apparent reduction in U.S. support for China in the wake of the Chinese incursion could have been seen as poorly timed inasmuch as it came at the very time when Peking was facing massive Soviet military pressure on the northern border and unprecedented Soviet naval and air activity along China's eastern and southern periphery.

The possible dangers of this kind of behavior for future Sino-American relations are not difficult to

imagine. In particular, as Chinese leaders withdrew
from Vietnam without a clear military victory, they may
have been inclined to look abroad for an explanation for
their lack of success. From one perspective, the United
States could be made to take the blame -- after all,
U.S. leaders first encouraged China's tough stance
against Vietnam and then appeared to pull back support
when the Soviet Union began to apply strong pressure on
China.

This type of U.S. behavior could also be interpreted
as American "weakness" vis-a-vis the Soviet Union -- a
development that might have a substantial impact on
China's future interest in closer relations with the
United States. In particular, many analysts have argued
that Peking's prime interest in closer relations with
the United States is the support that relations with the
United States provides China in the face of Soviet pressure. If American support is seen as "weak," then the
Chinese interest in better relations with the United
States could be adversely affected. Indeed, some analysts have claimed that U.S. actions during the China-
Vietnam crisis and other developments caused Peking to
become greatly disillusioned with U.S. willingness to
help China against Soviet "hegemony" in Asia and prompted
the Chinese to begin a new course of action designed to
ease Soviet pressure by seeking Chinese accommodation
with the U.S.S.R. in talks begun in fall 1979.[46]

Fortunately for the future development of Sino-
American relations, the Soviet invasion of Afghanistan
in December 1979 put at least a temporary stop to this
kind of deterioration and disillusionment between
Peking and Washington. Faced with what they now both
saw as a common and immediate threat from the U.S.S.R.,
China and the United States forged a markedly closer
strategic relationship in 1980 designed to foil Soviet
or Soviet-backed expansion, including efforts by Vietnam
to dominate Indochina and spread its influence elsewhere
in Southeast Asia.

Peking reacted strongly to the Soviet invasion,
stating that it posed a direct threat to Chinese security
and marked the most serious escalation of Soviet "expansionism" in over a decade. The Chinese reaction implied
that Peking wished to see the United States adopt a more
active approach to the Middle East, South Asia, and
Southeast Asia in order to counteract the Soviet
"threat"; and it signaled what some saw as an even keener
Chinese interest in pursuing closer strategic cooperation
with the United States than in the past -- an interest
that was reflected during Chinese discussions with
Defense Secretary Brown in Peking in January 1980. It
also demonstrated stronger Chinese suspicion of Soviet
motives in international affairs -- a development that
resulted in Chinese suspension on January 20, 1980, of

the Sino-Soviet talks which began on China's initiative in 1979.

The Soviet action and resulting furor in the United States undercut the arguments of those American policy-makers who had favored an evenhanded approach toward the Sino-Soviet powers. It also offset the arguments of those Americans who had been suspicious that China could not be trusted to maintain a reliable foreign posture in coordination with the United States against the U.S.S.R., thereby opening the way for greater U.S.-PRC cooperation against Soviet and Soviet-backed expansion, especially Vietnam.

A new American approach to the Sino-Soviet powers -- and the apparent demise of the former evenhanded strategy -- were apparent in Secretary Brown's weeklong visit to China in January 1980. Although the full details of the visit were not readily available, several of its accomplishments strongly indicated that the United States would side closely with China in common efforts to offset Soviet power in Asia, including Southeast Asia. According to various press accounts:

1. The United States agreed to sell a groundstation enabling China to receive data of possible military use from American satellites.
2. The United States told China of its willingness to sell the PRC an array of non-lethal military equipment, which could be expanded in the future.
3. The United States and China coordinated closely their parallel strategies in support of Pakistan and in backing other unspecified efforts -- perhaps including support for anti-Soviet Afghan forces -- to thwart Soviet expansion in Southwest Asia.
4. And, most importantly for Southeast Asia, the United States informed China that it would welcome Chinese military help against Vietnam in whatever form Peking might choose, if Vietnamese forces crossed from Cambodian territory into Thailand.[47]

NOTES

1. For background see, A. Doak Barnett, China and the Major Powers in East Asia (Washington: Brookings Institution, 1977). Robert Sutter, Chinese Foreign Policy After the Cultural Revolution (Boulder, Colo.: Westview Press, 1978). Robert Sutter, "China's Strategy in Asia Following the U.S. Defeat in Indochina," paper presented at the Seventh Sino-American Conference on Mainland China, Taipei, June 1978. For further information on Chinese foreign policy during this period, see, U.S. Government, Foreign Broadcast Information Service

(FBIS), <u>Trends in Communist Media</u> (a weekly publication analyzing the media content in China and other Communist countries. The publication is available on microfilm at the Library of Congress.)

2. For further discussion, see, Sutter, <u>Chinese Foreign Policy</u>, p. 42-60, 113-120.

3. For further discussion of this period see, Sutter, "China's Strategy in Asia."

4. See FBIS, <u>Trends</u>, June 22, 1977.

5. <u>Ibid.</u> September 8, 1977.

6. <u>Ibid.</u> November 23, 1977.

7. <u>Ibid.</u> July 20, 1977.

8. <u>Ibid.</u> October 5, 1977.

9. <u>Ibid.</u> January 25, 1978.

10. <u>Ibid.</u> January 11, 1978.

11. See in particular <u>A New Realism, Factfinding Mission to the PRC, July 3-13, 1978. Report by the Subcommittee on Asian and Pacific Affairs to the Committee on International Relations, U.S. House of Representatives</u> (Washington, U.S. Government Printing Office 1978).

12. Note for instance Huang Hua's trip to Zaire in June 1978 and the visit of a Chinese military delegation to Congo in late June.

13. See speeches of Huang Hua and Chen Chu before the U.N. disarmament session in late May and June.

14. See, for instance, <u>Far Eastern Economic Review</u>, November 24, 1978.

15. See, for example, <u>Far Eastern Economic Review</u>, March 2, 1979.

16. New China News Agency (NCNA), May 20, 1978.

17. For further analysis, see FBIS, <u>Trends</u>, June 1, 1978.

18. <u>Ibid.</u> June 14, 1978.

19. <u>Ibid.</u> June 28, 1978.

20. For further analysis, see <u>Ibid.</u> July 6, 1978.

21. <u>Ibid.</u> July 26, 1978.

22. See <u>Far Eastern Economic Review</u> analysis of this period.

23. See note 11.

24. NCNA, January 1, 1979 (emphasis added).

25. NCNA, December 23, 1978 (emphasis added).

26. <u>Kwangming Daily</u>, December 19, 1978.

27. <u>People's Daily</u>, December 30, 1978 (emphasis added).

28. NCNA, December 13, 1978.

29. NCNA, December 28, 1978 (emphasis added).

30. NCNA, January 8, 1979.

31. NCNA, January 13, 1979.

32. NCNA, January 13, 1979.

33. Personal, informal survey of several China specialists.

34. See FBIS, <u>Trends</u>, January 24, 1979.

35. NCNA, May 20, 1978.

36. *Christian Science Monitor*, June 15, 1978.
37. NCNA, July 25, 1978.
38. A *Washington Post* editorial supported this argument.
39. See note 11.
40. *Washington Post*, December 4, 1978.
41. NCNA, December 16, 1978.
42. New York Times, February 7, 1979.
43. Washington Post, February 18, 1979.
44. New York Times, February 21, 1979.
45. See article by Richard Burt in *New York Times*, March 15, 1979.
46. See, H. Lyman Miller, "From the Third Plenum to the April Adverse Current: The Domestic Politics of Sino-Soviet Detente." Paper presented at the Annual meeting of the New England Regional Conference of the Association for Asian Studies, October 20, 1979. See also, Daniel Tretiak, "China's Vietnam War and Its Consequences", *China Quarterly* No. 80, December 1979; and Banning Garrett, "A That in Sino-Siviet Relations?", *INTERNEWS*, June 18, 1979.
47. U.S. Library of Congress, Congressional Research Service, Issue Brief 76053 "China-U.S. Relations," (periodically updated).

6

The Strategic Triangle and the Indochina Crisis

Banning Garrett

The triangular relationship among China, the Soviet Union and the United States affected developments in the Indochina crisis in at least three ways; first, the triangle was a decisive factor in actions of the three powers in Indochina -- if the relationship had been configured differently in 1978-79, it is likely that the conflict would not have escalated to a Vietnamese invasion and occupation of Kampuchea and a Chinese invasion of Vietnam. Secondly, the Chinese action against Vietnam was in part aimed at manipulating the triangular relationship to China's advantage. Soviet and U.S. actions -- and non-actions -- in response to the Chinese invasion can be explained largely by reference to the triangle rather than to the specific realities of Indochina. Thirdly, the triangular relationship structured the aftermath of the crisis and will continue to have a major impact on decisionmaking of the three powers toward Indochina, especially with regard to possible future escalation of the Sino-Vietnamese conflict.

The triangular relationship among the three powers has been extraordinarily important for all three. In the most general sense, the leadership in each country has looked over its shoulder at the third country while making policy toward or interacting with the second on key issues of national strategy, military posture and diplomacy. The basic dynamic of this relationship has been each power trying to prevent collusion against it by the other two. Although each power always faces the possibility of collusion against it, different periods have been dominated by one of the powers feeling the most vulnerable. In the 1950's, the U.S. faced Sino-Soviet collusion (and failed to capitalize on Sino-Soviet differences that would soon erupt into an open, bitter split). In the 1960's, the Chinese feared U.S.-Soviet collusion against them including possible joint action against China's emerging nuclear capability. And in the

1970's, the Soviets feared Sino-American collusion
including possible military cooperation between Washington and Beijing.

The Chinese opening to the United States in the
early 1970's was aimed in large part at ending China's
untenable strategic isolation between two hostile superpowers, and at heading off collusion against China
between Washington and Moscow. The Soviets saw the
nascent Sino-American rapprochement as potential anti-
Soviet collusion and sought to prevent such an alignment
through improving relations with the U.S. while hedging
against the prospect of a two-front coordinated military
threat. Although some U.S. officials worried about a
Sino-Soviet rapprochement at U.S. expense, this collu-
sion/anti-collusion dynamic of the last decade, put the
U.S. in the best position in the triangle, with the other
two powers competing for improved relations with Washington. But that dynamic also led to an inherent instability. The Chinese viewed U.S. efforts to develop
detente with the Soviet Union as "appeasement" and
potential anti-China collusion. They also feared that
detente would allow the Soviets to strengthen their military presence in Central Asia and the Far East, thereby
increasing Soviet pressure on China. The Chinese sought
to use their American connection to strengthen their own
position vis-a-vis Moscow in several ways: by exacerbating U.S.-Soviet relations and thus diverting the
Soviets to other areas of military competition as well as
undermining detente; by developing a global united front
against the Soviet Union with the U.S. taking the lead;
and by encouraging the United States to build up its
military power and to wage a "tit for tat" global struggle against Soviet expansionism.

For the Soviets, U.S. ties with China portended unacceptable anti-Soviet collusion from the beginning of
the rapprochement -- including the possibility of military links between Washington and Beijing -- and a
potential encirclement of the Soviet Union by the U.S.,
Japan, China, and NATO. The Soviets warned that such a
combination would undermine detente and jeopardize
future arms control negotiations. They sought to convince Washington that U.S.-Soviet relations were more
important than Sino-American ties, that the Chinese were
dangerous and aggressive, and that the U.S. should deal
with the Chinese on a bilateral basis, not an anti-Soviet
basis.

The dynamic produced by these conflicting demands
on the United States led to instablility in the triangular
relationship because neither the Soviets nor the Chinese
were willing to accept a U.S. policy of evenhandednesss
toward Moscow and Beijing and instead each actively
sought to undermine U.S. policy toward the other power.

These efforts played into -- and upon -- deep policy disputes in Washington, which aggravated the tendency toward instability.

Although Carter took office in January, 1977, with U.S.-China relations far down the list of foreign policy priorities, the "China card" was soon pushed to the front of the presidential agenda.

The dynamics of the strategic triangle and their impact on policy disputes in Washington propelled the Carter administration toward closer military ties with China as U.S.-Soviet relations deteriorated. Washington's moves toward Beijing further exacerbated U.S.-Soviet tensions, thus contributing to the overall worsening of relations. The initial intention of the administration, however -- under the influence of then-Secretary of State Cyrus Vance and of President Jimmy Carter's own inclinations -- had been to put top priority on improving U.S.-Soviet relations, especially on finalizing a second strategic arms limitation (SALT II) agreement. At the same time, Sino-American ties were put low on the list of priorities as a bilateral matter between China and the United States. But National Security Adviser Zbigniew Brzezinski was pushing for a strategic relationship with China to counter the Soviets from the first days of the administration.

Carter's outspoken human rights policy toward the Soviet Union, including a personal letter to Soviet dissident Andre Sakharov, and a new SALT proposal calling for major reductions in weapons from the previously agreed-upon totals of the 1974 Vladivostok accord (which the Soviets were hoping to finalize quickly with the new administration), led to the bitter failure of a mission to Moscow by Secretary Vance in late March. Carter responded to the impasse with the Soviets by flirting for the first time with the notion of improving U.S. ties with China to pressure the Soviet Union on SALT and other issues. The Soviets indicated their concern over possible Sino-American collusion in the most important assessment of triangular relations in this period, contained in a May 14 Pravda article signed by I. Aleksandrov, a pseudonym representing the Party Central Committee. The Aleksandrov piece indicated the Soviet leadership had concluded that (1) the United States was seriously considering support for a Western effort to supply China with modern arms and military technology, (2) such arms transfers would threaten Soviet security, at least in the long run, and (3) there was a danger China might succeed in pulling the United States toward an anti-Soviet alliance. The Aleksandrov article warned that any Western military aid to China would be used not only against the Soviet Union but eventually against the West as well, and called on the West to join the Soviet Union in containing

Chinese ambitions. It also implied that the Soviets would not sit idly by if the West began arming China, [1] although it did not specify what action Moscow might take.

The struggle within the administration over whether to tilt toward China by selling military-related technology to the Chinese and other moves raged for several months. The Vance/State Department faction--which opposed what they viewed as a provocative, high-risk China card policy--won the first round of the battle in the spring of 1977, although returning the China card to the deck after considering whether to play it did not resolve the issue.

In a major Asia policy address in June, 1977[2] Vance indicated that U.S.-China relations would be dealt with primarily in a bilateral rather than triangular context, and that the United States had at least temporarily ended its flirtation with playing China against the Soviets. He promised that a constructive U.S. relationship with China "will threaten no one. It will serve only peace." At the same time, Vance assured the Chinese that the U.S. "will not enter into any agreements with others that are directed against the People's Republic of China." Vance not only disclaimed any U.S. intention of playing one country against the other, but also dealt with the problem of normalization of relations between Washington and Beijing as strictly bilateral. He emphasized the administration's commitment to move toward full normalization of relations with the Chinese based on "the view expressed in the Shanghai Communique that there is but one China." He also said, however, the progress toward normalization "may not be easy or immediately evident" and he called for "reciprocal efforts" on China's part to "normalize further our bilateral relationship."[3]

While the administration was signaling to Moscow that the United States would not play its China card at that time, it was also taking other steps to ease tensions with the Soviet Union. Carter backed off his tough SALT proposals and toned down his statements on human rights, which had rankled the Soviets. This policy trend culminated in a speech on U.S.-Soviet relations by Carter on July 21 at Charleston, South Carolina. Carter, who later characterized the speech as "a move toward better understanding," said he believed that "an atmosphere of peaceful cooperation is far more conducive to an increased respect for human rights than an atmosphere of belligerence or warlike confrontation."[4]

The trend toward cooling the rhetoric and signaling Washington's interest in improving ties with Moscow was initially reinforced by a National Security Council Presidential Review Memorandum (PRM 10), the main conclusions of which were leaked to the press during the summer. PRM 10, a major interagency review of the global balance of power and U.S. strategy, concluded that the growth in

Soviet military and economic power was slowing down and
that long-term trends favored the United States. PRM 10's
conclusions took a more relaxed view of the Soviet Union
than Ford administration studies, which had warned of a
continuing Soviet military buildup outstripping the
United States and a Soviet reach for nuclear superiority.[5]
The massive study concluded that the U.S.-Soviet military
balance was roughly equal at present, but contrasted the
strength and scope of the American economy and capacity
for technological innovation with forecasts of impending
Soviet capital and labor shortages. In addition, PRM 10
noted Moscow's problems with political succession, agricultural failures, and the continuing Sino-Soviet split
as factors compounding Soviet long-term weakness and
tilting the balance of power toward the United States.

The NSC study produced an initial sense of relief
among arms controllers and pro-detente experts and officials who were concerned that "alarmist" claims about
Soviet intentions were damaging prospects for a new SALT
agreement and the overall tenor of U.S.-Soviet relations.
PRM 10 seemed to suggest that the United States could
take a more relaxed view of the "Soviet threat" and
proceed with SALT and other efforts to increase Soviet-
American cooperation.

The PRM 10 strategic assessment, however, created
immediate problems for Sino-American relations, which
were apparent during and after Secretary Vance's trip to
Beijing in late August. Chinese leaders attached
great importance to the Vance visit, which was to be
their first direct contact with a Carter Cabinet-level
official and was scheduled to begin just after the close
of the Eleventh Party Congress.[6] However, the Chinese
quickly made it clear that they were disappointed with
the outcome of their talks with the secretary of state.
Vice-Premier Deng Xiao-ping charged that the United
States had regressed from the Ford administration's
position on normalization, setting back efforts to
establish full diplomatic ties between Washington and
Beijing.

U.S. officials worried that the failure to move
forward in relations with China resulting from Vance's
trip was more a function of fundamental differences in
strategic views than of the highly publicized impasse
over normalization. The conclusions of PRM 10 were a
direct challenge to China's view of the United States as
a declining superpower with the Soviet Union as the
superpower on the ascendancy. The Chinese view provided
the strategic and ideological rationale underlying
Beijing's efforts to establish an informal working alliance with the United States against the Soviet Union. To
the Chinese, PRM 10 also raised questions about the usefulness of America as an ally if Washington failed to see

the need to take a strong aggressive global stand against Moscow.

Chinese fears that the Carter administration would not take a hard line against the Soviets but would seek a more cooperative relationship with Moscow seemed justified by progress in the SALT negotiations reported after Gromyko met with Vance and Carter in Washington in September 1977. The President and Secretary of State indicated that they were optimistic and that the Soviets had made concessions in the talks.[8] Carter told the U.N. that the U.S. and the Soviet Union were within sight of a new SALT agreement, and on October 27 the President said that the general terms for a new SALT accord might be reached "within the next few weeks."

Carter's prediction was wrong. By the end of the year, hardliners inside and outside the government had combined to pressure the administration to take a new, tougher line in the SALT talks, which ultimately led the United States to withdraw compromise proposals made earlier, setting back the negotiations. Congressional and public reaction to deepening Soviet and Cuban involvement in Ethiopia's war with Somalia over the Ogaden Desert further complicated U.S. - Soviet relations, which in early 1978 were in another downhill slide.

In the winter of 1977-78, the Chinese were also pressuring Carter to take a tougher line toward Moscow, suggesting that the administration was following the path of "appeasement" of the Soviet Union. Members of Congress visiting China in January were told by Vice-Premier Deng that the global military strength of the United States vis-a-vis the Soviet Union and Washington's determination to stand by its commitments to its allies were of more immediate concern to China than normalization of relations with America.[9] The Chinese told their foreign visitors they had been very disappointed with the development of Sino-American ties under Carter, and they viewed Vance as "anti-Chinese."[10]

The Chinese also questioned U.S. credibility and usefulness as an ally in major press articles. The reliability of the American commitment to Western Europe, and by implication to China, was challenged by Peking Review: "Today, Western Europe comes under the U.S. 'protective umbrella,' but if the Soviet Union plunges Western Europe into a blitz-krieg, no one can be sure what the U.S. reaction will be... Shouldn't this make people think and take precautions.?" [11] If it is doubtful that the United States would come to the defense of Western Europe in a crisis, the article implied, Washington is even less likely to risk war with the Soviet Union by aiding China in the event of a Sino-Soviet conflict.[12] People's Daily went further, charging that "advocates of appeasement" in the West--apparently including at least some members of the Carter administration if not the President--"hope they can divert the Soviet Union to the East so as to free themselves from this Soviet peril at the expense of the security of other nations."[13]

In these attacks on the Carter administration's policy the Chinese accused the United States of

1. Underestimating "the scope and magnitude of Soviet expansion"--a clear reference to PRM 10's assessment of the global balance of power.[14]

2. Trying "to use disarmament as a means to check the speed of Soviet arms expansion and war preparations," although "neither the talks on the reduction of forces in Central Europe nor the SALT talks can stop the Soviet Union from building up its military strength."

3. Hoping to use "technical expertise, loans, and sales of grain" to "curb the Soviet Union," by making it dependent on the West. But "in so doing, (the Americans) greatly speed up the process in which the Soviet Union is catching up with and surpassing the U.S. and Western Europe in arms and equipment."

People's Daily also hinted that Chinese leaders had hopes American policy would change[15] -- hopes that brightened in early 1978 as U.S. - Soviet relations again deteriorated. In response to growing domestic pressure for action to check Soviet involvement in Ethiopia, Brzezinski began hinting that SALT and other bilateral U.S.- Soviet issues might be linked to Soviet behavior in Africa. The issue of linkage produced a major battle within the administration, with Vance publicly rejecting the idea of tying SALT to Soviet activity in Africa. Although President Carter decided to harden U.S. policy toward the Soviet Union, he decided to exempt the SALT talks from linkage -- a move that made the "China Card" an attractive alternative option for pressuring the Soviets. While Vance won his way in Carter's decision to continue the SALT dialogue, Brzezinski took control of China policy, as Carter gave the go-ahead for moving toward strategic ties with Beijing.

BREAKTHROUGH TOWARD U.S. - CHINA NORMALIZATION: THE STRATEGIC CONTEXT

Carter decided to send Brzezinski to Beijing in late May. On the eve of his departure, the NSC leaked to the press the White House's intention to allow sales to China of quasi-military U.S. advanced technology. It was also revealed that the U.S. would not interfere with Western European arms sales to China. The White House officially denied that Brzezinski's trip was intended to send any signals to Moscow, but administration officials said privately that the visit's primary purposes were: to reassure the Chinese about U.S. defense policies vis-a-vis

the Soviet Union, reaffirm Washington's desire to pursue
parallel interests with China globally, keep the Soviet
Union "off balance" by holding out the possibility of
increasingly close Sino-American cooperation if U.S.
relations with Moscow deteriorated further, reassure the
Chinese about American concern for their security vis-a-
vis the Soviets, and reaffirm U.S. interest in normalizing
relations with China.[16]

Many of these issues were addressed publicly by
Brzezinski during his Beijing stay. In his opening toast
he told his Chinese hosts: "We approach our relations
with three fundamental beliefs: that friendship between
the United States and the People's Republic of China is
vital and beneficial to world peace; that a secure and
strong China is in America's interest; that a powerful,
confident and globally engaged United States is in
China's interest." Brzezinski said that "the United
States does not view its relationship with China as a
tactical expedient, "but rather as "derived from a
long-term strategic view" as "reflected in the
Shanghai Communique." He said the United States recognizes and shares "China's resolve to resist the efforts
of any nation which seeks to establish global or regional
hegemony." Brzezinski's reference to resistance to
"regional" hegemony indicated U.S. support for Chinese
action against Vietnam, viewed by China as a Soviet
surrogate. Brzezinski also mentioned Africa, Europe, the
Middle East, and Asia as areas where "we can enhance
the cause of peace through consultations and, where
appropriate, through parall pursuit of our similar
objectives."[17]

Brzezinski's visit provided the breakthrough that
set the two countries on the path to normalization of
relations seven months later. But the context of that
rapid movement toward a final compromise on a formula
for establishing full diplomatic ties was clearly the
mutual U.S. - China interest in countering the Soviet
Union on a global scale, the primary theme of Brzezinski's
discussions with Chinese leaders. The anti-Soviet
tenor of his mission was underscored by the not uninten-
tionally over-heard anti-Soviet jokes he made to his
Chinese hosts as they climbed the Great Wall together, to
the effect that whoever got to the top last would have
to fight the Russians in Ethiopia.[18] Brzezinski also
stressed that President Carter "is determined to join
you in overcoming the remaining obstacles in the way to
full normalization of our relations within the framework
of the Shanghai Communique. The United States," Brzezinski
added, "has made up its mind on this issue."[19] And
Brzezinski aides said that "the basic significance of the
trip was to underline the long-term strategic nature of
the United States relationship to China," and to serve
the broader strategic aim of countering the Soviet Union.[20]

Brzezinski also departed significantly from Vance's
formulation the previous June that the U.S. relationship
with China "will threaten no one." In both his opening
and departing toasts, Brzezinski said that "only
those aspiring to dominate others have any reason to
fear the further development of American Chinese relations." As both Brzezinski and Chinese leaders clearly
believed the Soviets' desire to "dominate others,"
the statement was an obvious warning to Moscow and suggested an anti-Soviet tilt in U.S. policy in contrast with
Vance's earlier "evenhanded" approach.

Brzezinski and his NSC staff added to Soviet concern
about his visit by leaking to the press that the sale to
China of U.S. dual-purpose, military-related technology
and Western arms had been discussed in Beijing, and that
Chinese leaders had been given detailed briefings on the
SALT negotiations and on PRM 10. (Brzezinski's view of
the policy implications of PRM 10, which contrasted
sharply with Vance's, was that Soviet weaknesses and
long-term U.S. advantages should be exploited to extract
greater concessions from the Soviet Union and to
contain its influence, even at the expense of possible
deterioration in U.S. - Soviet relations -- a view that
was far more amenable to the Chinese and suggested
greater American willingness to pursue a potentially
provocative informal alliance with Beijing against
Moscow.) An NSC official in Brzezinski's delegation also
discussed expanding technological exchanges and U.S.
help in achieving China's goal of becoming a modern
industrial state by the end of the century.[21] Chinese
officials, who had expressed dissatisfaction with Vance's
Beijing visit, termed the talks with Brzezinski
"beneficial," and were clearly pleased.[22]

The intended message to Moscow resulting from
Brzezinski's Beijing consultations was clear: the United
States had begun to "play the China card," and the Chinese
had succeeded in drawing the U.S. closer into an informal
global anti-Soviet alignment. How far the relationship
would go was uncertain, especially considering the unpre-
dictable politics of the Carter administration and the
rollercoaster relationship between Washington and Moscow.
But Brzezinski's trip signaled a new era in Sino-American
cooperation, at a time of near cold war tension in U.S. -
Soviet relations.

For Vietnam, there was also a clear message: the
U.S. was now backing China in its dispute with Hanoi
as part of common Sino-American opposition to "global and
regional hegemony." One member of Brzezinski's
delegation, according to an informed source, went so far
as to offer a toast to China's victory over the Vietnamese. The two sides apparently discussed Indochina in
some detail. Reuters reported from Beijing May 22 that
Chinese officials "had been harshly critical of Vietnam."

Reuters added that "informed sources" -- apparently in the
U.S. delegation --" said the Chinese side had abandoned
any pretense of neutrality in the Cambodia-Vietnam dispute
and had lumped Vietnam by implication with Cuba as a tool
of the Soviet Union."

An indication that the Chinese believed they had
received U.S. backing for escalation of the conflict with
Vietnam, is the fact that China chose May 24, the day
after Brzezinski left Beijing, to publicly denounce the
Vietnamese for the first time for "ostracizing, persecuting and expelling" ethnic Chinese. Only two days
later, the Chinese announced they were sending ships to
repatriate Chinese from Vietnam, which was viewed as a
provocative act by the Vietnamese, and the open Sino-
Vietnamese split was underway as Gareth Porter details
(see chapter III). By June, there were reports of border
clashes and Vietnamese preparations for war.

While the Chinese began their public campaign
against the "regional hegemonists," Brzezinski returned
to Washington to step up his attacks on the "global hegemonists." A few hours after a tense White House meeting
May 27 between Carter and Gromyko, attended by Brzezinski
and Vance, the President's national security adviser
publicly charged the Soviets with violating "the code of
detente" and called for "an international response" to
Soviet and Cuban military activity in Africa. Carter had
charged in his talks with Gromyko that the Soviets bore
responsibility for the invasion in early May of Zaire's
Shaba Province by Katangese rebels -- a charge Gromyko
denied to reporters on the White House steps. Brzezinski
also stressed in an interview on NBC's "Meet the Press"
that the United States and China have "parallel interests"
and said he was "troubled" by the buildup of conventional
forces by the Soviet Union, including efforts "to strength-
en the concentration of its forces on the frontiers of
China."23

President Carter also stepped up his attacks on Moscow at a NATO summit meeting in Washington on May 30,
charging that the Soviet's military buildup in Eastern
Europe "far exceeds their legitimate security needs" and
calling for major increases in NATO defense spending. A
week later, at Annapolis, the President challenged the
Soviets to "choose either confrontation or cooperation,"
saying that "the United States is adequately prepared to
meet either choice." Soviet President Brezhnev warned of
a possible return to a "lukewarm war" if not a cold war,
and the Soviet press labeled Brzezinski a "foe of detente,"
warning that his "basically aggressive 'tough line'" --
which it viewed as expressed in Carter's Annapolis speech
-- is "not only fraught with the danger of a throwback to
the Cold War," but also "harbors the dangers of a confrontation."

The Soviets made it clear that they were upset over

Carter's China policy as well. On June 25, Brezhnev made
his strongest attack to date on U.S. policy toward China,
charging that "recently attempts have been made in the U.S.
at a high level, and in quite cynical form, to play the
China card against the USSR" -- a charge Carter denied
two days later, although his denial was part of the game,
assuming he sought to avoid unnecessarily antagonizing the
Soviets or admitting that the United States was using the
Chinese. Brezhnev called U.S. policy "short-sighted and
dangerous," and warned that "its authors may bitterly
regret it." A week earlier Pravda had stated more explicitly that U.S. "alignment with China on an anti-Soviet
basis would rule out the possibility of cooperation with
the Soviet Union in the matter of reducing the danger of
a nuclear war and, of course, of limiting armaments." Over
the following few weeks, Pravda, Izvestia, and the Defense
Ministry's Red Star declared that American collusion with
China would backfire against the United States and that
Western military aid to Beijing would ultimately be used
against the West; that playing the China card would lead
to a harsh Soviet reaction; and that the Chinese aim was
to provoke a war between the United States and the Soviet
Union.

In the summer of 1978, Soviet officials privately
told Western journalists that they were increasingly concerned that the Carter administration had decided to
shelve detente in favor of forging closer ties with China.
They said that Washington -- in search of a short-term
advantage -- seemed to have abandoned pledges of increased
trade and transfer of technology promised in the early
1970s by Kissinger to entice the Soviet Union into detente.
Soviet experts also suggested that Moscow would have to
make foreign and domestic policy adjustments in response
to the situation, which portended a shift in the balance
of power and alignment of forces against the Soviet Union.[24]

These concerns were indicated publicly in a highly
unusual Politburo statement August 25 that cautioned the
West against supplying arms to China, and clearly suggested that such a move would undermine efforts to reach a new
SALT agreement and to negotiate the reduction of forces
in Central Europe at the Vienna talks. The statement was
also a response to the unprecedented trip which Chinese
Communist Party Chairman Hua Guo-feng was then making to
Romania, Yugoslavia and Iran. The Politburo accused China
of being a "serious threat" to peace, working for "an
uncontrollable arms race," and "advertising their hostility
toward the Soviet Union" in order "to gain access to NATO
military arsenals."[25]

Soviet concern over the course of U.S.-Chinese relations increased during the fall of 1978 as Washington and
Beijing edged closer to normalization. In an unprecedented interview with the London Observer November 12, Brezhnev adviser Arbatov warned that if China were to become

"some sort of military ally to the West, even an informal ally," then "the whole situation would look different to us. We would have to re-analyze our relationship with the West. If such an axis is built on an anti-Soviet base then there is no place for detente, even in a narrow sense (presumably including SALT)." The pursuit by the U.S. of rather short-term benefits of gaining leverage over the Soviet Union, Arbatov said, "could lay the cornerstone of an absolutely new set of international relationships that would make nobody very happy." Asked at what point the Soviets would decide that a Chinese alliance with the West had become operative, Arbatov would say only "it is very difficult to draw the line." Soviet analysts also indicated concern over the possibility of a "NATO for Asia" consisting of China, Japan, and the U.S., directed against the Soviet Union.[26] The Soviets responded to this situation, however, by seeking to head off further U.S.-China collusion against them by trying to improve relations with the United States.[27]

During this same period, the Vietnamese were finalizing their Peace and Friendship Treaty with the Soviet Union, while the U.S. had put normalization of relations with Hanoi on the backburner (see Porter). On November 3, 1978, the Soviet-Vietnamese treaty, with its mutual security clause, was announced in Moscow. And Secretary of State Vance held a press conference in Washington where he revealed that the U.S. had decided not to oppose Western European arms sales to China.

The process set in motion by China and the United States in May of 1978 culminated in the announcement on December 15, 1978, that the two countries would normalize diplomatic relations on January 1, 1979, and that Chinese Vice Premier Deng Xiao-ping would visit Washington. The joint communique announcing establishment of diplomatic ties included an "anti-hegemony" clause which both the Chinese and the Soviets viewed as directed at Moscow. Officially, the White House maintained the position that normalization of relations with China was not aimed at the Soviet Union and should not interfere with improvement of relations with Moscow, including finalization of SALT II. Privately, however, some administration officials, especially at the NSC, believed that "playing the China card" -- including normalization and the recent decisions to sell military-related technology to China and to allow Western European arms sales to Beijing -- had put pressure on the Soviets to complete the SALT II treaty.[28]

The announcement that China and the United States would soon normalize relations was made less than a week before Vance and Gromyko were scheduled to meet in Geneva for what was billed by the American side as the final round of SALT talks before a Carter Brezhnev summit to be held in Washington in mid-January. Carter said December 19, two days before the meeting, "I can say without any doubt that our new relationship with China will not put any additional obstacles in the way of a successful SALT agreement and also will not endanger our good relationship with the Soviet Union.[29] The Soviet news agency Tass, however, replied, "the Soviet Union will follow most closely what the development of American-Chinese relations will be in practice and from this will draw appropriate conclusions for Soviet policy."[30]

The two sides failed to reach agreement at the December 21-23 Geneva meeting, however--a failure attributed by some administration officials, notably at the State Department, as in large part the result of Soviet concern over U.S.-China policy.[31] State Department officials said in interviews that although there were details of the agreement that had been more difficult to resolve than either side had expected, the Soviets appeared to want to put off finalization of the accord--and a Carter-Brezhnev summit--until after Deng's visit to Washington to assess how the United States dealt with the Chinese leader.[32] President Carter acknowledged January 18 that Soviet concern about Sino-American ties may have interfered with the completion of the SALT II treaty.[33] Soviet sources privately confirmed Moscow's wait-and-see posture, but also claimed that the U.S. was responsible for the impasse in Geneva because it had hardened its negotiating position.[34] Pravda made a similar charge January 6 in response to reports from the U.S. side that the Soviets had raised new issues in the December talks.[35] The Soviets publicly denied that U.S.-Chinese ties were the cause of the delay in the arms negotiations, apparently because they did not want to acknowledge a linkage between SALT and China.[36]

The Soviets received mixed signals from a summit of four Western leaders held in Guadeloupe January 5-6, three weeks before Deng's visit to Washington. President Carter, British Prime Minister James Callaghan, West German Chancellor Helmut Schmidt, and French President Valery Giscard d'Estaing strongly endorsed a new SALT agreement and reassured the Soviets concerning U.S. normalization of relations with China. He told reporters that "we are determined to insure" that relations with China "never become an obstacle to detente."[37] But Callaghan also took the opportunity to announce that Britain would go ahead with plans to sell 50 to 80 Harrier vertical-takeoff jet fighters to China as part of a $2 billion trade package.[38] British sources at the summit insisted that the planes were "defensive" in the context of the Sino-Soviet conflict. But Schmidt, representing a party and government opposed to West German arms sales to China reportedly said the Harrier sale would "come close to the alarm line,"[39] and cautioned the other three leaders at the summit against going too far in arms sales to China for fear of undermining East-West detente.[40]Schmidt reportedly

said that it would do no good to "poke a stick into the
cage of the bear."[41] According to a West German account,
the four leaders agreed that detente should not be en-
dangered by overplaying the China card.[42] Carter reportedly informed Brezhnev a few days after the summit that
the United States has no plans to sell arms to China but
would not interfere with Western European efforts to do
so, and he said publicly January 27 that "we certainly
have no intention to sell weapons to the Soviet Union
or China."[43]

DENG TAUNTS THE POLAR BEAR FROM WASHINGTON, THEN INVADES
VIETNAM

Depite President Carter's reassurances to the Soviets
of the U.S. commitment to SALT and to limits on Sino-
American military ties, Deng's dramatic visit to the
United States January 29 to February 5, 1979, left the
Soviets anxious about U.S. intentions. On the eve of
Deng's visit, Carter said the United States would try to
avoid having "an unbalanced relationship between China
and the Soviet Union."[44] And Vance had said two weeks
earlier, "Our policy toward them will be balanced and
there will be no tilts one way or the other, and this is
an absolutely fundamental principle."[45] State Department
officials were stressing that the administration intended
to avoid the appearance during Deng's visit of siding with
the Chinese against the Soviets.[46]

But the administration conspicuously failed during
Deng's visit to reject outright a call by the Chinese
leader for an anti-Soviet alliance embracing China, the
United States, Japan, and Western Europe. "If we really
want to be able to place curbs on the polar bear, "Deng
told Time in an interview published the day he was
welcomed to the White House, "the only realistic thing
for us is to unite."[47] As the final compromises for
normalization were being made in early December, Deng had
told columnist Robert Novak explicitly that Beijing and
Washington should ally against Moscow: "Only when there
is an alliance between the United States and China, then
peace and stability in the world are assured."[48] At the
White House, January 29, Deng said that because the United
States and China view their bilateral relations in a
"long-term strategic perspective," the two sides "easily
reached agreement on normalization."[49] Deng had also
stressed to Novak that he viewed an alliance with the
United States as far more useful for bringing stability
to the world than any number of SALT agreements between
the U.S. and the Soviet Union. Deng repeated this point
in his interview with Time, saying that he agreed with
a recent open letter in the New York Times signed by 178
retired U.S. generals and admirals which charged that the
Soviets were seeking military superiority, not parity.

Arguing that the United States was in"strategic retreat,"
Deng said that in "seeking world peace and world stability, such agreements (as SALT II) are neither as significant nor as useful as the normalization of relations
between China and the U.S. and the peace and cooperation
treaty signed between China and Japan."

During his stay in the United States, Deng backed
off from the word "alliance" in describing his call for
"common efforts" against the Soviet Union, but he pressed
his case for an informal grouping of China, the U.S.,
Japan, and Western Europe to encircle and contain the
Soviets.[50] He also toned down his remarks on SALT, saying
that "there is maybe a need" to reach a SALT II accord,
although it would not restrain the Soviets,[51] but he continued his attacks on "Soviet hegemonism" and the Soviet
"polar bear" throughout his visit.

The administration's reaction to Deng's visit was
ambiguous--perhaps reflecting the White House's desire to
move as close as possible to China without decisively
antagonizing the Soviets, as well as reflecting differences among officials. The policy struggle within the
administration was evident in the events surrounding the
"Joint Press Communique" issued at the end of Deng's visit
to Washington. At the beginning of Deng's stay, Vance
had announced that no formal communique would be issued.
The State Department hoped, by eliminating the occasion
for a joint condemnation of "hegemony" from the U.S.
capital, to avoid unnecessarily irritating the Soviets.
But President Carter evidently changed his mind, and a
compromise "Joint Press Communique" was issued February 1.
The communique, drafted under Brzezinski's auspices by
China experts without consulting Vance's Soviet expert,
reportedly left officials at the State Department "angry
and dispirited."[52]

In the communique, the two sides reaffirmed that "they
are opposed to efforts by any country or group of countries to establish hegemony or domination over others."
White House officials explained that the addition of the
phrase "or domination" indicated that the anti-hegemony
clause was not directed at the Soviet Union alone, but
was broadened to include Vietnam's domination over
Cambodia as well.[53] The communique also failed to include
the balancing disclaimer of the two previous Sino-American
joint statements--the 1972 Shanghai Communique and the
1978 normalization announcement--which noted that neither
side is prepared "to enter into agreements or understand-
ings with the other directed at other states."

Carter did, however, manage to distance himself somewhat from Deng. While the two sides "agreed that in many
areas they have common interests and share similar points
of view," the Communique said that they "also discussed
those areas in which they have different perspectives."
The day before, during a ceremony for the signing of

scientific and cultural exchange agreements, Carter said that the U.S. and China "have agreed to consult regularly on matters of common global interest (presumably the Soviet Union)." But at the same time he said: "the security concerns of the United States do not coincide completely, of course, with those of China. Nor does China share our responsibilities" -- suggesting that SALT was an area of differing "perspectives," "security concerns," and "responsibilities."[54]

Carter did not explicitly reject the Chinese proposal for an informal alliance against Moscow, however. This led the Soviet news agency Tass February 1 to call for a "clarification" of the administration's attitude toward the "incendiary statements by the Chinese guest of the White House, to the slandering of the policy of relaxation of tension, to the condemnation of efforts to restrict the arms race, to calls to create a 'united front against the Soviet Union'." Brezhnev adviser Georgi Arbatov said in a CBS television interview during Deng's visit that the Chinese leader was attempting to "hammer into the minds of Americans an illusion that ... an improvement of relations and a military-political alliance with China can be a sound alternative to detente, to arms control, to development of cooperation in the world ... This illusion, I think, "Arbatov warned, "is dangerous even in the era of conventional warfare." He added, however, that he thought the United States was "rather far" from an alliance with China, and that he had hopes for the "common sense and political wisdom of Western countries and the American people."[55] Brezhnev had said in an interview with _Time_ published two weeks before Deng's visit: "There are some in the U.S. and other Western countries who have found the course hostile toward the Soviet Union followed by the present Chinese leadership so much to their liking that they are tempted to turn Beijing into an instrument of pressure on the world of socialism. Such a policy appears to me to be adventurous and highly dangerous for the cause of universal peace."[56] _Izvestia_ commented February 7, after Deng left the U.S., that the struggle within the Carter administration over policies toward the Soviet Union and China was likely to continue. "The present administration is apt to vascillate. Going on within it is a confrontation between belligerent and more moderate tendencies."[57]

The Soviet's worst fears about Sino-American collusion appeared to be justified when Chinese troops launched a massive invasion of Vietnam, less than two weeks after Deng left the United States. Deng had warned during his stay in Washington that China might have to teach "some necessary lessons" to the Vietnamese, who he called the "Cubans of the Orient."[58]

The Chinese action was the first major test of the triangular relationship following the normalization of ties between the U.S. and China. It posed a major challenge to the Soviets by threatening their ally, Vietnam, and taunting them to retaliate against China itself. For the Soviet Union, it was also an important test of Sino-American and U.S. - Soviet relations that China had provoked. Brezhnev had said following the announcement of Sino-American normalization in December that the Soviet Union would wait and see whether the U.S. relationship with China was developing on an anti-Soviet basis. Now, the initial U.S. policy statement on the invasion seemed to give backhanded support for China's action. The State Department called for "the immediate withdrawal of Vietnamese troops from Cambodia and Chinese troops from Vietnam," a formulation which implied that the U.S. would not object to the Chinese staying in Vietnam as long as the Vietnamese were in Cambodia.[59] The U.S. also warned the Soviets not to attack China, seeming to give further cover to the Chinese action.[60]

The Soviets reacted by charging U.S. complicity with China. Tass said February 20 that "the war against socialist Vietnam was practically prepared by Peking with the tacit consent of Washington." The next day the Soviet Literary Gazette charged that "this is what the adventurist games of some Washington politicians with the Chinese militarists lead to." And Pravda said February 28 that the U.S. had given Deng the green light for the invasion by not objecting.[61]

Besides charging U.S. "collusion" or at least tacit approval of the Chinese invasion, the Soviets warned China of possible unspecified Soviet retaliation. A government statement on February 18 warned China to withdraw "before it is too late," a position given added emphasis by Soviet Foreign Minister Gromyko ten days later. Gromyko said: "The Soviet Union decisively demands that the Peking leadership stop its aggression against the Socialist Republic of Vietnam before it is too late--I repeat, before it is too late."[62]

While the Soviets took the line that "Vietnam will not be abandoned in its time of trials,"[63] they also stressed that "the heroic Vietnamese people, who have become the victims of a fresh aggression, are capable of standing up for themselves this time again."[64] This put the Soviets in the position of standing by their ally and appearing ready to intervene if the Chinese went for the jugular by attacking Hanoi, while at the same time showing restraint in the face of Chinese provocation. The Chinese, of course, could term the Soviets a "paper polar bear," while Moscow could say that China heeded its warnings and pulled back before "going too far."

The Soviets also used the Chinese invasion to argue that it is China (and not the Soviet Union) that poses

the greatest threat to world peace. The February 18
government statement claimed "China's attack against
Vietnam is added proof of Peking's grossly irresponsible
attitude to the destinies of peace, and of the criminal
ease with which the Chinese leadership turns to arms."
Brezhnev, in a major address March 2--near the end of the
conflict--condemned China as the "most serious threat to
peace in the whole world."

At the same time, the Soviet President took a conciliatory line toward the United States, and portrayed the
SALT II treaty as almost complete and ready for signing
at a summit between himself and President Carter. In
addition, Brezhnev was conciliatory toward Western Europe
and made a new offer for a no-first-use pledge of
conventional force as well as nuclear weapons as part of
arms reduction efforts in Central Europe between NATO
and the Warsaw Pact, which, he said, would be given a new
impetus by SALT II.

Brezhnev's remarks indicated that an assessment
had been made in Moscow that the U.S. was not entirely
behind China's action, and that, consequently, it was
still possible to head off further Sino-American collusion by finalizing SALT II and taking other steps to
improve relations with Washington. The extent of U.S.
collusion with China in the attack on Vietnam apparently
had been a point of dispute in Moscow from the beginning,
with some analysts arguing in the Soviet press that such
collusion may have been more apparent than real as a
result of Deng's adroit maneuverings, and that President
Carter may have in fact tried to talk Deng out of the
action as claimed by the State Department.[65] _Pravda_
March 5 suggested that the Chinese invasion had led to
second thoughts in the U.S. about Washington's relationship with Beijing. "The Americans," _Pravda_ said, "are
beginning to understand that their new 'ally' is perhaps
dragging them to the brink of a dangerous precipice."[66]

For the Chinese, the invasion of Vietnam served as a
test of their new relationship with Washington. Some
U.S. officials speculated during Deng's visit to the U.S.
that China might use the normalization agreement and the
Vice Premier's visit as a sort of security guarantee
against Soviet retaliation for an attack on Vietnam. This
would be similar, the officials said, to the advance
insurance the Vietnamese took out before their December
25,1978, invasion of Cambodia in the form of a peace
and friendship treaty with the Soviet Union, signed
November 3.[67] China began to strengthen its forces on the
Sino-Vietnamese border within days of the December 15
announcement of normalization between Beijing and Washington. Normalization allowed the Chinese to redeploy
a large number of its troops away from Fujian province
opposite Taiwan to bolster their strength in the south
on the Sino-Vietnamese border and in the north and

northwest Sino-Soviet frontier regions.

China officially justified the February 17 invasion as retaliation against Vietnam for "wanton incursions into Chinese territory." The Chinese rationale allowed a retreat at any time the government decided to announce it had succeeded in teaching Vietnam a lesson, although China's actual goals in launching the attack on Vietnam went far beyond the border conflict. Deng reportedly said in Beijing two days after the invasion was launched that it was necessary to demonstrate that China "cannot be pushed around." Chinese officials indicated that the attack was in response to Vietnam's humiliating, swift takeover of Cambodia, which was seen as part of a Soviet-sponsored effort to demonstrate China's inability to defend its allies.[68] The attack also was aimed at forcing the Vietnamese to withdraw their estimated 100,000 or more troops from Cambodia, and at "exploding the myth" of Vietnamese "claims to be the third strongest military power in the world."[69]

The Chinese apparently hoped the action against Vietnam would further exacerbate U.S. - Soviet relations[70] and push the U.S. closer toward an alliance with China. The Chinese may have calculated that Soviet suspicions of Sino-American collusion over the invasion would increase Moscow's distrust of the U.S. and deepen its fear of a growing alliance between Beijing and Washington. A Soviet attack on China in response to the invasion-- a widespread fear among U.S. officials--could drag the U.S. into the war on China's side. At the very least, U.S. - Soviet relations would reach a crisis point, the SALT talks would be undermined in their final stage, and the U.S. would be pushed closer to an alliance with China.

The invasion also served to "test" the new Sino-American relationship to see if the U.S. would back up China. The Chinese also may have calculated that their move against Vietnam would enhance their reputation and usefulness as a potential ally to Western Europe, Japan, and the United States.[71]

For China, the outcome of the military action against Vietnam was at best a draw.[72] The Vietnamese did not prevent China from seizing several provincial capitals and creating widespread punitive destruction of tremendous cost, and they suffered heavy casualties. But Vietnam also inflicted heavy casualties on the Chinese-- who themselves put the figure of their losses at 20,000 while claiming 50,000 Vietnamese casualties--and put up a fierce and effective resistance with regional forces, committing only a small number of regular troops toward the end of the fighting. The Chinese forces looked bogged down in the fighting rather than overwhelmingly powerful in their punitive role, while the Vietnamese gained the political advantage of being the defenders of their homeland. The Chinese also failed to force

Vietnam to withdraw from Cambodia. Furthermore, China
agreed to negotiate with Vietnam without a prior pullout
of Vietnamese troops from Cambodia, although Vietnam
did drop its demand for a total withdrawal of Chinese
troops from what it insisted was Vietnamese territory
on the border still occupied by the Chinese.

The Chinese action against Vietnam generally provoked
nervousness and opposition in Western countries and Japan
rather than strong support and a push for closer military
or even closer political ties with Beijing.[73] Although
the Chinese demonstrated they could attack a Soviet ally
without retaliation from the "paper polar bear," the
Soviets generally won public praise in the West for
their restraint rather than ridicule for not attacking
China. West German Chancellor Helmut Schmidt termed
Soviet behavior "wise" and said he hoped the Chinese
invasion would not harm SALT or detente.[74] The invasion
also led to second thoughts by foreign investors about
Chinese internal stability and external behavior--doubts
compounded by China's simultaneous reexamination of its
ambitious modernization plans and temporary suspension
of some $2 billion in pending deals with Japanese firms.[75]
New doubts were also raised in the West about the wisdom
of selling arms to China.[76]

The United States knew several weeks prior to the
invasion that China was preparing to take military action
against Vietnam.[77] In January, the U.S. sent five messages to the Soviets and six to the Chinese expressing
concern over possible widening of the war, with an
expression of grave concern over the January 5-6 weekend
of the Guadeloupe summit, according to an excellent
inside account by Don Oberdorfer of the Washington Post.[78]
A senior Chinese official told a Senate delegation
visiting Beijing on January 8 that the Vietnamese
must be taught a lesson, that there would be war.
According to Oberdorfer, U.S. intelligence had also issued
an "alert memorandum" on January 5 predicting an imminent
Vietnamese takeover of Cambodia, which occurred two days
later, and suggested that the Chinese would react with
"a strong, localized demonstration of power" along the
Vietnamese border.

U.S. officials told Oberdorfer that they had feared
China would attack Vietnam during Deng's visit to the
United States, thereby suggesting U.S. connivance and
approval of the action. They said that on January 25,
shortly before Deng departed for the United States,
China's ambassador in Washington, Chai Ze-min, was
called to the State Department to receive a plea for
restraint, which he was pointedly told must reach Deng
before he departed from Beijing. Shortly after Deng
arrived at the White House, according to Oberdorfer's
sources, President Carter warned him that an attack
against Vietnam risked a wider war. Although Deng

reportedly insisted that the Vietnamese must be taught a
lesson, he agreed to take Carter's objections back to
the Chinese Politburo, thus indicating that no action
would be taken during his visit to the United States.
President Carter said nothing publicly about the danger
of war between China and Vietnam while Deng was in the
U.S., and continued to maintain that Deng's visit and
the normalization of relations between Beijing and
Washington would enhance peace and stability in the
Pacific.

Carter also proceeded with a scheduled trip to
Beijing by Treasury Secretary Michael Blumenthal after
China attached Vietnam February 17. Blumenthal's mis-
sion--which some State Department officials argued
should be postponed--was to improve trade relations,
including the negotiation of a settlement of frozen
assets claims by the two sides, and to participate in
the ceremony to open the U.S. embassy in Beijing March 1.
He was instructed to deliver a public message from
President Carter to Chinese leaders, however, which
included the statement that "even limited invasions risk
wider wars and turn public opinion against the transgres-
sor."[79] Although Blumenthal's remarks were considered
mild and he reportedly did not use any leverage to
pressure the Chinese to withdraw from Vietnam, he did
put public distance between the U.S. and China on the
Vietnam issue.[80]

Chinese leaders responded to Blumenthal's statements
by defending their action against Vietnam and reiterating
that it was to be limited in scope and duration. Reporters traveling with Blumenthal said that Deng seemed
to make light of the U.S. concern that the war could
expand into a wider conflict involving the Soviet Union.
"Both the Cuba of the Orient and the Cuba of the West,"
Deng said, "seem to be emboldened by the so-called
tremendous backing force behind them. Now some people in
the world are afraid of offending them. Even if they do
something terrible, these people wouldn't dare to take
action against them. It's a question of being afraid of
them. We cannot tolerate the Cubans to go swashbuckling unchecked in Africa, the Middle East and other areas.
Nor can we tolerate the Cubans of the Orient to go
swashbuckling unchecked in Laos, Cambodia or even
China's border areas.[81] Deng's words seemed to be a
criticism of the Carter administration, both for its past
failure to take what Beijing considered a strong enough
stand against the Soviets and Cubans, and for its failure
to give full backing to China's attack on the Cubans of
the Orient.

While Blumenthal's visit to China during the
height of the war may have given mixed and worrisome
signals to Moscow,[82] President Carter resorted to personal diplomacy to reassure the Soviets that the United

States was still commited to finalizing the SALT II agreement, and, by implication, to detente.[83] Negotiations for the SALT treaty continued during the Chinese invasion, and in the end the Soviets decided to accept U.S. reassurances, as indicated by Brezhnev's March 2 speech calling for finalization of SALT II and a summit meeting with President Carter. At the same time, however, the Soviets conducted large scale maneuvers on the Chinese border in mid-March, after China had withdrawn from Vietnam, apparently as a warning against future Chinese actions against the Vietnamese.[84]

One State Department official, interviewed in May 1979, acknowledged that the Soviets may have initially feared that the U.S. would be dragged into the Sino-Vietnamese conflict on China's side or had even "egged on" the Chinese. But, he argued, the Soviets could see that the Chinese action could not have come at a worse time for President Carter, who was trying to sell normalization with China to the public and Congress as a move to increase stability in Asia. Carter's problem, the official said, was getting congressional approval of the Taiwan bill, "not tweaking the bear." The Soviets, the official said, "could see the U.S. being taught a lesson on how little it could control China." The State Department official added that the long term impact of China's attack on Vietnam was to put a "more realistic tone" into Sino-American relations and to reduce the euphoria that had been building between the two countries.

In a seemingly contradictory development, Chinese leaders offered to open negotiations with the Soviet Union to improve relations less than a month after Chinese troops were pulled out of Vietnam. The Chinese initiative set off a series of moves and counter moves with triangular implications as the two sides probed each other's intentions and sought to influence Washington through the emerging Beijing-Moscow dialogue.

The Chinese informed the Soviet Union April 3 that they would not extend the thirty-year treaty of friendship, alliance and mutual assistance between them which expires in 1980. But at the same time, the Chinese proposed negotiations without preconditions "for the solution of outstanding issues and the improvement of relations between the two countries.[85] China's decision to drop preconditions for the talks was a major concession. For the previous decade, China had demanded that the Soviets first withdraw their troops from disputed border areas before negotiations to improve relations could even begin.

Moscow's initial response was to ignore the call for negotiations and to denounce the decision to terminate the treaty as "contrary to the will of the Chinese people."[86] The Soviets warned that Chinese leaders must

assume "all responsibility" for their action and that
Moscow would "draw proper conclusions." The Chinese
persisted however. In a People's Daily commentary, the
ending of the treaty was portrayed not as a hostile act
but rather as recognition of the outmoded nature of the
agreement.[87] The commentary noted that the Sino-Soviet
treaty, which was signed in 1950, was the product of a
different historical period and was "mainly directed
against Japan," with which both China and the Soviet
Union now have normal relations.

The Soviets finally responded positively to the
Chinese offer on April 17, asking for more concrete
terms for opening talks.[88] On May 5, China suggested that
the two sides seek to eliminate obstacles to the
development of trade, cultural and other exchanges and to
define relations between them--an apparent reference to
a formal document sought by both Beijing and Moscow to
replace the 30-year treaty.[89] On June 4, the Soviets
suggested that the two sides hold talks on normalization
of relations at the deputy foreign minister level in
Moscow in July or August. The Soviet note to the
Chinese also said that the two sides "should agree to
deny recognition of anyone's claims whatsoever to special
rights or hegemony in world affairs, and should build
relations with each other of the basis of peaceful
coexistence."[90] The surprising use of the Chinese codeword "hegemony" seemed to be a Soviet concession
aimed at avoiding a wrangle over using the word in any
future agreement reached on the conduct of Sino-Soviet
relations. During this period, both sides also toned
down somewhat their public attacks on each other.

Suspicion and hostility continued, however. Deng
said in May that China "will hold talks and negotiate"
with the Soviet Union, but, he added, there will be no
real improvement in relations "unless Russia gives
up its hegemonism and social imperialism," which he indicated he thought was unlikely.[91] Deng's attitude toward
negotiations with the Soviets was further elucidated
when he was asked for his reaction to the announcement
May 9 that the U.S. and the Soviet Union had finally
reached agreement on SALT II. "We don't think you
should put your trust blindly in any such agreement --
not only this agreement but all other agreements will
not serve to restrain the expansionism of the Soviet
Union," Deng said.[92] But, he added, "we are not against
this agreement, we're not against negotiations." Deng's
statements suggested that while Chinese leaders were not
opposed to negotiating with the Soviets (and they had
just opened talks with the Vietnamese the previous month),
they did not expect Sino-Soviet talks to be a substitute
for efforts to organize a global anti-Soviet front.
China's willingness to hold talks on the basis of the
Soviets' June 4 proposal was indicated by Hua Guo-feng

in his political report to the second session of the
National People's Congress June 18. Hua ridiculed the
Soviets' use of the word "hegemony," however, and said
that "the prospects for Sino-Soviet negotiations depend
on whether the Soviet Government makes a substantive
change in its position.[93]

The Soviets also indicated suspicion and skepticism
about the talks while holding open the door for negotiations. Brezhnev had said June 1 in a speech over
Hungarian television that the Soviet Union was ready to
"approach seriously and positively the organization of
Soviet-Chinese talks" if the "Chinese side manifests a
real goodwill."[94] But he also accused China of being
"a serious source of military danger," and charged that
"Chinese requests to the West for the most up-to-date
weapons are growing with every passing day." The
Soviets apparently hoped to gain triangular leverage over
China through the improved relations with the U.S.
seemingly signalled by the Carter-Brezhnev summit in
Vienna June 15-18 and the signing of the SALT II accord.
In a press conference a week later, Foreign Minister
Gromyko accused the Chinese of opposing the SALT II
agreement for "narrow considerations."[95] He said that
although "practically all the world is now applauding
the treaty," China "does not like it" because it prefers
tension and even "heated" relations between the Soviet
Union and the United States. Gromyko also tried to
raise Chinese fears of potential U.S. - Soviet collusion
against Beijing by revealing that Brezhnev and Carter
had talked about China during the summit. The Soviet
Foreign Minister claimed that Carter had agreed with
Brezhnev that "it was inadmissable for any power, in this
case the reference was to the United States, to use its
relations with China to the detriment of the Soviet
Union, to the detriment of its security interests."

The U.S.-Soviet summit and the signing of SALT II
after seven years of negotiations did not signal a new
upswing in relations between Washington and Moscow, however. The summit was low-keyed and confined almost
entirely to SALT II, and the cool atmosphere and limited
results likely eased Chinese concern that U.S. - Soviet
relations might improve significantly at their expense.
By early July, the Chinese still had not responded to the
Soviets' June 4 offer--despite Hua's statement in the
interim indicating the Chinese would agree to hold talks--
and Moscow apparently became impatient for a formal reply
to set a time and place for the talks and increasingly
suspicious about Chinese intentions. An article in
Pravda July 11 by I. Alexandrov--a pseudonym for the top
leadership--said that "certain Chinese leaders would be
quite satisfied if the very fact of Soviet-Chinese talks,
or talks about talks, would help them get political and

economic concessions and military aid from the United
States, Japan and their capitalist allies." But the
Alexandrov article also said "if the Chinese display
goodwill and realism, the Soviet Union will not keep them
waiting long," and that what is needed is a "serious and
positive Soviet-Chinese dialogue which would lead to
detente..."[96]

The next day, Chinese Vice Premier Geng Biao said
his country would soon formally accept the Soviet proposal for talks, and on July 16, it was reported that the
Chinese had offered to send envoys to Moscow in mid-
September for talks at the Deputy Foreign Minister level.[97]
Also on July 16, however, an armed clash took place on
the Sino-Soviet border between China's Xinjiang province
and Soviet Kazakhstan which was described as the most
serious in more than a year. One Chinese was killed and
another wounded in the incident, which was first disclosed by China July 24. The border clash may have been
instigated by opponents of the talks in either China
or the Soviet Union who hoped to derail the negotiations,
an effort by the Chinese to gain a tactical advantage
before the meeting in Moscow and to lay the basis for
raising the border issue in the talks--or simply an
accidental coincidence.[98]

Recriminations and mutual denunciations continued
between Moscow and Beijing right through the opening of
talks in late September, with both sides saying publicly
they expected little to result from the negotiations.[99]
Not until mid-October, after five preparatory meetings,
did the Soviet and Chinese negotiators agree to the first
full session. On October 25, the Soviets reportedly
offered a draft joint statement which would endorse the
principles of peaceful coexistence and be a general non-
ideological document to govern Sino-Soviet relations like
the one on "basic principles of relations" that the U.S.
and the Soviet Union signed in May 1972.[100]

It was reported that the Soviets had offered to withdraw some of their forces from Mongolia in exchange for
Chinese agreement to join a non-aggression pact.[101] And
it was also reported that the subject of ideology had
come up at the talks--which most observers had expected
to be confined to improving state-to-state relations--
and that the two sides had decided in theory that they can
agree that both are socialist states, and that neither
will attack the other's ideology any further or question
the legitimacy of the other's system.[102] Some analysts
suggested that this could lead to a breakthrough in the
talks, although not to a rapprochement or even a major
improvement in relations. The Sino-Soviet talks adjourned
November 30 without any publicly announced agreement,
however, except that the discussions would resume in
Beijing at an undetermined date.[103] They were indefinitely

postponed by the Chinese after the Soviet invasion of
Afghanistan.

As this Sino-Soviet drama unfolded in the spring and
early summer, U.S. officials and government China watchers
were divided on the significance of the developments for
triangular relations. White House China experts attached
little importance to the diplomatic maneuverings, arguing
that it is unlikely anything substantive would result
from the contacts and that the Chinese were not dissatis-
fied with the recent course of Sino-American relations
and therefore were not seeking to pressure Washington
through the threat of Sino-Soviet rapprochement. Other
officials and analysts argued that there were indications
that the flirtation was more serious than at any time in
the past decade and could result in a major improvement
in relations between the two powers. Some of these
analysts pointed to Chinese "disillusionment" with the
Carter administration's "appeasement" of Moscow, including finalization of SALT II, and suggested that the
momentum of improved relations between the Soviets and
the Chinese might go "too far," reducing U.S. leverage
over both China and the Soviet Union. Others suggested
that an improvement in Sino-Soviet relations is virtually
inevitable at some point--while any renewed alliance
against the West is extremely unlikely--and that it would
benefit the U.S. if there were a Sino-Soviet mini-detente
which would reduce the risks of a Soviet-Chinese war.[104]

Soviet China experts interviewed in Moscow in mid-
August were more optimistic about the upcoming talks than
official statements and press commentaries. They said
that it was an excellent time for holding the talks and
that the negotiations could resolve some problems and
ease tensions with China, which would be in both countries'
interest. At the same time, they stressed that they had
absolutely no hope for close relations again with China
in the foreseeable future. The Soviets also pointedly
claimed that the Soviet Union was not entering into
the talks with China to gain triangular leverage over
the United States. They said that Moscow objected to
the U.S. using the Chinese against the Soviet Union and
would not seek to reverse the situation, insisting that
only bilateral issues would be discussed in the Sino-
Soviet talks and no agreements directed against the U.S.
or its allies would be reached.

For the Soviets, the possibility of improved
relations with China provided them with a potential "China
card" for triangular leverage against the U.S., while
at the same time giving them renewed hope for heading off
a Sino-American alliance. Besides political and diplomatic benefits, an easing of tensions with Beijing could
allow the Soviets to cut back on defense expenditures or
to divert military resources to the western front.[105] The
Soviets also would benefit from increased trade with China

and could hope to increase their influence within the country through expanded cultural contacts and scientific exchanges. Moscow also indicated that it placed a high priority on reaching agreement on a new document to replace the thirty year treaty governing Sino-Soviet relations before it was to expire in 1980.

For the Chinese, the decision to open talks with the Soviets could have had the following aims:

1. To restrain Soviet support for Vietnam and to create suspicions in Hanoi about Soviet intentions.[106] The Chinese also may have sought to mitigate the chances of a two-front war by dividing their adversaries and keeping them off balance.[107]

2. To ease Soviet military pressure while gaining time to carry out the Four Modernizations, including military modernization. The poor showing by China's armed forces in Vietnam dramatized the country's potential weakness in a war with the Soviet Union. One result was a twenty percent increase in the Chinese defense budget announced at the National People's Congress in June and explained as necessary to pay for the war with Vietnam and to strengthen China's border defenses.[108] Nevertheless, Chinese officials told visiting Americans that military modernization would be kept at the bottom of the Four Modernizations, although they indicated that they were still interested in importing limited amounts of Western military technology.[109]

3. To increase, as a side benefit, trade with the Soviet Union. Trade between the two countries in 1978 totaled $516 million, a record high since relations deteriorated between the two countries in the 1960s and up thirty-six percent over 1977.[110]

4. To pressure the United States. This may have been a primary motivation of China's initiative toward the Soviet Union. Chinese leaders, throughout the spring and early summer of 1979, expressed their disappointment with the course of Sino-American relations since normalization and with U.S. policy toward the Soviet Union. Deng warned a group of U.S. Senators in mid-April that congressional legislation on Taiwan had come close to nullifying the normalization of relations agreement between China and the United States.[111] In talks with Henry Kissinger, Chinese officials reportedly complained about U.S. policy toward the Soviet Union, including the SALT negotiations which were about to be completed, and about what the Chinese viewed as Soviet global gains at U.S.

and Chinese expense.112

The Chinese also reportedly were disappointed with the failure of the U.S. to support their attack against Vietnam. Columnists Evans and Novak reported in May that there had been "backtracking" on Sino-American relations in both Washington and Beijing because of the U.S. failure to support the Chinese action in Vietnam.113 The columnists based their report on a confidential State Department study by several China experts arguing that Deng was in political trouble following the Sino-Vietnamese war and had been forced to retreat from many of his policy initiatives in liberalizing the political system and carrying out economic reforms. They also noted that in Washington, "official enthusiasm for the Chinese connection has diminished considerably more than is admitted." Soviet China experts interviewed by the author in August 1979 viewed the Carter administration as having backed away from a tilt toward China during the latter stages of its attack on Vietnam--which they viewed as the "tail wagging the dog"--and as resuming a push toward finalizing the SALT II agreement, much to China's disappointment. This more "evenhanded" U.S. approach, they said, left China "disillusioned" with the Carter administration and may have been a motivation behind China's interest in opening talks with the Soviet Union.

Senator Henry Jackson said in Beijing in late August, on the eve of a visit to China by Vice President Walter Mondale, that Chinese leaders were frustrated and unhappy at the slow pace of improvement in Sino-American ties in general and, in particular, by the administration's inaction on the trade agreement the two countries had signed July 7 that included granting most-favored-nation (MFN) status for Chinese imports.114 Jackson, for whom the Chinese showed unusual support by arranging meetings with both Deng and Hua, said that "there is a feeling of frustration (in Beijing) and this is a state of mind that the Vice President will face when he comes."115

Whether or not China's playing of its "Russia card" and its expressions of disappointment with the Carter administration's policies toward both Beijing and Moscow pressured Washington is not clear. But Sino-American relations were pushed forward significantly by the U.S.-- and once again this push was given an added boost by deterioration in U.S. relations with the Soviet Union.

The administration changed its policy on "evenhandedness" in dealing with China and the Soviet Union just before Mondale left for China. A new administration "tilt" toward Beijing on economic matters was indicated by Mondale's announcement in Beijing that the Sino-American trade agreement, reached July 7, would be submitted to Congress before November and that "its submission is not linked to any other issue"--that is, to equal treatment for the Soviet Union.116 U.S. officials traveling

with Mondale played down the Triangular implications
of this policy shift -- previously the administration had
said it would seek most-favored-nation (MFN) status,
included in the trade agreement, for both China and the
Soviet Union simultaneously as part of an "evenhanded"
policy -- denying to reporters that this represented
any tilting toward the Chinese and said that "evenhandedness" did not mean "a mechanical one-for-one
treatment."[117] The officials disclosed, however, that
the preceding week Vance had quietly signed papers
certifying China to be a "friendly country" and not part
of any international communist effort to dominate the
World,[118]a status unlikely to be obtained by the Soviet
Union. This cleared the way for Mondale to announce
that the Army Corps of Engineers would help China with
construction of huge hydroelectric power projects, and
to hint at possible U.S. involvement in other major
Chinese infrastructure projects such as ports and high-
tension power transmission lines.[119] Mondale also
announced that the U.S. would extend $2 billion in Export-
Import Bank credits for sales to China over the next five
years -- an amount, he said, that could be increased if
necessary -- and that U.S. corporate investment in
China would be encouraged by providing government
guarantees.

These administration measures to improve economic
ties with China and deepen U.S. involvement in China's
modernization efforts, contrasted sharply with stagnating
U.S.-Soviet trade and administration wariness about
encouraging U.S. involvement in the Soviet economy. Some
analysts also suggested that the limited supply of credit
and of high technology for export put the West in the
position of having to choose between the Soviet Union and
China, and that China was now likely to have the more
advantageous position as a result of normalization of
U.S. - Chinese relations and the commitment of the U.S.
government to China's modernization effort.[120]

Mondale made these economic announcements in the first
speech by an American leader broadcast throughout China
since Liberation in 1949.[121] The speech, delivered
August 27 to students and faculty of Peking University,
indicated a U.S. tilt toward China in its dispute with
the Soviet Union as well as on economic matters. Mondale
also implied an even wider although unspecific U.S.
security guarantee for China than that indicated by
Henry Kissinger in October 1976. The Vice President told
the Chinese that "any nation which seeks to weaken or
isolate you in world affairs assumes a stance counter to
American interests." U.S. officials refused to specify
what actions Washington would be willing to take to carry
out the implied commitment to China's security, although
they did deny that the U.S. was extending a military
umbrella over China.[122]Soviet diplomats interviewed after

Mondale's trip were quick to point to this statement as
implied backing for future Chinese military action against
Moscow's ally, Vietnam, which China says is a surrogate
for the Soviet Union in its efforts to weaken and isolate
the People's Republic. In any case, Mondale's statement
went beyond Kissinger's warning that the U.S. would
view a direct threat to China as a threat to U.S.
security interests.

Mondale also pointed to the "unprecedented and friendly relations among China, Japan and the United States,"
which, he said, "bring international stability to
Northeast Asia" -- a statement likely to be interpreted
in Moscow as suggesting closer Sino-Japanese-American
cooperation against the Soviet Union. Mondale's
statement was made only a few weeks after the director-
general of the Japanese Defense Agency, Ganri Yamashita,
had visited NATO headquarters in Brussels. He reportedly
told NATO military planners that the buildup of Soviet
forces globally was making it more vital for Japan to
share military information with the Western alliance[123]
raising the spectre in Moscow of the linkage of a U.S.-
China-Japan axis to cooperation with NATO. Mondale's
trip laid the basis for a virtual lurch forward toward
a quasi-alliance with Beijing as U.S. - Soviet relations
went through another major crisis, this time over U.S.
intelligence reports of a Soviet combat brigade in Cuba.
Even as Mondale went to China in late August, the
political atmosphere between Washington and Moscow was
soured by mini-confrontations over the delayed departure
from New York of a Soviet ballerina whose husband had
defected and over Soviet censorship of several American
books at the Moscow International Book Fair. The two
incidents occurred just as sentiment in the Senate seemed
to be swinging in favor of ratification of the SALT II
agreement. Even before those two incidents were defused,
the confrontation over an alledged Soviet "combat brigade"
in Cuba began, threatening to scuttle chances for Senate
approval of SALT and possibly lead to a direct conflict
with Moscow.

A major battle was set off within the administration
about what response should be taken against the Soviets
and Cubans. Vance and the State Department apparently
felt the first priority was to protect SALT II
and avoid further deterioration of relations with the
Soviet Union, while seeking to appease domestic critics
by taking actions primarily aimed at isolating and
containing the Cubans. Brzezinski and the NSC
apparently saw the crisis as an opportunity to press a
global counteroffensive against the Soviets and Cubans,
while also not linking SALT II to a Soviet pull-out from
Cuba.

There were numerous leaks to the press that the
administration was considering a "tough list" of options

drawn up by Brzezinski and his staff. Once again, the
"China card" popped to the top of the deck of presidential options, which included: a slowdown or even halt
in sales of advanced technology to the Soviet Union
while forging closer economic ties with China; stepped
up political pressure around the Soviet periphery, from
Eastern Europe to Afghanistan to China; aid to the
Chinese in their efforts to obtain advanced weapons,
including U.S. encouragement of Western European arm sales
to Beijing rather than indifference to such deals; sales
of U.S. military-related technology to China; and sales
of actual U.S. weapons and military technology to the
Chinese; intelligence sharing with China and providing
training and technical assistance for the Chinese
military. Also included in Brzezinski's list reportedly
were the options of formally breaking off the moribund
Indian Ocean talks with the Soviet Union and scuttling
the Vienna talks on force reductions in Central Europe,
and making highly visible demonstrations of U.S.
military power in Europe and in the Caribbean.[124]

Carter's public response to the troops issue, made
in a major speech October 1, drew primarily from the
State Department's recommendations and included
only the less threatening global options recommended
by the NSC. The President emphasized the importance of
avoiding a return to the Cold War and a confrontation,
possibly nuclear, with the Soviet Union, and made a strong
plea for Senate ratification of SALT II. At the same
time, he outlined a series of steps aimed largely at
Cuba, including intensified reconnaissance of the island,
added U.S. military presence in the Caribbean and
more economic aid to poor Caribbean nations to help
them "resist social turmoil and possible communist
domination." Carter also said the U.S. would increase
its naval presence in the Indian Ocean, step up efforts
to create a Rapid Deployment Force, and improve
intelligence capabilities for monitoring Soviet and
Cuban activity around the world.[125]

The President's relatively dovish public response
to the crisis generated over the issue, however, was
coupled with other unacknowledged moves taken from the
options menu served up by Brzezinski--options with far
more serious implications for U.S. - Soviet relations.
Within days of Carter's speech, there were indications
that the U.S. would tighten the screws on the flow
of high technology to the Soviet Union. Secretary
of Defense Brown reversed a decision that would have
allowed Control Data to sell the Soviet Union a Cyber 73-2
computer to upgrade a similar system sold in 1976
to the Soviet siesmic center in Naro-Fominsk near Moscow.[126]
More importantly, the administration made a number of
moves regarding U.S. - Chinese military ties. It
was leaked the day of Carter's speech that Secretary of

Defense Brown would make an unprecedented visit to
China in late 1979 or early 1980. Administration
officials continued to insist publicly that the U.S.
would not sell arms to China, but said that did not
rule out providing military training and technical
assistance.[127] It was also reported that the administration was considering "widening contacts in the security and intelligence fields to provide Peking with information vital to their own and to world security." [128]
In the same few days after Carter's speech, an important
Pentagon study was leaked to the New York Times which
recommended that the U.S. bolster China's
military potential so that Beijing could assist the
West in the case of a war with the Soviet Union.[129] The
study, which was prepared in April and entitled
"Consolidated Guidance No. 8: Asia During a Worldwide
Conventional War" (CG8), recommended possible steps
to provide military assistance to China, including
provision of advanced technology and intelligence data,
sale of advanced arms, Chinese production of American
weapons and joint military exercizes. The secret study
said that in view of China's "pivotal role" in the
global balance of power, it would be to the United States'
benefit "to encourage Chinese actions that would
heighten Soviet security concerns. Such encouragement
could include arms transfers or the employment of U.S.
forces in joint operations."

Although State Department officials tried to publicly
minimize the impact on U.S. - Soviet relations of Carter's
decisions and the administration leaks, in interviews
conducted during November and early December they predicted that relations with Moscow would continue to
worsen. They also said it was likely that the U.S.
would move closer toward an alliance with China, and
would sell military-related technology to the Chinese,
and possibly even U.S. arms as well.[130] Several officials
said that the "China tilters"-- Brzezinski and
his China specialist, Michel Oksenberg, in particular --
had won the battle for military ties with China.
Nevertheless, these officials said, a major fight still
was underway to at least slow the pace of development of
those relations.

But the Soviet invasion of Afghanistan in late
December sent U.S. relations with Moscow into a tailspin
and sharply weakened the position of those in the State
Department who hoped to limit the substance of Brown's
trip to prevent further damage to detente. A "senior
official" told the New York Times on the eve of
Brown's departure for China that the Soviet invasion had
given Brown's mission a "new dimension," and asserted
that "the Soviets have forced us and the Chinese into a
posture in which we both see the world in the same way."[131]

The official added that closer security ties with Beijing
were viewed by many officials as a principal way the
United States could respond to Soviet actions in
Afghanistan. A consensus on this issue was not formed
among senior officials, however, as indicated by Cyrus
Vance's comments on China policy in June 1980, after
his resignation as Secretary of State. After making a
strong plea for ratification of the SALT II treaty and
condemning the "new nostalgia" for "simplistic solutions,"
he urged that U.S. "think anew about how to manage our
affairs with the People's Republic of China in relation
to those with the Soviet Union. Even as we act to
develop nonmilitary ties with China we should strive to
restore a more balanced approach to both countries."[132]

Vance, however, was out of power, and the move
toward a deeper military relationship with China continued. Only a week before Vance's speech, China's
defense chief and Deputy Premier, Geng Biao, where he
joined Defense Secretary Brown for a press conference in
Washington announcing that China would be allowed to buy
"non-lethal" military equipment such as air-defense radar,
helicopters and transport planes, and that U.S. companies
would be allowed to set up electronics and helicopter
factories in China. Brown denied the U.S. was moving
toward a defense alliance with China, but Geng, asked if
China would like to buy arms from the U.S., replied: "I
don't think there is such a possibility at present. But
I believe there might be such a possibility in the
future."[133]And the day before Vance's statement, his
former deputy, Assistant Secretary of State for East
Asian and Pacific Affairs, Richard Holbrooke, suggested
that future aggressive behavior by the Soviet Union could
lead China and the United States to forge an alliance and
engage in joint military planning and that the U.S.
might sell arms to China. [134]

Ironically, what China's invasion of Vietnam failed
to achieve in pulling the U.S. closer into a military
alignment with Beijing, was accomplished for China by
the Soviet Union's invasion of Afghanistan. The United
States did not want to be dragged into a confrontation
with the Soviet Union by China's actions, and President
Carter wanted to finalize the SALT II agreement. He
therefore sought to distance the U.S. from the Chinese
invasion of Vietnam. But when Carter looked for a way
of punishing the Soviets over Ethiopia the troops in Cuba
issue and finally in response to the invasion of
Afghanistan -- he looked to a closer military link with
China to play on the Soviet's fear of Sino-American
collusion.

Just as triangular concerns and strategies of the
three powers were key factors in determining their
orientation toward the Indochina crisis before and during
the Vietnamese invasion of Cambodia and the Chinese

invasion of Vietnam, those factors continued to be
important in the post-crisis period and are likely to
shape reactions in the future. On the one hand, the
forging of a closer U.S. - Chinese military relationship
seemed to signal to Moscow that the U.S. would give firmer backing to the Chinese if they invaded Vietnam
again. The "non-lethal" military equipment the
U.S. agreed to sell China included trucks and communications gear that would help redress major deficiencies
revealed in the invasion in PLA mobility and tactical
communications. The broader security guarantee given
by Mondale in August 1979 also suggested that the U.S.
would shield the Chinese if they sought to teach Vietnam
another "lesson."

Yet, on the other hand, it was far from certain that
either the Chinese wanted a replay of the 1979 invasion,
much less a larger scale conflict that could have even
greater negative consequences for Chinese security
and economic modernization -- or that Washington would
encourage or even support another Chinese action against
Vietnam which had an even greater chance of escalating
to Sino-Soviet and U.S. - Soviet confrontations.

The deterioration of U.S. - Soviet detente increased
the likelihood of a Soviet military response to another
large-scale Chinese military action against Vietnam.
The invasion of Afghanistan may have accelerated the
already burgeoning Sino-American military relationship,
but it also indicated that the Soviets might be more
willing to take aggressive action when the constraints of
detente were stripped away. By December 1979, the
promise of detente for the Soviets had virtually
disappeared: Senate ratification of SALT II was indefinitely delayed: NATO had decided, under U.S. pressure,
to proceed with deployment of new theater nuclear weapons
capable of hitting the Soviet Union from Western Europe
for the first time; the administration had indicated it
would begin blocking the transfer of advanced technology
to the Soviet Union; Carter had decided to seek MFN
status for China but not for the Soviet Union; and the
U.S. had signalled Moscow it was about to enter a new
stage of military ties with China by sending the
Secretary of Defense to Beijing. In addition, Soviet
efforts to improve ties with China had come to an impasse
by the end of November. The final Soviet decision to
invade Afghanistan thus came when the Soviets had already
been punished by denial of the main fruits of detente
and by increasing U.S. - Chinese collusion against them.

Although the Chinese have been the most vehement
critics of detente, it seems likely that Soviet fear of
damage to its relations with the United States that would
result from an attack on China was an important restrain-
ing factor in the 1970s, and especially during the Chinese
invasion of Vietnam in 1979 when Moscow was hoping to

finalize the SALT II agreement. But in a future
Chinese invasion of Vietnam, the Soviets might not feel
such constraints as long as U.S. - Soviet relations remain near Cold War tension. Thus, the dynamics of the
triangle might actually deter the Chinese from another
attack, despite the implication of firmer U.S. support.
But those dynamics also suggest an eventual renewal of
the U.S. - Soviet dialogue and attempts to build a new
detente-type relationship. At that point, the Chinese
could again see an attack on Vietnam as a way of undermining U.S. - Soviet relations and calling on the
implied U.S. commitment to Chinese security. Such
possibilities add to the importance of a new U.S.
policy that seeks to de-escalate the Indochinese and
Sino-Vietnamese conflicts.

NOTES

1. New York Times, 15 May 1977; for complete text
see Pravda 14 May 1977.
2. Delivered to the Asia Society in New York, 29
June 1977.
3. Vance also said that U.S. relations with China
are a "central part" of U.S. foreign policy and are important for "global equilibrium," a slight watering-down
of Carter's statement at Notre Dame on May 22 (written
by Brzezinski) that "we see the American-Chinese relationship as a central element of our global policy, and China
as a key force for global peace." Carter's statement was
the first time a President had termed relations with
China a central element in U.S. global, rather than regional, policy--a statement calculated to worry the
Soviets as well as to reassure the Chinese. The Soviets
would also be disturbed by Carter's description of the
Chinese as a "key force for global peace," since Moscow
had a week earlier accused China of seeking to provoke a
new world war.
4. The speech reportedly was written by Vance's top
Soviet adviser, Marshall Shulman, who wrote in the January 1977 issue of Foreign Affairs that he thinks the
United States is more likely to get what it wants from
the Soviet Union through reduced tensions and increased
cooperation rather than through confrontation and pressure tactics.
5. The key document presenting the hardliners' point
of view on Soviet intentions and the strategic balance
was the so-called "Team B" report done for the CIA by a
group of conservative outsiders which concluded that the
Soviets were seeking nuclear superiority over the U.S.,
not parity. See the New York Times, 26 December 1976 and
the Washington Post, 2 January 1977; see also IB, Vol. 4
no. 1, 14 January 1977, for the unfolding debate over the
Soviet military threat that faced the new administration.

6. See _Issues and Studies_ (Taipei), January 1978, pp. 109-116, for the possibly authentic text of a secret speech by Foreign Minister Huang Hua delivered a month before Vance's visit to Beijing. Huang reportedly said "far from being a coincidence, the schedule of the (Vance) tour was arranged to show that we have attached special importance to the mission, and to checkmate the Soviet revisionists. If you want to ask who will be the most nervous and uneasy about Vance's trip, in my view, it will be the Soviet revisionists, and Taiwan comes next." p. 114.

7. The Chinese were prepared to assure the United States they would not use force to liberate Taiwan for ten years, according to Huang Hua, ibid., pp. 112-13. But the Vance mission nevertheless led to Chinese denunciations of reports they were willing to be flexible on the Taiwan issue. See _New York Times_, 7 September 1977, and also 29 August 1977, for Harrison Salisbury interview with Li Xian-nian. U.S. officials said privately later that there had been no discussion of arms sales or even military ties with China during Vance's visit. This may have contributed to China's displeasure, and it contrasts sharply with the content of Brzezinski's discussions with Chinese leaders during his visit to Beijing nine months later.

8. At a press conference on 29 September 1977, Carter also said that the Soviets had been "fairly flexible in their attitudes."

9. Senator Gary Hart (D-Colo.) to Reuters in Peking, 9 January 1978, for example.

10. K. S. Karol, cited in the _Christian Science Monitor_, 30 January 1978.

11. Jen Ku-ping, "The Munich Tragedy and Contemporary Appeasement," _Peking Review_, no. 50 (9 December 1977). This was apparently a reference to leaks from Washington that PRM 10 advocated NATO abandonment of one third of West German territory in the event of a Warsaw Pact attack--a report denied by the administration. See the _New York Times_, 6 January 1978, which says PRM 10 does not advocate such a policy.

12. The Carter administration had not yet publicly reaffirmed the commitment to China's security made by Kissinger in October 1976, although there is no public indication whether Kissinger's statements at that time had actually reassured the Chinese.

13. "Chairman Mao's Theory of the Differentiation of the Three Worlds is a Major Contribution to Marxism-Leninism," by the editorial department of _People's Daily_, translated in _Peking Review_, no. 45 (4 November 1977). Chairman Hua made a similar statement on the eve of Vance's visit to Peking in August. Hua said in his "Political Report to the Eleventh National Congress of the Communist Party of China, August 12, 1977": "There is a

trend toward appeasement among those people in the West who cherish the illusion that peace can be maintained through compromises and concessions, and some even want to follow in Chamberlain's footsteps and try to divert the peril of the new tsars to the East in order to preserve themselves at the expense of others." The repetition of this line more than two months after Vance's visit indicates the Chinese were not reassured by the secretary of state on this question. See also the New York Times, 6 January 1978, on the "Military Posture and Force Structure Review" section of PRM 10, which cited the document saying that the notion of "establishing close links with China in an effort to divert Soviet military resources to Asia," had been considered and rejected as not feasible "in the near future," suggesting that Western military ties with Beijing could also result in greater Soviet military pressure on China.

14. Hua said in his "Political Report" that "the current strategic situation in their contention is that Soviet social imperialism is on the offensive and U.S. imperialism on the defensive."

15. People's Daily cited comments by Mao Zedong during World War II that the United States had shifted from following a "Munich policy" in the Far East that undermined China's resistance to Japan to a policy of support for the Chinese resistance.

16. New York Times, 27 April 1978; and U.S. News and World Report, 8 May 1978.

17. China publicly indicated support for the U.S. role in aiding the Western intervention in Zaire (see Washington Post, 20 May 1978), and Secretary Vance consulted with Chinese Foreign Minister Huang Hua in New York on 2 June before Huang left for Kinshasha to demonstrate Chinese support for the beleagured Mobutu regime. Carter's tough stand on Zaire, blaming an invasion of Zaire's Shaba province by rebels based in neighboring Angola on the Soviet and Cubans, apparently was intended partly as a show of toughness by the Carter administration to impress the Chinese on the eve of Brzezinski's visit.

18. See Time and Newsweek, 5 June 1978, for the prominence given to the jokes by Brzezinski, who some Chinese sailors dubbed the "Bear Tamer."

19. The Carter administration explained the final negotiations for normalization of relations with China as a tenuous, difficult process with last minute negotiations and concessions, and that they had to move quickly in December 1978 to finalize agreement with the Chinese-- even if the timing upset the SALT talks. But according to a Japanese source, interviewed in August 1979, Brzezinski and Chinese leaders agreed to set January 1, 1979 as their target date for normalization. The source attended a small, private meeting with Brzezinski and his

aide, Samuel Huntington, in Tokyo immediately following
their trip to China. Brzezinski told the group that the
U.S. and China would normalize relations on January 1,
1979--which, in fact, was the case. The State Department
11 June 1978 denied a report from the Washington correspondent of the Mainichi Shimbun that White House sources
had told him that Brzezinski and the Chinese had set
January 1 as the target date for normalization. The
paper also said that the U.S. would meet China's three
conditions for normalization and would abandon its
demand that China pledge not try to annex Taiwan by force.
A State Department spokeswoman said "We have never fixed
a time schedule or deadline" for completion of the normalization process. (San Francisco Examiner, 12 June
1978).

20. New York Times, 28 May 1978. Chinese officials
later made the same point to Rep. Lester Wolff (D-N.Y.)
He returned from leading a congressional delegation to
Beijing in mid-July saying that the Chinese, who told
him they were willing to negotiate directly with Nationalist Chinese leaders, said that they want to move
rapidly in normalization, which they see as a "key
strategic and political move in the world arena, specifically against the Soviet Union."

21. New York Times, 28 May and 25 June 1978. See
Evans and Novak, Washington Post, 22 June 1978, on administration decision-making on the issue. The Times reported on 18 May that administration officials were inclined to approve the sale of certain defensive arms to
China by Western European countries. On 9 June 1978 the
Times reported that the administration had agreed to a
Chinese request to buy airborne geological survey equipment (with military uses for antisubmarine detection) that
it will not sell to the Soviet Union. U. S. Officials
also told Reuters, 9 June 1978, that the same equipment
would be denied the Soviets because of its potential
military uses.

22. Reuters, 29 May 1978; New York Times, 24 May 1978.

23. The "Meet the Press" interview was taped on
Saturday, 27 May and aired on Sunday, 28 May 1978.

24. See Soviet World Outlook, 15 August 1978. See
also New York Times, 18 June 1978, for excerpts of a
major Pravda statement on triangular relations. Soviet
sources also told reporters, however, that China's
hostility toward the Soviet Union was so great that
Moscow could not allow emergence of a China modernized
and armed by the West. Pravda warned the Chinese of the
consequences of a war with the Soviet Union. See
Washington Post, 5 September 1978.

25. Washington Post, 27 August 1979.

26. See the New York Times, 20 December 1978;
Washington Post, 19 September 1978; and an article by
Soviet journalist Ernst Henry in West German's Der Speigel,
15 January 1979.

27. Washington Post, 5 November 1978; New York Times,

29 November 1978.

28. See the New York Times, 20 December 1978,
"Chinese Card: How to Play It," by Richard Burt. Burt
also says officials acknowledged that U.S. arms sales to
China are possible but could lead to the end of detente.

29. Interview with Walter Conkrite, CBS News, 19
December 1978. See the New York Times, 20 December 1978.
The Times reported that Brzezinski had briefed Soviet
ambassador Anatoly Dobrynin on Sino-American normalization
on December 15, telling him that Carter desired to continue improving relations with the Soviet Union and as-
suring him that normalization was not directed at any
third nation.

30. Washington Post, New York Times, 22 December 1978.

31. See the New York Times, 25 December 1978 and 24
January 1979, for attribution of this view to members of
Vance's party to the Geneva talks. Also see Don Oberdorfer's account of triangular relations and the Vietnam
invasion, Washington Post, 1 April 1979.

32. See the Wall Street Journal, 26 December 1978
and the International Bulletin, Vol. 6, No. 1, 15 January
1979.

33. Washington Post, 19 January 1979; see also
Jonathan Steele, Manchester Guardian, 28 January 1979.

34. See International Bulletin, Vol. 6, No. 1, 15
January 1979, and the New York Times, 12 January 1979.

35. See the New York Times, 28 December 1978, for a
report that the U.S. sought changes at the Geneva summit,
apparently on demand from the Pentagon and NSC, which
would suggest that the normalization announcement was not
entirely responsible for the failure to reach final agreement on the SALT II accord. A White House official was
quoted as saying that the Soviets thought the U.S. was so
eager for an agreement that they could get last minute
concessions from the Americans. "A typical example of
eleventh hour negotiating by the Russians," the official
said.

36. New York Times, Washington Post, 27 December
1978.

37. New York Times, 7 January 1979.

38. Washington Post, 6 and 7 January 1979; Los
Angeles Times, 6 January 1979.

39. Boston Globe, 21 January 1979, which also notes
the nuclear capability of the Harrier.

40. See International Bulletin, Vol. 6, No. 1, 15
January 1979 and Reuter, 24 January 1979. On Schmidt's
reaction to the Harrier deal, see Die Zeit, 12 January
1979. Brezhnev had warned Callaghan against the Harrier
deal in a letter to the British Prime Minister in November, which was similar to letters sent to other Western
European leaders. See the Washington Post, 19 September,
27 October and 24 November, 1979.

41. New York Times, 7 January 1979. Schmidt said January 12 that under no circumstances would West Germany sell arms to China. New York Times, 13 January 1979.

42. In a detailed report on the summit, Kurt Becker wrote in Die Zeit, 12 January 1979: "None of the four statesmen in Guadeloupe underestimated Soviet sensitivity in regard to arms deliveries (to China). After China's opening toward the West, Brezhnev had already pointed out-- in identical letters to several West European governments, including Bonn--the fragility of detente in the event that the West should supply arms to Peking. Immediately before the summit meeting, Brezhnev in letters to all four participating heads of government had increased this warning in even more severe tones. And this had its effect. When it comes to arms supplies, Moscow is guided not by quantity but by principle and has made it clear from the start that a Western arms alliance with China would affect East-West relations. Thus, whoever tries to play the China card has to keep in mind the old Soviet encirclement trauma and take the possibility of endangering detente into account." Becker's analysis is representative of Western European, pro-detente views, expecially those of West Germany ruling Social Democratic Party (SPD).

43. New York Times, 26 January 1979; Los Angeles Times, 28 January 1979.

44. New York Times, 27 January 1979. For full text of January 26 press conference, see the State Department Bulletin, March 1979, pp. 30-31.

45. Full text of Vance's 11 January 1978 press conference, State Department Bulletin, February 1979, pp. 7-11. See also Vance interviews with Asian Wall Street Journal, 19 January 1979. For contrasting views on U.S.-China relations between Vance and Brzezinski, see the texts of their respective statements at a special State Department briefing for business executives trading with the PRC and with Taiwan, held 15 January 1979. See State Department Bulletin, ibid., pp. 14-21, and the New York Times, 16 January 1979.

46. See the New York Times, January 1979 and 24 January 1979; Washington Post, 28 January 1979. Business Week, 12 February 1979, reported a Vance-Brzezinski split on the issue of "evenhandedness" in dealings with Moscow and Beijing. The magazine reported that Vance had been promoting an evenhanded policy "which simply means that the U.S. won't give the Chinese anything in the way of aid, technology, or trade preference that it doesn't give Moscow. Vance's opponent, as usual, is National Security Adviser Zbigniew Brzezinski, who believes that strengthening China at Soviet expense is the whole point. Explains one congressional ally: "The concept of evenhanded treatment amounts to abrogation of the Administra-

tion's China policy; its purpose is to extract acceptable behavior from the Soviet Union.'"

47. Time, 5 February 1979.

48. Novak's first report of his interview with Deng appeared in the Evans and Novak column, Washington Post, 4 December 1978, without direct quotation. Novak quoted Deng directly in Look magazine, 19 February 1979.

49. Baltimore Sun, 30 January 1979.

50. In an interview with the Public Broadcasting Service, 1 February 1979, excerpts of which appeared in the Washington Star, 4 February 1979.

51. Los Angeles Times, 1 February 1979.

52. The Los Angeles Times reported 3 February 1979 that the communique was drafted on the U.S. side by Michel Oksenberg of the NSC, and Richard Holbrooke, Assistant Secretary of State. See also the Times, 19 February 1979, on the lack of consultation with Vance's Soviet advisers.

53. Robert Pierpoint, CBS News, 1 February 1979.

54. See the New York Times, 1 and 2 February 1979, for the various statements, cultural exchange agreements and the Joint Press Communique.

55. Interview with Marvin Kalb, CBS Evening News, 2 February 1979, excerpts of which were printed in the Washington Star, 3 February 1979.

56. Time, 22 January 1979. Brezhnev, who said he was "sick and tired of talking about China," also said: "The point is not at all the establishment of diplomatic relations. The point is that attempts are being made to encourage in every way and to stimulate with economic bait and now, gradually, also with deliveries of modern weapons, material and military techonology, those who, while heading one of the biggest countries in the world, have openly declared their hostility to the cause of detente, disarmament and stability in the world, those who lay claims to the territories of many countries and stage provocations against them, those who have proclaimed war inevitable and mounted active preparations for war. Is it really difficult to understand that this means playing with fire?"

57. Cited in Soviet World Outlook, 15 February 1979, which also noted that Radio Moscow, 4 February 1979, commented that Deng's visit to the Beijing aircraft plant in Seattle was a hint of possible future Sino-American military cooperation but concluded that "there is still quite a long way to go before any direct organization of such cooperation could be implemented."

58. Washington Post, 1 February 1979.

59. William Beecher, Boston Globe, 19 February 1979, said the statement gave a "compelling rationale" for the Chinese invasion.

60. New York Times, 18 February 1979.

234

61. Soviet World Outlook, 15 March 1979; see also
Survival, May-June 1979, for full text of Pravda article,
28 February 1979, "Peking's Agression Must Be Resolutely
Rebuff ّd."
62. New York Times, 2 March 1979. If Don Oberdor-
fer of the Washington Post, 1 April 1979, is correct, the
Soviets already knew the Chinese were withdrawing from
Vietnam when Gromyko made this statement. Nevertheless,
the Soviet leadership could probably mobilize almost
universal support for a war with China, according to
Soviet dissident Roy Medvedev, writing from Moscow for
In These Times ("Medvedev Tells of Soviets' China Fears,"
28 March-3 April, 1979). Medvedev wrote during the Sino-
Vietnamese war, when a Soviet attack on China seemed a
possibility: "If there has been any area without major
differences between dissident circles and official Soviet
policy, it has been the problem of China. ...The signs
of national unity in the face of the threat of war were
apparent....All this contributed to the climate of opinion that converted the Sino-Vietnamese conflict into a
portent of major war."
63. New York Times, 2 March 1979.
64. Soviet World Outlook, 15 March 1979, citing a
Soviet government statement of 18 February 1979.
65. Izvestia, 20 February 1979, for example, con-
ceded that the U.S. might have tried to dissuade Deng
from the Vietnam action, but said that he "could not care
less about the delicate calculations of Brzezinski and his
strategic team." Cited in Soviet World Outlook, 15 March
1979. A detailed analysis of conflicting Soviet views of
the strategic triangle and the Sino-Vietnamese war has
been done by Gerald Segal, in "The USSR and the Great
Power Triangle: A Case Study of the Sino-Vietnamese War,"
unpublished.
66. Cited in Soviet World Outlook, ibid.
67. Washington Post, 1 February 1979. Article VI
of the Soviet-Vietnamese treaty says: "if one of the
sides becomes the object of attack or of a threat of attack, the contracting parties will quickly move to mutual
consultations with the goal of removing the threat and
taking appropriate effective measures for the preserva-
tion of the peace and security of their countries." This
article could provide the basis for Soviet intervention
in a Sino-Vietnamese conflict, but it does not obligate
Moscow to come to Hanoi's direct assistance. U.S. envoy
to China (later ambassador) Leonared Woodcock said in
Beijing on January 1, 1979, that China had begun to move
troops away from the coastal province that faces Taiwan:
"from everything that we know, the movement of troops has
been to the north and to the south, completely away from
the coastal areas adjacent to Taiwan." Los Angeles Times,
2 January 1979. The Christian Science Monitor reported

2 January 1979 from Hong Kong that a "usually reliable
Chinese source said that "Normalization means China is in
a better position to handle the Vietnamese because
thousands of Chinese soldiers stationed opposite Taiwan
can now be moved to strengthen China's border with Vietnam
and the Soviet Union ....This means it will be harder for
the Soviet Union to attack China if China attacks Vietnam."
The Monitor also reported that "one Chinese representative has asked this correspondent if the United States
will aid China in a war with Vietnam and the Soviet
Union. At least one American diplomat has also been
asked this question in China."

68. New York Times, 18 February 1979; Los Angeles
Times, 20 February 1979.

69. Wall Street Journal, 28 February 1979.

70. See, for example, the report in the Christian
Science Monitor, 22 February 1979.

71. Deng had admitted in Washington that there was
nothing that China could do to help the U.S. in Iran
(Washington Star, 4 February 1979). But in Tokyo, on his
way back to China and in the wake of the collapse of the
Shah's regime in Iran as the U.S. stood by helplessly,
Deng pointed to indecision and lack of direction in U.S.
Iran policy. He reportedly said that the U.S. "is
allowing the Soviet Union to place a lot of pawns on the
world's chessboard," adding that "things cannot be allowed
to go on this way." (Washington Post, 8 February 1979;
see also Boston Globe, 16 February 1979.) Dennis Blood-
worth of the London Observer wrote 25 March 1979 that the
Chinese invasion of Vietnam "has reset the board in
Southeast Asia, established China as a major piece,
earned a few sideline glances but lost the Chinese none
of their friends, and indicated Deng's 'forward strategy'
....It proved that Peking was ready to risk war with the
USSR, even global conflict, to back up protest with
punitive action." Joseph Kraft, writing in the Washington Post 22 February 1979, interpreted the attack as
China's bid for a place among the great powers. See also
U.S. News and World Report, 5 March 1979, and "Why Did
China Invade Vietnam?", Internews International Bulletin,
by Banning Garrett, Vol. 6, no. 4, 26 February 1979.

72. For a detailed analysis of the war, see Harlan
Jencks, "China's 'Punitive' War on Vietnam: A Military
Assessment," Asian Survey, August 1979, Vol. XIX, No. 8.
See also Drew Middleton's running analysis of the fight-
ing in the New York Times, 20, 21, 22, 24, 25, 26, 27
February and 1 March, 1979; Wall Street Journal, 1 March
1979; and Los Angeles Times, 22 February 1979. For a
report on the Chinese aims and their view of the
accomplishments of the invasion, see Air Force magazine,
June 1979.

73. See Banning Garrett, "West Germans Fear Damage
to Detente," Internews International Bulletin, 26 March

1979, Vol. 6, no. 6, which included a report on my interviews with West German politicians during the invasion about the impact of China's invasion of Vietnam on Western European attitudes toward the "China card." Peter Corterier, a center-right Social Democratic Party leader and a party spokesperson on foreign affairs, said: "There is concern all over Europe that the China-Vietnam conflict might get out of hand. There is also new concern that arming China is more dangerous than previously thought. Overall, there is some disillusionment with the China connection."

74. The Soviet press noted Western praise for Moscow's restraint. The Soviet magazine New Times editorialized in March, 1979 (issue no. 12), that "Peking has let it be understood that it hoped to place our country in a difficult position by attacking its ally. But in this respect too the Chinese strategists have been disappointed. The Soviet Union is living up to its treaty commitments to the Socialist Republic of Vietnam and has warned the aggressor of the severe penalty in store for him if he persists in engaging in international brigandage. The Soviet position has been duly evaluated by the world community. The Russians come out looking like 'a force for moderation,' the Wall Street Journal has commented. The London Financial Times, 16 March 1979, however, evaluated the Chinese action and Soviet reaction differently: "The invasion of Vietnam was the first occasion on which the Chinese tested how far their new relationship with the West had raised the threshold beyond which the Russians would attempt punitive action them. The result was satisfactory. The Russians huffed and puffed, but they were not willing to endanger the SALT negotiations in order to support Vietnam in a quarrel with China. The Chinese could thus conclude that they might count on at least some Western protection, in spite of the determination of NATO members to approach Moscow and Peking with evenhandedness."

75. See for example the New York Times, 23 February 1979. U.S. Treasury Secretary Michael Blumenthal said in Beijing February 28 that "Obviously, if there were a wider war to develop here, that clearly would have an impact on businessmen's attitudes and on the economic situation." Wall Street Journal, 1 March 1979.

76. The pending sale of Harrier jet fighter bombers to China, which British Prime Minister Callaghan had announced at the Guadeloupe summit in early January, was challenged by Labour Party MPs during the invasion. Energy Secretary Anthony Benn broke with official government policy by voting against the sale at a meeting of the Labour Party International Committee on February 13. (See the London Financial Times and Guardian, 14 February 1979). The government had hoped to include the Harrier sale in a $14 billion trade agreement negotiated with China during

the invasion, but decided to delay the decision to assess the outcome of the Chinese action. (See the Daily Mirror, Daily Telegraph, Guardian, Financial Times, 20 February 1979). Industry Minister Eric Varley finally signed a trade agreement March 4 that did not include the Harrier. (Daily Mail, 4 March 1979)

77. Representative Les Aspin of the House Intelligence Subcommittee on Oversight released a study 26 February 1979 commending the intelligence community for its excellent job in foreseeing the Chinese invasion of Vietnam.

78. 1 April 1979.

79. New York Times, 19 February 1979.

80. Blumenthal also publicly endorsed China's military modernization program by voicing support for the Four Modernizations, saying it was in the interest of the United States and the world that "the Chinese people succeed in their four modernizations." (Washington Post, 2 March 1979).

81. New York Times, 28 February 1979. Asked whether he expected the Soviet Union to intervene militarily, Deng said: "We estimate that the Soviet Union will not take too big an action. If they should really come, there is nothing we can do about it. We are prepared against them. I think our action is limited and will not give rise to a very big event."

82. See for example the analysis of Frederick Moritz in the Christian Science Monitor, 26 February 1979.

83. Strobe Talbott, Endgame, op. cit., p. 248, says that President Carter, at Vance's urging, held a private meeting with Soviet Ambassador Dobrynin at the White House two days before Brezhnev's March 2 speech. Carter reportedly denied U.S. complicity with the Chinese invasion of Vietnam and stressed "that relations between the U.S. and Russia must be set right before the strain got out of control; Sino-American normalization and the Sino-Vietnamese border war must not determine the course of Soviet-American relations; and most immediately and urgently, SALT must be concluded." See also Oberdorfer Washington Post, 1 April 1979, and Priscilla Johnson MacMillan, "The Secret U.S. Effort to Save SALT," San Francisco Chronicle, 6 June 1979, for an analysis also based on interviews with U.S. officials.

84. New York Times, 17 March 1979; Washington Post and Boston Globe, 28 March 1979.

85. Washington Post, 4 April 1979; Beijing Review, No. 14, 6 April 1979.

86. Soviet Government Statement, Tass, 4 April 1979.

87. "What Reason is There for Moscow to Fly into a Rage?", Renmin Ribao Commentator; reprinted in Beijing Review, No. 16, 20 April 1979.

88. UPI and Reuters, 18 April 1979. Foreign Minister Gromyko personally handed the note to the Chinese

ambassador in Moscow--just as the Chinese and Vietnamese representatives sat down in Hanoi to begin negotiations for a settlement of their border war.

89. According to "official Chinese sources," cited by Reuters, 10 May 1979.

90. Tass, cited in the New York Times, 6 June 1979. Again the Soviet note was handed to Chinese embassy officials by Gromyko.

91. New York Times, 23 May 1979.

92. Washington Post, 11 May 1979. See also the interview with Vice Premier Li Xian-nian in Newsweek, 16 July 1979. Li takes a hard line on Soviet expansionism and warns of the possibility of a second Sino-Vietnamese war.

93. Hua's full report was printed in Beijing Review, No. 27, 6 July 1979.

94. Pravda, 2 June 1979. Some excerpts in the New York Times, 6 June 1979.

95. The full text of Gromyko's Moscow press conference was translated in Soviet Life, August, 1979.

96. Quoted in the Baltimore Sun, 12 July 1979; and Christian Science Monitor, 26 July 1979.

97. Washington Star, 13 July 1970, citing a report from Japan's Kyodo news service on Geng Biao's statement. China's offer to send envoys to Moscow was reported by Reuters, 16 July 1979 and Financial Times, 18 July 1979.

98. Washington Post, Los Angeles Times, New York Times, 25 July 1979; Los Angeles Times, 27 July 1979. See also William Beecher, Boston Globe, 26 July 1979 for a report based on U.S. intelligence sources saying that the Soviets may have added as many as three divisions to the forces along the border with China and in Mongolia, and that they are now sending their best conventional weapons to the Far East as well as to the Central European theater in response to the Sino-Vietnamese war.

99. See Christian Science Monitor, 14 and 27 September 1979; Washington Post, 19, 24, and 27 September 1979; Los Angeles Times, 16, 24, and 27 September 1979; New York Times, 15, 24, 28 and 30 September 1979; and Financial Times, 24, 25, and 27 September 1979.

100. New York Times, 1 December 1979; see also the Christian Science Monitor, 13 November 1979.

101. New York Times, 10 November 1979.

102. New York Times, ibid. The Times also reported that the Chinese Communist Party has circulated a document to officials that concludes that the Soviet party should no longer be viewed as revisionist. The document, according to the Times'"knowledgeable Chinese sources," says the Soviet Union is still socialist because its means of production are owned by the state, and that the main threat from the Soviets now is military expansionism. "The sources say the document indicates that China is preparing to drop the ideological part of its longstanding

quarrel with the Soviet Union, and they believe that this could result in a significant breakthrough in the current talks between the two Governments in Moscow."

103. New York Times, 1 December 1979. The Soviets had originally insisted that the talks be held only in Moscow since the border talks are held in Beijing. (Reuters 25 July 1979; Financial Times, 26 July 1979).

104. Based on interviews and press reports. See Banning Garrett, "Thaw in Sino-Soviet Relations?", Internews International Bulletin, Vol. 6, No. 12, 18 June 1979. See also "Playing the China Card: Implications for United States-Soviet-Chinese Relations," report prepared for the Subcommittee on Asian and Pacific Affairs, House Committee on Foreign Affairs, by Robert Sutter and Michael Baron of the Congressional Research Service, pp. 10-12.

105. Garrett, ibid. For discussion of future prospects for Sino-Soviet relations, see "China and the Soviet Union," in A. Doak Barnett, China and the Major Powers in East Asia (Washington, D.C.: Brookings, 1977); William G. Hyland, "The Sino-Soviet Conflict: A Search for New Security Strategies," in Strategic Review, Fall 1979; and Alex Alexiev, "Sino-Soviet Relations: Prospects for Accommodation," Contemporary China, Vol. 2, No. 2, Summer 1979.

106. Brezhnev apparently was seeking to reassure the Vietnamese of continuing Soviet support when he said in his June 1 speech that better relations with China "cannot be at the expense of third countries." (Brezhnev, op. cit., note 13). This point was repeated in the July 11 Alexandrov piece, op. cit., note 14.

107. A point made by The Economist, 16 June 1979.

108. The budget was raised from $10.5 to $12.64 billion, according to the Washington Post, 30 July 1979. The budget increase was announced at the same NPC session that approved a "readjustment"--a scaling down--of China's ambitious modernization program, including a significant cutback in purchases of Western technology. See Banning Garrett, "China Shifts Economic Priorities," Internews International Bulletin, Vol. 6, No. 14, 16 July 1979.

109. This point was made to delegation from the National Defense University which visited China in May and met with senior Chinese defense officials, including Defense Minister Xu Xiang-qian. See the report by a member of the delegation, Capt. William R. Heaton, Jr. (USAF), Army, November 1979. See also the Financial Times 20 August 1979, on the low priority assigned to military modernization. "China Touches Tigers' Bottoms," by Maj. Gen. Robert Ginsburgh (USAF, ret.) in Air Force Magazine, June 1979 cites PRC officials saying that the attack on Vietnam was necessary to secure a future peaceful international environment to realize the Four Modernizations.

110. The Chinese import nonferrous metals, timber and some agricultural machinery from the Soviet Union, and in 1978 reportedly were seeking hydoelectric power generators, transport planes and helicopters. China exports to the Soviet Union foodstuffs, some metals and textiles, which have faced protectionist barriers in the U.S. and Western Europe. In addition, China has a favorable trade balance with the Soviet Union and carried out most of its trade through barter, thus conserving scarce foreign exchange. For reports on Sino-Soviet trade, see the New York Times, 23 May 1979 and 30 September 1979; Business Week, 4 June 1979; Reuters 9 June 1979; and The Economist, 16 June 1979.

111. New York Times, Boston Globe, 20 April 1979. See earlier official Chinese reaction to the terms of U.S. legislation on future official Chinese reaction to the terms of U.S. legislation on future relations with Taiwan (Washington Post, Los Angeles Times, 25 March 1979; New York Times, 26, 27 and 29 March 1979.) See also Robert L. Downen, The Taiwan Pawn in the China Game (Washington, D.C.: Center for Strategic and International Studies, Georgetown University, 1979).

112. See Joseph Kraft, "China's Disappointment," Washington Post, 6 May 1979. Maj. Gen. Ginsburgh, op.cit, footnote 28, writes that Chinese officials said "they wish that in dealing with Cuba we would learn from their experience in dealing with Vietnam. They wish that we were better negotiators in dealing with the issues of strategic arms limitations." Chinese Vice Premier Li Xian-nian, in an interview with Newsweek, 16 July 1979, implicitly criticized the Carter administration's policies toward the Soviet Union and Cuba and warned of another Chinese strike into Vietnam.

113. Washington Post, 23 May 1979.

114. See the New York Times, Los Angeles Times, and Washington Post, 25 August 1979, for coverage of Jackson's trip to China.

115. Carter administration officials travelling with Mondale to China discounted reports that Chinese leaders were dismayed by the slow pace of development of Sino-American relations since normalization. They noted that the administration had sent seven cabinet level officials to China in the previous eight months, that a joint commission had been established to coordinate the transfer of technology, and that progress had been made on a textile agreement. (New York Times, 26 August 1979). But U.S. Ambassador to Beijing Leonard Woodcock disclosed after Mondale's visit had clearly been successful in forging closer Sino-American ties that Chinese leaders had been "extremely suspicious" of the U.S. just prior to Mondale's trip because of the failure of the administration to submit the trade agreement for approval by Congress. Woodcock said Mondale's explanation of "a

delay caused by a congressional logjam won the Chinese over." Washington Post, New York Times, 1 September 1979.

116. New York Times, 28 August 1979.

117. Ibid.

118. The Times, ibid., noted that "This certification is a legal requirement for providing services and commodities to other nations under the Foreign Assistance Act. Yugoslavia is the only other communist country so certified."

119. New York Times, 1 September 1979.

120. The Economist, 23 December 1978, noted that "although most of the non-military things both China and Russia want to buy from the west are available in quantities enough to satisfy them both, some things are not, notably some of the fruit of high technology industries, such as computers and oil-drilling equipment. To expand the total output of such things takes time and a lot of capital. Meanwhile, with China and Russia competing for the same limited supply, more for China means less for Russia. It is also possible that China's entry into the credit market will mean that Russia will be able to finance fewer of its imports from the west on the buy-now-pay-later principle."

121. U.S. officials urged the Chinese to broadcast Mondale's speech on national radio and television shortly after he was invited to address the students and faculty at Beijing University. But the Chinese reportedly agreed only after having examined most of the text. See the New York Times, 23 August 79, which also printed excerpts of the speech. The full text and other remarks by Mondale are reprinted in the State Department Bulletin, October 1979, pp. 10-13.

122. Los Angeles Times, 28 August 1979.

123. See the Christian Science Monitor, 24 and 29 August 1979.

124. Consideration of various options for action against the Soviets, including closer ties with China, appeared in the following reports prior to Carter's policy speech on October 1: ABC news, 17 September 1979; New York Times, 19, 23, and 25 September 1979; Los Angeles Times, 19, 29, and 30 September; Washington Star, 26 September 1979; Evans and Novak in Washington Post, 24 September 1979; and Boston Globe, 25 September 1979. William Beecher of the Globe reported that the administration was considering whether to allow Boeing to provide China with the extremely precise navigation equipment usually sold with the 747 jetliner when delivering three 747SP's contracted for earlier with the Chinese government. Beecher points out that a major shortcoming in China's nuclear weapons systems is their lack of accurate navigation equipment. "If the technology in the 747 navigation system could be adopted to China's missiles," one administration official told

Beecher, "it would overcome the biggest deficiency in those weapons."

125. See the New York Times, 2 October 1979 for the text of Carter's speech and a background on the crisis.

126. New York Times, 4 October 1979; Wall Street Journal, 5 October 1979; and Aviation Week, 8 October 1979.

127. Washington Post, Baltimore Sun, 2 October 1979.

128. Henry Brandon, Washington Star, 7 October 1979.

129. New York Times, 4 October 1979, "Study Urges U.S. Aid to Chinese Military," by Richard Burt and "Louder Than Words," by columnists William Safire.

130. Drew Middleton of the New York Times reported 11 November 1979 that "it is evident" that the Chinese hope Secretary Brown's visit to China "will result in some form of direct or indirect military assistance for their military forces." Administration sources, although denying that Brown would hold talks with the Chinese on U.S. arms sales, pointedly told reporters that the agenda for Brown's trip had not yet been set, suggesting to the Soviets that good behavior on their part might mitigate the damage to their interests from the Secretary of Defense's visit to China. See the Los Angeles Times, 3 November 1979 and the Boston Globe, 3 October 1979.

131. New York Times, 3 January 1980.

132. The speech was Vance's first public address since he had resigned after opposing the ill-fated U.S. rescue mission in Iran, and was delivered at the Harvard commencement exercises. For the full text, see the New York Times, 6 June 1980.

133. New York Times, 30 May 1980

134. New York Times, 5 June 1980

7

Conclusion

David W.P. Elliott

The preceding essays have traced the Third Indo-china Conflict from border tensions to open polemics to large scale invasion, and from a localized set of bilateral disputes to a confrontation involving the super-powers. Will a better understanding of the process of escalation be of use in facing problems of the future in this region, or is it of historical interest only? Even if it were possible to identify the precise sequence of cause and effect culminating in the diplomatic impasse that followed the Vietnamese occupation of Kampuchea and the Chinese invasion of Vietnam, it is not certain that the problem could be untangled simply by reversing the escalatory sequence of events. The diplomatic map of Southeast Asia has been irretrievably altered by what has happened, and a return to the status quo ante is impossible.

Nevertheless, as Jean Monnet observed when asked how to reconcile France and Germany within the framework of a united Western Europe in the face of the heavy burden of past antagonisms, in order to find the solution it is necessary to change the context in which the problem is set. If the problem is defined in terms of Vietnamese domination of Kampuchea, the obvious solution is the withdrawal of Vietnamese troops and the restoration of full Kampuchean sovereignty. This remedy is, however, unlikely to materialize for two related reasons. First, there does not seem to be any prospect for an initial process of self determination in Kampuchea that would lead either to stability or that would reflect the wishes of the majority of Kampucheans. Second, the analysis presented in this study suggest that the problem is not simply Vietnam and Kampuchea, but also the larger regional and global implications of the conflict.

In the eyes of many of the parties who might be involved in a comprehensive settlement in Southeast Asia, Vietnam emerges as the main source of conflict. To a greater or lesser extent China, the United States, and various members of the Association of Southeast Asian

States (ASEAN) share the view that Vietnam's aggressive actions and intentions lie at the root of the problem and, thus, the solution rests on an initiative from Hanoi to undo what it has done.

The analysis presented here suggests a somewhat more complex picture. Almost certainly the Vietnamese did not in 1975 envision themselves bogged down in a costly occupation of Kampuchea and diplomatically isolated a few short years later. It seems unlikely that this situation was the result of an unfolding blueprint of agression whose sole architect was Hanoi. Indeed, what the foregoing essays suggest is that the Third Indochina Conflict was the result of an intricate combination of factors which cumulatively pushed the contending parties past the point of no return. Vietnam must bear responsibility for its considerable contributions to this process, but it was not the sole responsible party.

Three major conflict structures converged to form the essential ingredients of an explosive compound: Vietnam-Kampuchea, China-Vietnam, and the strategic triangle of the U.S., China, and the Soviet Union. Vietnam was the catalyst which fused these conflict structures together because it served as the geographical and political link between Kampuchea and China. Nevertheless, it is by no means clear that the initial escalation into armed hostilities between Vietnam and Kampuchea came from Hanoi's side. Much of the available evidence, in fact, points the other way. Nor is it apparent that it was Hanoi's behavior that goaded China into action. Several of the authors suggest that it was China that set out on a "collision course" with Vietnam, and there is some indication that China's invasion of Vietnam may have been aimed at larger foreign policy goals than the chastisement of Vietnam for its actions in Kampuchea.

Thus it is not entirely disingenuous of Hanoi to argue that any settlement of the Kampuchean problem must take into account all the factors that precipitated the conflict. And while Vietnam's desire to politically dominate Indochina has been abundantly demonstrated, it does not necessarily follow that the extension of Vietnamese power into Kampuchea constitutes irrefutable evidence of a desire to dominate the rest of Southeast Asia. If Vietnam's move into Kampuchea was not part of a predetermined blueprint of aggression or an inevitable consequence of an expansionist and bellicose nature, then its intentions with regard to the other states in the region cannot be confidently inferred from its occupation of Kampuchea. Any assessment of the future of Vietnam's relations with the rest of Southeast Asia must rest on a larger body of evidence than its invasion of Kampuchea, and must also take into account the effects of a settlement of the Kampuchea issue on the future course of relations between Vietnam and its neighbors.

One of the principle lessons of the Third Indochina Conflict is that polarization leads to escalation. It was the progressive elimination of alternatives to war that ultimately led to armed hostilities. A corollary lesson is that the linkages between apparently unrelated conflict structures cannot be ignored. The combination of polarization of actors with the fusion of different conflict structures was disastrous for all parties concerned. China's pressure on Vietnam and attempts to coerce Vietnam to sever its ties with the Soviet Union led to the opposite result. Vietnam's initial rigidity in dealing with ASEAN and the United States contributed to its progressive diplomatic isolation, and its lack of sensitivity concerning Kampuchea's historical fears of Vietnamese domination made it impossible for Hanoi to understand the sources of Kampuchea intransigence, and led to the conclusion that Beijing was behind it all. Pol Pot, in turn, could not see beyond the immediate problem with Vietnam, and failed to see what the regional forces set in motion the escalation of the bilateral conflict with the SRV would mean for Kampuchea. At the same time, his internal purges and repression presented the opening for Vietnamese intervention.

Perhaps the parties not directly involved had the greatest opportunity to break through the spiral of escalation. The United States did not adequately foresee the consequences of the polarization process, and was content to let events take their course rather than normalize relations with Vietnam and widen Hanoi's spectrum of diplomatic options. ASEAN, which became intensely concerned with the conflict after the Vietnamese invasion of Kampuchea, played a relatively passive role during the period of escalation in 1978. Thailand, the ASEAN member most directly involved, appears to have agreed with the Chinese position, and Thai support of Chinese assistance to Pol Pot both before and after the Vietnamese invasion constituted a major element of the problem -- though Thailand continued to regard itself as an uninvolved bystander in the conflict. Thailand on the regional level and the United States on the global level had the opportunity to play an important diplomatic role in decoupling the converging constellation of issues that escalated the conflict. Neither elected to do so.

Two complementary factors suggest an explanation for the failure of the United States to take a more active role in intervening to arrest the process of polarization. The first was the feeling that the problem was not important enough in a global perspective to incur the expected political costs, and the second was an ingrained tendency to rely on a militarized concept of deterrence. Because the United States had foresworn further military ventures in Southeast Asia, it would have to rely on a proxy -- the People's Republic of China. But China's approach to the problem was to give military aid to Kampuchea as a means of pressuring Vietnam and, when this approach backfired, China attempted to bring Vietnam into line by military intimidation. The policies of China and the United States aimed at preventing the expansion of Soviet influence in Indochina but achieved the opposite result, and the diplomatic efforts of Washington and Beijing were largely confined to maneuvers on the global chessboard that would reinforce a confrontationist policy rather than contribute to a resolution of the conflict.

This book presents a case study of the failure of diplomacy. The breakdown of negotiations between Vietnam and Kampuchea led to escalation which prompted Kampuchea to seek a Chinese deterrent which, in turn, caused Vietnam to look for ways to counter what it perceived as an impending military challenge from China. Hanoi's simultaneous diplomatic overtures toward Washington and ASEAN failed, leaving a Soviet deterrent to Chinese pressures the remaining option for the SRV. To the United States, there did not appear to be an effective middle ground between the earlier attempt at unilateral imposition of a framework of regional order and its later disengagement from the region and, consequently, Washington acquiesced to Beijing's confrontationist stance.

The tragedy of the Third Indochina Conflict is that everyone lost and no one gained -- with the possible exception of the Soviet Union. This suggests that the conflict was essentially the result of misperceptions and that the traditional prescriptions of better communications and more rational decision making might have prevented the outbreak of armed hostilities. But the essays in this book are not simply further illustrations of the burgeoning literature on perception and misperception in international relations. They imply that in order to understand internation conflict, the analysis must seek to decipher the patterns, structures, and processes of these conflicts. There are crucial linkages between the local, regional, and global dimensions of interstate politics, and it was the failure to discern the larger implications of the various sets of bilateral disputes that contributed to the escalation of the conflict as they merged in explosive combination. It is equally true, however, that many of those who did perceive connections between the various levels of the conflict did not understand the dynamics of the process of escalation, and attributed it to superpower intervention by proxy.

Effective diplomacy requires the careful analysis of the interplay between the dual processes of polarization and escalation. In this case it was the forces of polarization that locked the different conflict structures together, and pushed the war to broader and more threatening levels. The challenge of decoupling the conflict structures was not met by any of the parties, and the conflict momentum triggered responses not unlike the pattern of mobilization and countermobilization that led to the outbreak of World War I. Polarization led to long range consequences which could have been foreseen but were not, because the immediate reflexive response of confrontation had a simpler and more compelling attraction.

Analyzing and responding to complex conflict situation requires the contradictory elements of perspective and involvement, detachment and concern, patience and resolute action. The parties most closely involved lacked the perspective to see the consequences of their own actions and often misinterpreted the actions of others by failing to grasp the full spectrum of motivations -- including non-rational factors -- underlying their behavior. Those not immediately involved lacked the foresight to see that polarization would lead to escalation, and opted for policies aimed at gaining short term advantage. The primary objective of the preceding chapters has been to examine the motivation of the involved parties from their own perspective, to contrast this with the perception of these motivations by others, and to examine the linkages between different levels of the international system in the conflict. Hopefully this will help clarify the intricate interplay of cause and effect in the evolving conflict, and provide a useful background for conceptualizing the approaches to resolving the problems arising from it. The underlying aim of this study, however, is to further expand our understanding of conflict itself. Ultimately the utility of such studies should be (to paraphrase the historian Jacob Burckhardt) not to make men more clever for the next time, but to make them wiser forever.